The Business of Holidays

The Business of Holidays

Edited by Maud Lavin

With contributions by
Melanie Archer, Amy Tavormina Fidler,
Benjamin Finch, Alyson Priestap-Beaton,
and Jason Warriner

THE MONACELLI PRESS

First published in the United States of America in 2004 by
The Monacelli Press, Inc.
902 Broadway, New York, New York 10010.

Library of Congress Cataloging-in-Publication Data
The business of holidays / edited by Maud Lavin ; with contributions by
Melanie Archer, Alyson Priestap-Beaton, Amy Tavormina Fidler, Benjamin
Finch, and Jason Warriner.
p.   cm.
Includes bibliographical references.
ISBN 1-58093-150-2
1. Holidays—Economic aspects—United States. 2. Consumption
(Economics)—United States. 3. Popular culture—United States.
4. United States—Social life and customs. I. Lavin, Maud.
GT4803.B87   2004
394.26—dc22   2004008284

Editor: Maud Lavin
Associate Editor, Senior Writer, Designer: Melanie Archer
Production Manager, Designer: Amy Tavormina Fidler
Chief Designer: Benjamin Finch
Photography Editor, Senior Photographer, Designer: Alyson Priestap-Beaton
Chief Designer: Jason Warriner

Printed in China

Contents

NISSIN

NISSIN FOODS

Budweiser

SHERWOOD

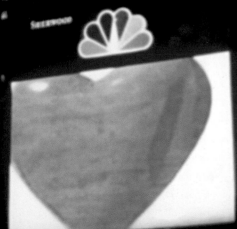

Panasonic

HICKORY FARMS®

HICKORY FARMS

Cub is Lower. Every Day
4.97

Cub is Lower. Every Day
STONE GROUND MUSTARD
1.98

Cub is Lower. Every Day
BEEF SUMMER SAUSAGE
2.98

HICKORY FARMS SPECIAL™

Cub is Lower. Every Day
SUMMER SAUSAGE & CHEDDAR
7.98

Cub is Lower. Every Day
BEEF SUMMER SAUSAGE
2.98

Cub is Lower. Every Day
CHEDDAR CHEESE
2.49

MAKE IT HICKORY FARMS SPECIAL

It's St. Patrick's Day...

It's Easter Sunday...

It's Opening Day...

It's Mother's Day...

It's Memorial Day...

It's Father's Day...

It's Graduation Day...

It's Race Day...

It's Game Day...

It's 4th of July...

It's Labor Day...

It's Tailgate Saturday...

It's Halloween...

It's Thanksgiving...

It's Christmas...

It's Every Day...

5.49

5.49

HICKORY FARMS

Cub is Lower. Every Day
BEEF STICK
5.49

HICKORY FARMS®

MAKE IT HICKORY FARMS SPECIAL™

The Business of Holidays

Introduction   Maud Lavin

If our holidays were a literary character, they would be Miss Marple, Agatha Christie's dithery, elderly sleuth with her hand-knitted shawls and gray, flyaway hair. Typically, no one takes Miss Marple seriously, since she seems vague and fusty. But time after satisfying time, Miss Marple proves herself the all-seeing, all-knowing force behind solving the crime.

It is the same story with the ever-present march of holidays through our retail economy. They come clothed in Hallmark cards, electric lights shaped like jack-o'-lanterns and Christmas trees, and wrapping paper decorated with flowers and polka dots. They carry heart-shaped cookies, bottles of Manischewitz wine, and Fanny Farmer cream-filled chocolates. They are still the province of women, particularly older women who mark their calendars and glue together family reunions. Holidays are somehow not fashionable, and yet they are celebrated by all—whether the celebrants take them seriously or claim not to. Gen-X and Gen-Yers, for instance, may not send cards or bake cookies, but they contribute to the surge of prepaid-phone-card sales and air-travel expenditure at holidays. In fact, the holidays are the most powerful fuel infusing the over $3.167 trillion U.S. retail economy.[1]

For instance, nearly one quarter of all yearly merchandise purchases are made in the Christmas season (set by the National Retail Federation as November and December).[2] Some of these are mainstays like food and alcohol, used for celebrating as well as surviving. Others are presents like CD players, which might have been purchased at other times of the year but are saved for holiday shopping. And still others are items whose sole raison d'être is the holidays. In the 2001 Christmas season, for instance, $6.4 billion was spent on house decorations, lights, and trees.[3]

Four of the five major retail seasons—Back to School, Halloween, Christmas, Easter, and Mother's Day/Father's Day—are holiday-driven.[4] And where money goes, culture follows. In deciding how a society or a group within a society represents itself to itself and others, market forces apply, including the economic tug between producing old products, popular because they are familiar, and competitive innovations. In Chicago's Loop, the river is dyed green on St. Patrick's Day; in New York's Greenwich Village, the Halloween Parade flaunts cross-dressing; on Valentine's Day, the country spends over $1 billion on candy.[5] These are cultural images and habits that we experience as traditions, but they have been invented only recently. In some cases, their claims to harmlessness and their shared clichés mask bids for acceptance. It was only a century ago that the Irish were among America's most despised and impoverished; these days, on March 17, everyone is Irish. In other cases, holidays speak to personal yearnings, yearnings that are pictured but not fulfilled. Valentine's Day means romance to some, heightened loneliness and depression to others. Holidays can remind people of what they feel they are entitled to but are lacking. And sometimes celebrants go about trying to find it—spirituality or connectedness or presents or just plain sex. Consumerism, in standard and less conventional forms, is one avenue for the search. Shannon Hughey has compared Chicago police statistics on crimes committed on major holidays and has discovered, for example, that Valentine's Day ranks the highest for prostitution.

To unpeel the holidays is to find layer after layer of invented traditions, images, and practices borrowed from immigrant groups, different religions, agricultural cycles, and government rulings. U.S. consumer culture does its best to mainstream these images for mass production and consumption. Design and marketing, tools that translate a shared visual vocabulary into salable goods, go to work. But holidays are quirky. They are the stuff not only of little old ladies but of children, for whom they are often made personal and bright. Many people have childhood holidays memories that they want to re-create, embellish, or perhaps erase in ways that beg for reinterpretations of those mass-produced plastic masks and lights. In short, holidays are the days when past meets present and public meets private, and holiday culture is made up of goods that are mass-produced yet individually tweaked.

Nowhere is that reinterpretation more evident than in the celebrations of adults without kids in tow who use holidays to let loose in ways companies who produce holiday props never imagined. Girls go wild at Mardi Gras, drink too much, and take off their tops. Jello travels to mysterious places on April Fool's Day. Boys go wild on New Year's Eve, shooting off guns. And sometimes trends that seem outside corporate culture are in truth carefully engineered by businesses to appear counter-cultural or spontaneous. Authentic and artificial twirl around in a Dionysian whirl until it is hard to see the difference. This raises a cynical question: have rituals and parades that used to be about upending the social order, or at least celebrating that idea, become mere consumer exercises? Can a holiday be both consumerist and challenge the status quo?

Some holidays, Gay Pride Day being a prime example, lend themselves more easily than others to messages that can promote egalitarian change or, at least, a degree of acceptance of minority cultures. Other holidays, like Halloween, allow celebrants to express a mix of messages, some constructive, some the opposite. Historian Nicholas Rogers, in his book *Halloween*, suggests that while license may be equated with liberation and transgression with opening the door to less-heard voices, unbridling can also encourage destructiveness and bigotry. Citing episodes of anti-Semitism and beatings of homeless people on Halloween, he concludes, "If Halloween can provide a space for cultural diversity and pluralism, it can also prompt community intolerance of the marginal."[6] Yet most of Rogers's examples of Halloween unboundedness are more positive, and in fact, he traces the influence of gay masquerade on a growing permissiveness for the general adult population, straight and gay, to engage in "deep play" on trick-or-treat night. Like other forms of mass entertainment, perhaps even more so, holidays serve to assimilate and spread popular values.

Whereas television and movies involve passive viewing, holidays invite active participation. Their messages are intimate as well as public. Rituals are learned by doing, so their values become more deeply integrated. Holidays are vehicles of mainstreaming. Traditionally, cultural commentators have viewed such mainstreaming with suspicion, as if the task of holidays was primarily to maintain long-established and often unfair cultural hierarchies. *The Business of Holidays*, however, argues that cultural mainstreaming is itself a process of change—both change and stasis. While holiday celebrations can slow cultural change by enforcing normative pressures or outdated goals, they can also accelerate change, using modifications of those same traditions to create new meanings. Commercial culture—tinsel, greeting cards, cake decorations, and the like—can smooth these ebbs and flows, making it all look and feel so familiar.

A case-by-case exploration of the cultural meanings in play during each of the major holidays, rather than an assumption that all mainstream holiday values are easily understood, static, or received without translation and a joyful scrambling, is at the heart of this book. Like the cultural critic Ernst Bloch, *The Business of Holidays* is more optimistic than not in looking for signs of hope in the everyday culture of celebrations; it also strives to be comprehensive in its understanding of how consumer culture capitalizes on and promotes that hope.

Holiday culture is hybrid. Christmas, for instance, is typically a mix of homemade and drugstore decorations, spirituality and commerce, pagan and Christian customs, familial and governmental rules, childish and adult fun, and schooltime habits. It is also one of the holidays that almost all Americans have come to share (even non-Christians may find themselves at a Christmas party), and that perhaps explains its continual surge as a consumer holiday. New cultural meanings mix in with the old, and it is only by looking at that montage that the complex communication of its messages can be understood. Consumerist Christmas, with its mainly enthusiastic (and sometimes unwilling) mass participation, also plays more heavily now in national identity, even if unintentionally so, than some of the holidays originally created to honor and encourage patriotism—like Presidents' Day, a day Matthew Dennis aptly calls "a time for forgetting, not remembering" in his *Red, White, and Blue Letter Days.*[7]

Cultural historians have recently turned a serious eye to what holidays have to say about Americans as a society and about what individuals are trying to say through them. Karal Ann Marling in her book *Merry Christmas!* spends an engaging chapter entirely on the history of wrapping presents for Christmas; along the way, she unveils not only how the wrapped present came to be what is expected but also the conditions of the people in stores and box factories who do that work. In *Consumer Rites,* Leigh Eric Schmidt looks at the fine and unstable balance of secular and religious practices in the history of holidays, particularly in the nineteenth century. In fact, most U.S. holidays in the forms we know them today were born in the nineteenth and early twentieth centuries when consumer culture made its leap from local retail to nationally transported, distributed, designed, and advertised goods. In *Celebrating the Family,* Elizabeth H. Pleck shows how holiday culture has continued to evolve as more women have entered the workforce and more subcultures have gained acceptance.[8]

The authors of *The Business of Holidays* took on this project because we wanted to examine the culture of holidays. But our entry point has been one that has made many other commentators uncomfortable: the commercialization of holidays. Accordingly, we have focused on U.S. culture as the one most adept and greedy at melding holidays with consumerism. (Although this book covers most of the major holidays celebrated in the U.S., some, such as Yom Kippur, were left out because they exist, for the most part, outside of consumer culture.) We have foregone the hand-wringing and instead accepted that not only are most of our holidays commercialized but that they drive our retail economy. We have questioned the ways in which design and commerce facilitate the spread of invented traditions and the mix of old and new holiday meanings. What is the business of holidays? What is made visible and what is not? What holiday cultures are being designed, marketed, and sold? What messages are being transmitted? What messages can be added?

In commenting on the business of holidays, we are highly entertained as well as critical, additive as well as reactive in our engagement with these celebratory days. Arranged along the lines of both natural and retail seasons, *The Business of Holidays* aims to reflect a combination of publicly harvested research and private concerns and humor. We follow the calendrical march of the holidays and explore the business of each one's retail culture. While the celebrating is going on, we are looking at who is footing the bill, how the holiday is being designed, what it is saying—and what it could say.

Business Quarter 1
Winter

Trimming Thighs, Fattening Wallets

New Year's Day   **Amy Tavormina Fidler**

The holidays unroll in glorious gluttony. Thanksgiving, the official holiday season kickoff, is a festival of food and family—with the emphasis on food. Then follows an orgy of holiday parties filled with tempting treats, the church's bake sale, the office party's buffet . . .

But all good things must come to an end—and the end is New Year's Day. If the holiday season is a time to binge, the twelve clock strikes on New Year's Eve represent a time to purge. Do penance for your sins. Atone for those accumulated eggnog and pumpkin-pie pounds. In fact, the majority of New Year's resolutions center around changing the body's appearance, via weight loss, exercise, or both. There are many companies out there that can help: the fitness and weight-loss industries have come to embrace this time of year.

New Year's resolutions date back to ancient Rome, when people would offer promises of good conduct to the dual-faced god Janus (also the namesake of the month January).[1] Today, people make New Year's resolutions with all sorts of intentions, from life changing to habit breaking. Many Americans assume that making resolutions is universal, but according to one end-of-year survey by the Marist Institute for Public Opinion, only 44 percent of people queried planned to make such a vow themselves.[2] Women are more likely to make New Year's resolutions than men, and also more likely to keep them; younger people are more likely to make resolutions, but those thirty-nine or older are more likely to keep them.

ANDERSONVILLE PHYSICAL THERAPY
MASSAGE   PILATES   BOXING
RESOLUTIONS RESOLVED HERE!

People vow to spend less money, get a better education, stop smoking, spend more time with their family, shape up, or lose weight. Some want nothing more than to stop biting their nails. The resolutions that tend to stick are direct and practical: to lose fifteen pounds, to attend one cultural event a month. More difficult to keep are those that are abstract and ambiguous about the amount of change required—to save time, to save money, to get more sleep. Generally, people resolve to improve their own lives and make themselves "better people." While the number-one resolution for men is to stop smoking, for women, the top resolution is to lose weight.[3]

A great number of people, especially women, wish to lose weight year round, so it is no wonder that so many feel guilty about their weight after the holiday season comes to a close. Americans tend to gain anywhere between one and ten pounds each holiday season.[4] Advertisements urge self-indulgence: buy your Christmas cheer and cappuccino here. Supersize is only an additional ten pounds, er, cents. In order to compete with the increased volume of products filling the market, ads during the holidays position their products as rare, seasonal, and luxurious. They try to send a message: "Buy now, because we're not available the other eleven months of the year"; in fact, most are. In the November-December 2002 issue of *Real Simple*, for instance, Rocher Chocolates (available year round) proclaims, "Rocher is perfect for Christmas: share more than just a smooch." Even Rice Krispies needs to make itself seasonally festive; one ad includes directives to add frosting and bows to Rice Krispies treats. It can be hard to not eat holiday treats, especially when egged on by each television commercial break, Internet pop-up window, or city storefront. In addition, with the extra commitments of the holidays, time devoted to the gym and other forms of exercise often creeps quietly into oblivion. People's healthy activities are often traded for after-work cocktail parties or weekends of holiday shopping.

Fortunately for those who have made diet resolutions, there is no shortage of businesses and products on the market to help people lose weight and get fit, and fortunately for those whose products can help people lose weight and get fit, there are many people who have made diet resolutions. Sadly, most break them.[5] Regardless, weight-loss programs and fitness centers are ready to receive their influx of customers every January.

Weight Watchers is one such business—the highest earner in a $39.8 billion industry.[6] From its humble beginning in a Queens, New York, living room, Weight Watchers has expanded into an international company, complete with Web site, magazine, and line of low-"point" frozen foods, Smart Ones. In an interview with CNN, Linda Huett, president and CEO of Weight Watchers, states: "Obviously January's a very busy time for us. There are over one million people attending a Weight Watchers meeting somewhere in the world, every week. I think there are certain cycles . . . to our year, as there are in most businesses . . . January is a natural time . . . for people to sort of take stock . . . A fresh year. A fresh start . . . We get very busy in January."[7]

Many people also join Weight Watchers around Thanksgiving, looking for a way to cope with the coming holiday feasts. Weight Watchers has tools and promotions to help people stay motivated through this time and also runs ads that motivate dieters to join as a part of that New Year's resolution. For the 2001 holiday season, Weight Watchers beefed up its Web site with special holiday resources. According to Sheila Kelly, M.S., R.D., director of products research and development for WeightWatchers.com, "Dieting during the holiday season may leave some people feeling out of control. With this in mind, WeightWatchers.com has developed a number of possible solutions to help every dieter enjoy the holidays."[8] Content includes holiday recipe makeovers and editorials titled "How to Approach Your Thanksgiving Table without Feeling Stuffed like the Turkey" and "Thanksgiving Dinner Deconstructed." The site also offers low-"point" menu suggestions for party planners: "Throw a Low-Points Holiday Bash."

One Weight Watchers print ad for Smart Ones pizzas proclaims, "You're bad . . . you're really bad! Being bad never felt so good." Another, advertising the new line of Smart Ones stuffed sandwiches, declares, "Now 'being stuffed' is a good thing." Each Weight Watchers print ad ends with the slogan, "When you're smart, it shows." A key marketing strategy is to convey the concept that Weight Watchers members are intelligent, implying that those who do not use the products may be inadequate. People already feeling inadequate, due to low self-esteem or poor body image, may be especially susceptible to this sort of advertising technique. The somber, albeit somewhat nasty strategy preys on people's natural tendencies for comparison and guilt.

Not to be left behind, Jenny Craig launched two ads on December 26, 2002, just in time to inspire resolutions and new memberships.[9] Designed by the firm Johnson/Ukropina, these ads feature provocative images with almost painfully direct captions. One ad depicts two pairs of underwear hanging on a clothesline, one large and frumpy, the other small and sexy. The tagline reads, "Want to change your underwear this year? Jenny Craig. It works." The other features a fast-food trio of extra-large burger, fries, and soda with the question, "Have you supersized yourself? Call Jenny Craig." In some markets, these ads were coupled with "Jenny's New Year's Promise," an offer to try the Jenny Craig Program with a guaranteed refund if no weight was lost the first week.

Along with the desire for weight loss comes exercise and time at the gym. In 2001, over one million people joined health clubs in January.[10] Bally's Total Fitness, the largest operator of fitness centers in North America, promotes itself at the new year with direct and humorous advertising strategies that are designed to motivate people to purchase Bally's memberships. One 2001 seasonal television ad showed a group of people opening presents—one person proclaimed, "Look, a double chin!" while another gleefully announced, "A big butt!" Satirizing the common holiday dilemma gets the viewer's attention; shots of an impeccably thin girl at the Stairmaster and an oiled-down, muscled hunk lifting weights soon follow. Holiday promotions offer, among other specials, one free membership with one paid membership.[11] Broadcasting these ads during the gluttonous holiday season tends to pique people's interest, putting weight loss on the brain and planting a bug that will be remembered when holiday festivities are over.

During the final week of 2002, Bally Total Fitness "launched a $5 million television, radio, and print campaign specifically timed for the new year," according to Bally's senior vice president of sales and marketing, John Wildman.[12] The campaign, titled "The Beauty of Pain," stresses "time and commitment over any quick-fix solution" as a strategy that aims to maintain members past the January rush.

According to Bally's, "Each year 100 million Americans resolve to get fit, and 40 percent break their resolutions by February."[13] Clubs realize that people join on impulse, after noticing the holiday weight gain. To help people stick to their resolutions, Bally's director of training, Steven Boggs, attempts to "keep people who

took up exercise with the new year from giving up." Regarding excuses, Boggs has heard them all: "The number one excuse I get is time . . . The second is a lot of folks don't see the results as quickly as they want."

Interviewed on NPR's "All Things Considered," Samara Williamson, Crunch Fitness membership sales representative, agrees that January is the busiest month of the year, while December is the slowest: "We will triple our sales this month compared to last month." The topic under discussion was the impulse to sign up for a health club as part of a New Year's resolution but quit within six months. Responding to the question "Do the health clubs prey on that a little bit?" Williamson responds, "Of course we do . . . this is how we make our money. But we are here to help and we try to offer better specials in the month of January. But of course, we are looking out for ourselves as well."[14]

Nor are consumers spared the New Year's promotional push in the grocery store. Quasi–health foods and other convenience foods are beginning to compete at this time of year in helping the consumer to keep resolutions. During 2002, Kellogg's Nutri-Grain cereal bars were advertised as healthful alternatives to sweets, and Kellogg introduced a series of ads making literal the phrase "You are what you eat." Baked goods depicted different body parts, such as an ad with cinnamon buns as buttocks and the tagline "Respect Yourself in the Morning." The timely New Year's ad in this series states, quite simply, "Don't Have a Hip-py New Year. Respect Yourself in the Morning."[15]

In a perverse way, the cycle of gaining weight at the holidays and trying to lose it in January repeats itself year after year, and businesses follow the cycle. Many people do manage to shed some pounds as the result of their resolution and approach the new year with enthusiasm and vigor, which is good for them—but even better for business.

Commerce and Meaning in the Celebration of Martin Luther King Jr. Day

Martin Luther King Jr. Day   Maud Lavin and Shayla Johnson

Of the ten official federal holidays in the U.S.,[1] Martin Luther King Jr. Day, the third Monday of January, is the only one devoted to a single person.[2] Created in 1983, it is also the most recently established federal holiday. It commemorates the work of an African-American activist, a man who preached and practiced nonviolent mass civil disobedience to fight racist cruelties and anti-democratic discrimination across the country. Not surprisingly, it is a holiday that was born in controversy and after a long labor—the push for the legislation began four days after King's assassination in 1968 and took a number of congressional attempts and the gathering of petitions with millions of signatures until it became such an unarguable, will-of-the-people inevitability that Ronald Reagan (a known opponent of King's politics) had no choice but to sign it into law.[3]

The debates around the foundation of Martin Luther King Jr. Day raised questions about how the country defined heroism and how it continued to struggle with issues of racial equality. Often, though, these were thinly masked behind a discussion of expense. Federal holidays are created so rarely because they are expensive—banks and many businesses are closed, and all federal employees receive a paid vacation day. But in the case of Martin Luther King Jr. Day, proponents of the holiday were quick to point out that the arguments about cost were smokescreens for larger cultural issues. For instance, Senator Birch Bayh commented in one congressional debate: "The cost? What are the costs of a national holiday? Perhaps more rightly, what are the costs of not having a holiday? What are the costs of second-class citizenship? What are the costs of a little black boy or a little black girl . . . not having the opportunity to share in a national holiday of some great leader that happens to look like them, to come from the same heritage that they came from?"[4]

A brief history of the effort to create a federal King Day begins with U.S. Representative John Conyers Jr., who in 1968 introduced a bill to make King's birthday a federal holiday. This bill was defeated. In the late 1960s and thereafter, many African-Americans commemorated King's birthday on January 15, regardless of whether or not it was declared an official holiday. By 1971, the Southern Christian Leadership Conference had gathered petitions, three million signatures strong, supporting the creation of a federal holiday to honor King. In 1973, then–State Assemblyman Harold Washington (later mayor of Chicago) introduced successful legislation for a state holiday in Illinois. Over the decades, most but not all states followed suit. In 1979, Coretta Scott King and then-President Jimmy Carter appealed to Congress to pass a King Day bill, but their effort was defeated in a floor vote in the House. In 1982, Coretta Scott King testified before Congress about the importance of establishing a King holiday. She and Stevie Wonder, both longtime activists for the cause, delivered to Congress petitions gathered by the King Center in Atlanta and carrying more than six million signatures. In 1983, the House finally passed a King holiday bill; over 750,000 marchers on Washington, D.C., expressed support for the idea; the Senate passed the bill; and Reagan signed it into law.[5]

Politically, the question ultimately centered not on whether the government could afford to create a federal holiday honoring King's memory but on whether it could afford not to. But how has the holiday evolved since its inception? The Reverend Dorris Roberts of Chicago, now president of the NAACP Southside Chapter, recalls his work in Nashville as a youth in 1955, which was focused on political and economic growth for African-Americans. He remembers that, at that time, Martin Luther King Jr. had visited several college campuses to speak with fraternities, ROTC, and religious organizations. Today the Rev. Roberts expresses frustration that young people seem to have little reverence for the King holiday. He himself, however, is still actively involved with the observance through NAACP events and believes the ceremonies that have been most effective focus on "advocacy for employment and restoration" of communities.[6]

Questions of commerce impact the holiday in regard to the licensing of King's image. In 1982, the King family won a suit against American Heritage Products, which had been making statuettes of King without the family's permission.[7] Since then, the family has become increasingly diligent in protecting the ownership of King's image—only nonprofit and educational institutions are allowed to use it free of charge. In 1997, the family signed a lucrative deal with Time Warner to produce King-related media ranging from books of his collected writings to CD-ROMs of his speeches.[8]

Martin Luther King, Jr. (1929-1968) delivering his "I have a Dream" speech at the 1963 March on Washington.

The family's tight control over King's image and litigious tendencies may be part of the reason why gift-store windows in January are not stuffed with Martin Luther King Jr. T-shirts, mugs, and posters. Another, more interesting reason is that, at this point in history, the celebration of the day has not yet been calcified into ritual—commercially oriented or otherwise. Some people go to church, others watch television specials, still others ignore the holiday. Historian Matthew Dennis reports that some "Americans have used the occasion to organize gun buy-back programs, volunteer at food banks, refurbish schools, clean up trash and plant trees, and engage in other community activities with liberal political agendas."[9]

Dr. R. L. White, president of the Atlanta chapter of the NAACP, sees, however, that there is still some resistance to and "no full honoring of" the holiday. He interprets this lack of "reverence" as a "denial of [Dr. King's] importance."[10] The arguments around how the day should be celebrated and what it means are enlightening.

There is a general hope that King Day does not become just another excuse for a three-day weekend, emptied of other meaning, as Presidents' Day has become. Otherwise, debate roils. Some want to avoid the canonization of King, his representation as saintly, pure, and uncomplicated. Michael Eric Dyson, professor, Baptist preacher, and author of *I May Not Get There with You: The True Martin Luther King, Jr.,* has written:

> Whether involving his image as a patriot (or traitor), a meritocrat, a saint, or an icon, King has been fashioned to calm rather than trouble the waters of social conscience in the post–civil rights era. But he was no Safe Negro . . . Predictably, the King holiday, while bringing just recognition to King and the civil rights movement, has often been used to sweeten his bitter presence as a searing prophet of edifying rage.[11]

Dyson argues that it is important to commemorate the complex brilliance of King's anti-racism strategies—his brave marches and sit-ins, his hard-headed economic boycotts and strikes, and the angry eloquence of his speeches. The author points out that King's sweetly inspiring phrases of 1963—"I have a dream my four little children will one day live in a nation where they will not be judged by the color of their skin but by the content of their character"—are quoted often, while his angrier and economically astute points are cited far less frequently:[12]

> We are now making demands that will cost the nation something. You can't talk about solving the economic problem of the Negro without talking about billions of dollars. You can't talk about ending slums without first saying profit must be taken out of slums. You're really tampering and getting on dangerous ground because you are messing with folk then. You are messing with the captains of industry . . . Now this means that we are treading in difficult waters because it really means that we are saying that something is wrong . . . with capitalism . . . There must be a better distribution of wealth and maybe America must move toward Democratic Socialism.[13]

The counterargument to such worries about oversimplification suggests that collective memory inevitably works to make complexity plain, and that some broad strokes are needed in order to teach King's history. Another concern expressed by Dyson is that the history of King's frailties is likewise repressed in overly sugary celebrations, thus rendering him difficult for others to identify with. He advocates representing King as a complex man, one who can be identified with and whose strategies can be reused, translated, and extended. This attitude raises various questions: What are empowering ways to celebrate Martin Luther King Jr. Day? How can King's complexities be remembered and his activism be renewed and carried forward through the celebrations? How can King be put in the context of the Civil Rights movement so that it becomes clear it was (and still is) a collective effort as well as the work of leaders? How can the joy of King's eloquence be injected into solemn ceremonies? How can translations and inevitable simplifications from generation to generation avoid turning King into St. Martin?

It is schools and the African-American church community that have embraced these questions in efforts that transcend the commercialism associated with most major U.S. holidays. And it is scholars and church activists who are proposing uplifting and strategic ways to celebrate the holiday. White feels that one way to celebrate is for speakers at a church service or holiday event to challenge parents to become "more persistent in teaching and raising awareness." He notes, "They should tell the story in a meaningful way" and follow through on King's principles with, for instance, education on voting. Critics advocate a larger-scale global manifestation in appreciation of King's views on global equality. Dr. White participated in the bus boycotts in Macon, Georgia, as a youth. He observes what he considers a more keen awareness and respect for King's efforts in other countries among groups that shared a similar struggle. Today, he asserts, in America, more enthusiasm for the celebration is found in Atlanta than elsewhere in the country. White suggests that to celebrate the King holiday is to participate in a celebration that is even more universal than Kwanzaa. He says, "This celebration is more reflective of what we have done as a people." He explains that, in Atlanta, "It starts an entire week before the day of his birthday." The first event is a march on Martin Luther King Jr. Boulevard and Peachtree Road to the Martin Luther King Jr. Memorial.[14]

Dr. Joseph Lowery, a leader of the Civil Rights movement, sees voting as a powerful means of celebrating Dr. Martin Luther King. He also comments that there should be a focus on taking back the neighborhoods by going into streets as well as businesses to advocate support of education and non-violence. As he travels across the country, Dr. Lowery speaks primarily about world peace and racial profiling, negotiating as well fair employment contracts with large corporations such as Publix and Shoney's Restaurants. He states, King "was a man of the streets, a man of the people."[15]

Groundhog Money

Benjamin Finch

A framed and matted color photograph of Punxsutawney Phil can be had for one hundred dollars. Phil fans can visit him year-round or buy pins, necklaces, and hand puppets in his image. They can also attend the annual week-long Groundhog Festival in Punxsutawney, Pennsylvania, held, somewhat incongruously, in mid-summer. But the true pilgrimage takes place on Groundhog Day, February 2, when the faithful trek (or shuttle) up Gobbler's Knob to watch Phil look for his shadow. If he finds it: six more weeks of winter. If there's no shadow: an early spring. Either way, the Chamber of Commerce is happy to welcome thousands of tourists every February, when the town of six thousand swells by approximately thirty thousand visitors.

The Punxsutawney Chamber of Commerce was likely glad to welcome the film crew of the hit 1993 Bill Murray–Andie MacDowell comedy *Groundhog Day*, which starred Phil and supposedly took place in the Pennsylvania town, although the movie was actually shot in Woodstock, Illinois. Even so, the movie, one of the top ten grossing films of its year, provided spectacular advertising for the Pennsylvania town. And it offered one of the few chances for a locally based groundhog in this or any burg to bring in holiday money on a national scale. (Phil has a lot of competition, but none of the others have made it onto the big screen. In Wisconsin, there's "Jimmy," the groundhog who does not seem to have much of a life—except for his occasional indulgence in the fine cheese offered in the greater Midwest—and yet still appears in the newspapers every year. And in 1998, after years of embarrassment due to its lack of an official groundhog, New York City adopted "Pothole Pete," who no doubt has his own publicist.) Otherwise, despite quasi-desperate attempts by such groups as the

Committee for the Commercialization of Groundhog Day, dedicated to exploiting February 2 for profit (the committee claims it will not rest until there is a Groundhog Day Major Appliance Sale),[1] the groundhog is not a big money maker.

The groundhog can be considered an unpaid guest star in news weather segments for one day, often begrudgingly entertained by weathermen and -women across the country. Historically, meteorologists have not been the bearer of groundhog news, since most dismiss the predictions of their furry competitors as hocus-pocus. Usually the news anchor announces the groundhog's doings and then shifts the newscast to the meteorologist. In most cases, the meteorologist ends up disagreeing with the groundhog, stating his or her theory on the next six weeks of winter and then casually handing the broadcast back to the news anchor.

The accuracy rate of today's groundhog is the issue. What use is the groundhog if he is never right? According to one survey done in Quarryville, Pennsylvania, "Over a 60 year period the groundhog had been right only 28% of the time."[2] Rick DiMaio, a meteorologist for the Fox News affiliate in Chicago, when asked if the groundhog is ever right, quipped, "I can't comment on something that has only a fifty-fifty chance of accuracy. Of course, in the long run there will be times when he is right, but that doesn't mean there was any skill involved."[3] Still there are some people who are consumed by this holiday and will not budge from the belief that the groundhog is always correct. The chairman of the Board of Hibernating Governors, a board set up to oversee the groundhog's predictions, asserts, "Our records show that the groundhog has always forecast the weather with absolute, 100% accuracy."

As it turns out, weather forecasters do not need the groundhog's help to boost ad sales. According to DiMaio, the weather has such a great impact that "Morning snowstorms during the weekday usually triple the ratings, and heat waves also increase the ratings because more people tend to be inside with air-conditioning." On every day, not just on weather-oriented holidays, the newscast, specifically the weather segment, is marketed to viewers to maximize profits. Weather is "rationed out a tidbit at a time, usually two or three times a broadcast," and viewers are "forced to sit through the entire newscast" and, even more important, the commercials. More specifically, "The weather is usually broken up as follows: 9:08 for thirty seconds, 9:30 for three minutes, 9:55 for thirty seconds." Usually, the commercials just before and after the weather segment of the news cost more than those at other points in the newscast. Advertising during the weather is one of the most expensive times to advertise on television. Often commercials that run during the weather segments "reflect anything to do with outdoor chores or vacationing."

Not only do advertisers invest in commercials, but news stations and many other organizations have also tied their money to the weather. According to Commerce Secretary William Daley's 1998 congressional testimony: "Weather is not just an environmental issue; it is a major economic factor. At least $1 trillion of our economy is weather sensitive."[4] Specifically, news stations, both national and local, have invested more money in the weather than in any other part of the news. They have purchased costly and sophisticated animation programs and live doppler radar images to enhance presentation of the weather in order to increase viewership to sell more commercials. Satellites and computer technology are utilized to make fascinating and tantalizing graphics. Television news programs are, in essence, packaging the weather much like graphic designers package products, to make it more marketable to viewers. And perhaps the groundhog plays a small part, one day a year, in that marketing.

With today's sophistication in weather forecasting and presentation, the tradition of a small animal sniffing around sleepily in the sun or cowering back toward his hole has become just that—a tradition. The groundhog is not a media star based on his stellar prognostic ability; rather, with the understated popularity of the holiday every year, it is obvious that people concern themselves with tradition, not accuracy. The holiday is marked by a specific event that does not garner large consumer profits, but it is one that people look to for amusement, the occasional dinner conversation topic, and a television graphic. As Rick DiMaio comments, "Groundhog Day is there to promote enjoyment in weather. It also gives us something to look forward to while we are in the doldrums of winter."[5]

Dim Sum and Dragons

Chinese New Year   Melanie Archer

Dim sum, dragons, and a firecracker or two. For many people who visit U.S. Chinatowns to witness Chinese New Year celebrations, these are the only necessary ingredients. But the New Year is much more complex than a short checklist of items. According to an ancient legend, Chinese New Year was first celebrated to mark the disappearance of the Nian—a ferocious beast with an extremely large mouth, capable of swallowing several people in one bite. The celebration runs from the middle of the last month of the previous year (based on the Chinese calendar) to the middle of the first month of the new year—usually early to mid-February, according to the Western calendar. By the time the New Year arrives, families have already spent many days preparing for the event—purchasing gifts, cleaning house, and buying festive foods.[1] One popular custom is giving lishee—red envelopes filled with money. Another is visiting relatives' houses bearing gifts of oranges, always in even numbers for good luck. Upon leaving, the visitor receives the same number of oranges from the host.

The New Year celebration in the United States—for Chinese-Americans, the most important and frequently observed holiday[2]—has evolved since immigrants from Asia first arrived during the mid-1800s. These immigrants often joined their compatriots in established ethnic communities where a common language and culture made them feel at home. This resulted in the forming of the earliest Chinatowns.[3] At first, the Chinese were regarded as outsiders—they were hemmed in by intense racial hatreds and fears, by language barriers, and by stringent immigration laws that kept their families in China. In fact, the distinguishing feature of the first Chinese New Year celebrations in the United States was that a traditional family festival was being observed primarily by men without families.

Throughout the nineteenth century, most Chinese immigrants were men attracted to the United States by the discovery of gold in the hills of California.[4] According to U.S. law, these men were barred from bringing their wives over; then the Chinese Exclusion Act of 1882 reduced immigration to a small number of merchants, students, and tourists. Often these immigrants were not allowed to live in certain areas of the cities in which they settled. The Exclusion Act was repealed only in 1943, as China became a wartime ally.

Chinese-American holidays thus became a way to seek solace and preserve cultural ties to families and to China. Migrants would travel from smaller towns to cities such as Seattle and San Francisco to celebrate the new year.[5] But the American version of the Chinese New Year was different from that celebrated in southern China, original home of most of the migrants. Chinese men formed clans that functioned as the equivalent of the family. Clan members celebrated the new year by replacing the traditional family New Year's Eve feast with a banquet held at their headquarters in Chinatown. After the feast, the men would set off firecrackers or go to gambling houses, opium dens, or the Chinese opera or theater. No such tradition existed in China. During the 1880s, the few Chinese women who lived in the U.S. (in 1870, only 7 percent of the Chinese-American population was female) were mainly merchants wives' who were permitted by custom to leave their house only once a year—on the new year.[6] This reinforced the primary role that men played in establishing early American Chinese New Year customs—particularly interesting to note given the predominance of women in the practice of most holiday traditions in the U.S.

For the most part, the Chinese New Year was a festival celebrated in a segregated neighborhood; therefore, it was mainly the Chinese who created their own version of the holiday and thus drew white tourists to various Chinatowns. Merchants there, as early as the 1870s, discovered that these tourists enjoyed the sights, sounds, smells, and cuisine of what was to them an alien culture. Chinese merchants soon opened such New Year activities as the banquet and gambling to whites. As a result, the New Year holiday became a display of pride in cultural heritage and a quest for social tolerance. Eventually, in the 1920s, 1930s, and 1940s, more wives were allowed to immigrate, and with this movement, the New Year observance became longer and more traditional. The clan banquet remained an important event in the life of the community, and some married men even brought their wives. Chinatowns began to stage night parades with lanterns to celebrate the Feast of Lanterns, the holiday at the end of the New Year season.[7]

In the 1950s, the male-female immigration balance was equalized, and with this increased female presence, the New Year became more home-centered and the number of family occasions multiplied. Simultaneously and conversely, Chinese businessmen at this time, and later, welcomed the New Year as a commercial opportunity and made it into a staged event for tourists. Festival organizers in San Francisco hoped to encourage whites, as well as Chinese living outside the city, to attend that city's parade, and Chinese business leaders cooperated with city officials and members of the Chamber of Commerce. Thus, the "traditional" festival was one that combined mainstream American and Chinese ethnic elements and soon became seen, by all parties involved, as a way to generate tourism.[8]

There is a certain amount of ambiguity, however, that surrounds questions of authenticity in celebrating holidays such as Chinese New Year. The term *assimilation* is frequently used in reference to immigrant groups, but it is an ambiguous term—often viewed as pejorative, even though it has positive aspects. When one culture blends with another, it naturally goes through some form of transition. This transition, which softens sometimes harsh cultural lines, can lead to a better understanding and greater acceptance of new cultures, people, customs, and religions. A greater level of comfort is attained for both the new culture and the established one, and with this, the immigrant group gains increased mobility within the larger society. Also, often overlooked in this discourse are the contributions that other cultures have made to that of the U.S., and the ways in which many cultures have exchanged or intermingled ideas and practices. It may be said that the new culture has not really changed in a vitiating manner but that it has evolved in accordance with its changing role in the broader culture. Sadly though, assimilation can lead to both a slow extinction of old traditions and criticism of the new practices that arise. But to what degree does a culture have to be modified before it is deemed inauthentic? Immigrant groups are sometimes criticized for trying to blend into the larger society, a blending perhaps caused by the shame of being different in appearance and cultural practices. Are members of a new culture really attempting to cover up these differences by wearing the trendiest U.S. clothing and shoe brands or simply adapting to a new physical, social, and economic climate? Evolution over a period of time is inevitable, and eventually the new coexists with the old. In fact, this meeting of traditional and non-traditional has been the cornerstone of many of today's beloved holidays and observances.

One of the major factors in the acceptance of Chinese immigrants in the U.S. may once and for all verify the adage "The way to a man's heart is through his stomach." In the 1920s, with the coming of the Jazz Age, views regarding Chinese immigrants began to shift. Then with the end of World War II, a craving arose for all things

	Description	Price	QT.		Description	Pric
鮮明蝦餃	Shrimp Dumplings (4)	1.50		帶子腸	Scallop Funn Roll	1.75
韭菜餃	Shrimp, Vegetable & Meat (3)	1.50		羅漢齋腸	Vegetable Funn Roll	1.75

exotic.[9] Chinese restaurant owners in the United States learned to adapt their cuisine to American tastes. Chop suey and fortune cookies were invented to please white customers.[10] Restaurants serving these items and others became popular, and a few decades later, in the 1970s, dim sum rose as a veritable force in U.S. dining.[11]

Dim sum is a Cantonese term for "little snacks," a sort of Chinese version of hors d'oeuvres,[12] usually eaten as a festive brunch. Other translations include "to touch your heart"[13] and "heart's delight."[14] Originally a Cantonese custom, dim sum is linked to the Chinese tradition of yum cha, or drinking tea. Travelers journeying along the famous Silk Road needed a place to rest, and teahouses began to spring up along the roadside. Eventually, proprietors began offering a variety of snacks, and dim sum was born. Regardless of trendsetters' self-congratulatory opinions, dim sum was not new in America when it first became popular in the 1970s. The Chinese population in the U.S. had been eating dim sum from the beginning. But part of its popularity among non-Asians was the fact that most of the restaurants serving it were tucked away deep in Chinatowns. Navigating the narrow, twisting streets, dark corners, and rickety flights of stairs added a distinct cachet to brunch—and to the bruncher. Dim sum became popular because it was a delicious, exotic, and unique eating experience for Westerners.[15]

Although there are some exceptions, in most dim sum restaurants servers circulate through the dining area with carts topped with various dishes. The server marks the dish's number on an item-price list and calculates the total at the end of the meal. Some popular dishes include pork spareribs, char siu bao (steamed buns with roast pork), mini spring rolls, and har gao (shrimp dumplings with a translucent skin). Usually, there are more than fifty dishes on any one restaurant's list, and during the meal, tea flows like water. Dim sum for two can cost ten dollars and up, depending on the number of dishes and the stylishness of the restaurant.

To celebrate the Chinese New Year in 2003, I took a friend to dim sum at Won Kow restaurant in Chicago's Chinatown. Intermittent comments from our fellow diners—"Steamed duck feet. Are they serious?" "You know, they should really explain what these dishes mean"—were indications that the acceptance of Chinese culture and cuisine extends only as far as Western knowledge and comfort. I also observed that the list's more exotic items did not circulate on the carts. Was this an effort to have broader appeal to Westerners—to avoid appetites diminishing with the appearance of braised duck tongues? Was authenticity placed on the back burner for the sake of profits?

葱花炸兩腸	Steaamed Funn Roll with Fried Dough Fritter	1.75
三鮮餃	Seafood Dumpling	1.75
蝦土司	Shrimp Toast (3)	1.75

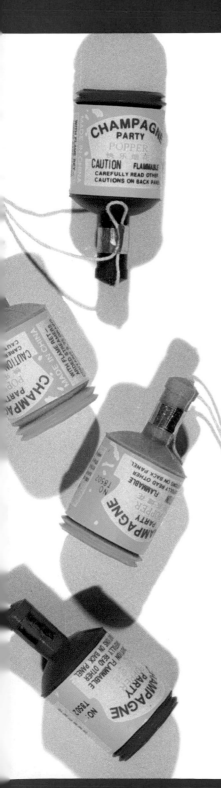

This question of authenticity is also relevant to today's Chinese New Year's parades, which usually consist of several brightly decorated floats, traditional Chinese drumming, dragon and lion dancing, firecrackers, marching bands, politicians, and Scottish bagpipers. Some of these elements seem vaguely incongruous. When the parade was first held in San Francisco around the 1920s, and for several decades after that, all of the participants and onlookers were Chinese, but in the mid-1980s non-Chinese people and groups were granted permission to participate in the San Francisco parade.[16]

California has the largest Asian population in the U.S.—40 percent or 3.7 million[17] of the estimated 10 million Americans of Asian ancestry.[18] In San Francisco, the site of the largest Chinese New Year parade outside of Hong Kong, Asian-Americans comprise 30 percent of the population.[19] In 2003 (4701 according to the Chinese calendar), the San Francisco parade welcomed some half-million revelers.[20] Wayne Hu, director of the parade, first got involved with it in 1970, twelve years after his father, Jackson Hu, first ran it in 1958 when the Chinese Chamber of Commerce took it over. The younger Hu commented, "What's neat about the parade is that there were none in China, just processions. It's Chinese American, a new thing."[21] A new thing that adds up to big bucks. Since 1971, the parade's budget has grown from $40,000 to $850,000, with $80,000 of that sum coming from the city's Grants for the Arts program and the rest from corporate sponsors and television broadcast fees. Parade critics say that it is too commercial and has spread too far from its roots. Also, feminists have attacked the Miss Chinatown USA pageant (the winners ride on a float in the parade), police have criticized firecracker use, and dueling envoys from Taiwan have been invited and uninvited.[22]

The two-hour San Francisco parade in 2003, the Year of the Ram, had about twenty sponsored floats, including ones for Harrah's casinos, Albertson's grocery stores, and the *San Francisco Chronicle*. Professional floats for the Chinese New Year parade can range from twenty-five to fifty thousand dollars. Portland Studio Concepts built a forty-three-foot structure for parade sponsor Southwest Airlines (a mechanical display of a young boy chasing a goat) in Portland over a two-week period and then transported it to San Francisco on the back of a truck. Finishing touches took just a day. Kendra Comerford, the firm's project manager, commented, "A parade is theater, it's just moving." Other floats included one celebrating the Lord of Wealth, with large gold coins piled around a model of an ocean ship; one featuring two giant China dolls; and a third resembling a diner, with a life-size Elvis Presley and a larger-than-life jukebox.[23] The connection between Elvis and China remains unclear.

But the parade is not always smooth sailing, so to speak. In 2003, the year's official posters proclaimed the Year of the Ram. But Ford, one of the parade's sponsors, cried bias, since the Dodge Ram pickup is made by a competitor. It was too late to recall the posters, but the official parade Web site changed the name of the celebration to the Year of the Sheep. According to Hu, "We were not as sensitive to the ram as Ford was."[24]

Dim sum, floats, and parade participants are not the only things that have been scrutinized as being somewhat assimilated into the broader U.S. culture. The dragon and lion dancing, which is meant to transport onlookers to China, returns them abruptly to the United States with the glimpse of a pair of Levi's or Adidas under the ornate costumes. Another segment of the Chinese New Year celebration that has been recently examined is the use of firecrackers.

According to Chinese tradition, setting off a firecracker scares evil spirits away, and the smoke rises up as a blessing. Shortly after the February 1, 2003, parade in Chicago's Chinatown, the streets were littered with streams of red pieces of paper from post-parade firecrackers. Shopkeepers tied strands of firecrackers with fruit and hung them outside their shops. Lion dancers, accompanied by musicians beating drums and cymbals, made their way around to the strands and set them off—a treat for the children nearby. As the strands sputtered, spewed, and popped, onlookers simultaneously ducked for cover, coughed, fanned the smoke, and covered their ears. It was, indeed, a celebration.

This was not the case six years earlier in New York City. In 1997, the Giuliani administration banned firecrackers at the celebration for safety reasons. But in 2003, several days before New Year celebrations, Mayor Michael Bloomberg's administration announced that it would relax the ban to allow a "pyrotechnic display" at a designated location in the city's Chinatown. Officials then scrambled to buy firecrackers, calling Fireworks by Grucci, the New York company that puts on the Macy's Fourth of July fireworks show over the East River. Grucci bought firecrackers from a Chinese company and quickly installed fuses on the belts of the firecrackers called red dragons so that they could be detonated by Grucci pyrotechnicians. There were some 38 strands, each with 5,200 firecrackers, and an estimated 197,600 bangs echoed through the streets.[25]

The display was not exactly the traditional setting off of firecrackers for the New Year, and reactions to the compromise were mixed. Karen Lew, a coordinator for an after-school program in Chinatown, spoke wistfully of the return of firecrackers: "I'm glad there were fireworks, but it was so structured. I grew up here and I remember seeing seas of red paper everywhere." She also commented on the lack of unbridled festivity seen in the past.[26]

It is only natural, however, that any culture introduced into another will face some degree of variegation. I grew up in the Caribbean, and so I notice and appreciate the ways in which segments of my culture are observed in the U.S., but I am simultaneously saddened to see the modifications or reinterpretations that make them a better "fit" for a wider audience. I can only imagine that these are sentiments shared by people of Chinese ancestry who are relative newcomers to the United States. How are events that surround the San Francisco Symphony's Chinese New Year Concert—with pre-concert reception featuring lion dancers, Chinese crafts, and dim sum—really observed? Probably more frugally—tickets ranged from $16 to $60 for the concert only and $250 to $2,500 for patrons.[27]

However Chinese New Year is celebrated, it is interesting to observe the syncretism and variations that have resulted from the immigration that first occurred some 150 years ago. The new traditions that have formed reflect the history and struggles of the Chinese in America. This factor in itself lends uniqueness and authenticity to today's celebration of the Chinese New Year. The floats (some of them) take on greater meaning, as do the lion and dragon dancers. Suddenly, oranges mean more than daily vitamin C; firecrackers more than noise. And perhaps in time, the steamed duck feet will not seem quite so off-putting.

Viagra and Valentines

Valentine's Day Ilivia Marin Yudkin

Old-fashioned romance is just that—old-fashioned. Sex, not love, dominates the news, from the nation's capital to the nation's bedroom. But not everyone has given up on romance. Not Pfizer.

Around Valentine's Day 2000, Pfizer ran an advertising campaign persuading women to give their partners Viagra instead of chocolates. Viagra, a treatment for erectile dysfunction (ED), formerly endorsed by Senator Bob Dole, is also aimed at a younger audience. Pfizer has fierce competition from two new drugs approved in 2003 to treat ED. A drug called Cialis is marketed through a partnership with Eli Lilly and Icos Corporation and Vardenafil is sold by Bayer A.G. and GlaxoSmithKline.[1]

So on February 14, 2000, a nationally broadcast, thirty-second television spot featured a romantic couple dancing as on-screen text said, "This February 14 . . . be sweet . . . be playful . . . be my Valentine."[2] This spot does not mention the drug until the end, nor does it state that it will make one's life better. Rather, it relies on its extraordinary name recognition at a sentimental time of the year. The *New York Times* even reported on February 13, 2002, that radio ads broadcast in Manhattan urged men to visit a Web site where they could get a prescription for Viagra in time for Valentine's Day.

By connecting a drug for erectile dysfunction with Valentine's Day, Pfizer is following a pharmaceutical-company trend of commercializing products during the holidays. Procter & Gamble has a history of tying ad campaigns to national holidays that reflect the image the company wants to portray. A representative from Eli Lilly asserts that "Every company wants a piece of the holiday pie." Other companies making this move include Schering-Plough, which has linked Claritin with the major-league baseball season.[3]

In 1997, the Food and Drug Administration relaxed its rules on mass-media advertising for prescription drugs. This made it easier for pharmaceutical companies to promote their products.[4] Before 1997, drug companies did not advertise on

Wishing you a happy Valentine's Day

VIAGRA
(sildenafil citrate) tablets
AN "OFFICIAL SPONSOR" OF VALENTINE'S DAY

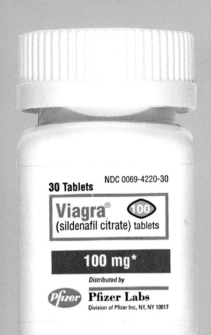

television, and most pharmaceutical companies directed their print marketing toward doctors and health-care providers. In 2000, though, the industry spent about $1.4 billion on television commercials.[5] To put that into perspective, each of the top seven most heavily advertised drugs beat out Nike's ad budget of $78.2 million for its top shoe.[6] "This is a very healthy industry," said Sheldon Silverberg, an expert on pharmaceutical companies at NDCHealth. "People are walking into doctors' offices after seeing commercials."[7] According to urologist Dr. William Schmied, the rise in drug advertisements has drastically changed the doctor-patient dynamic: "Patients come in asking for a specific drug because they have tried someone else's prescription, or because they saw an ad in a magazine." Yet according to the Henry J. Kaiser Family Foundation, while nearly a third of adults have talked to a doctor about an advertised drug, only one in eight adults has actually received a prescription in response to seeing a drug ad.[8]

Erectile dysfunction is a serious problem that affects nearly thirty million men in America. Prior to Viagra, there were few options for those suffering from ED. Treatment might have included the use of a cumbersome vacuum pump, injection therapy, or penile prosthesis. But medical researchers Earl Mindell and Virginia Hopkins write in their book *Prescription Alternatives,* "The anti-impotent drug Viagra (sildenafil) is one of the most over-hyped, misused, and misunderstood drugs in the history of pharmaceuticals." They continue, explaining that good food, regular exercise, and herbs like ginkgo biloba "[aren't] just great for improving blood flow to the brain and improving memory, [they] improve . . . blood flow everywhere."[9]

Interestingly enough, Viagra was invented by accident. In 1992, Pfizer was working on the drug UK 92-480, which was thought to improve blood flow to the heart. Patients reported side effects, including the ability for an impotent man to achieve an erection and for men whose erections had been short-lived to maintain their erections for a longer period.

As Pfizer prepared to market the drug in 1997, the name Viagra was chosen: "'We liked it because it sounded strong,' says David Brinkley, the head of Pfizer's Team Viagra. 'Another name that was in the name bank was Alond, which seemed kind of—I don't know.' He shrugs. 'It sounds like elong. And it just doesn't roll off the tongue as well.'"[10] Almost immediately after the launch of Viagra, the drug became a household name. And its appeal was not diminished by an FDA report that 130 men, most of them heart patients, had died after using it—27 of them "during or immediately after sexual intercourse."[11]

On March 27, 1998, the FDA approved the sale of Viagra, and shortly thereafter, Pfizer released the little blue pill by prescription only. Where Viagra was not sold, men would travel across international borders to get prescriptions. In Japan, a travel agency booked special Viagra tours to Hawaii and Guam. In Brazil, the mayor of a small town promised to distribute Viagra in an effort to boost population and thereby increase federal aid. In London, the *Independent* reported that black-market Viagra was selling briskly in the city's nightclubs at a hundred dollars a pill.[12] In Nevada, prostitutes at a brothel called the Moonlight Bunny Ranch reported that Viagra was rejuvenating geriatric customers: "They're paying more and staying longer."[13]

Cline, Davis & Mann, an advertising firm that specializes in pharmaceutical campaigns in New York, created the ads for Viagra. Carol DiSanto, vice president of Cline, Davis & Mann, said, "It was our job as advertisers to establish the image. It's not the sex drug."[14] (However, it has been reported that many men who do not suffer from ED use Viagra for recreational purposes.) After trying numerous concepts, "The Dance" was chosen by the agency as a vehicle to show how the pill could put a spark back in one's romantic life. Holidays impact consumer behavior, and this commercial acknowledges that Valentine's Day celebrates relationships.

Aside from the traditional hearts, roses, and chocolates, Valentine's Day has a dark side to it. When we place our hearts on the line, we fear rejection and pray that we do not get bruised. Its iconographic symbol a heart pierced by a cupid's arrow, love can be represented with imagery of vulnerability and death intermingled with that of romance. The penetrated heart can also be interpreted as the male and female, the heart representing the reproductive organs and the arrow the phallic symbol. The combination may represent the union of these two forces in sexual coitus—this reading of the symbols is especially apt in the context of Valentine's Day's roots in ancient fertility-related festivals.[15]

Art Buchwald cites a marketing man as saying, "'If you present your boyfriend with a dozen Viagra tablets on Valentine's Day, you are sending him more than a message. You are telling him how much you love him, particularly if you give him a refill for the prescription on George Washington's birthday.'"[16] If this is true, will prescription drugs be the new fad in gift giving? Anyone prefer Humalog to Halloween treats? Will St. Nick leave Prozac on the mantel? Does Viagra come in a heart-shaped box?

Love, Hate, and Cover-Ups

Valentine's Day　Shannon Hughey

Valentine's Day is the holiday that infatuated people love and singles love to hate. It is the day that is designated as the opportunity for lovers to sweep their partners off their feet with acts of heroic romanticism. This perhaps explains why Valentine's Day could be considered the most competitive gift-giving holiday. The giver must outwit romantic surprises of Valentine's Days past—including his or her own. With this bombardment of love in the air, it is no wonder that Valentine's Day is also the day for bittersweet memories of lost loves.

With an estimated fifteen thousand tattoo shops in operation in the United States, what better way to prove that your love is forever than to tattoo your lover's name on your own flesh? Many people use such a method to show their dedication to their passions as well. According to *U.S. News & World Report*, tattooing has become one of America's fastest growing retail segments.[1] It has become a practice of commitment that is gaining acceptance.

But can the commitment to a loved one keep up with the permanence of a tattoo? Often tattooed couples intend to be together forever. But though the symbol of devotion will stand the test of time, it is difficult to say for sure that the relationship will have the same stamina. This is a common occurrence among celebrities and non-celebrities alike. The public has watched as many of the famous have gone through the relationship turmoil that may befall anyone. Angelina Jolie had "Billy Bob" tattooed on her upper arm after her marriage to Billy Bob Thornton— the tattoo was removed by costly laser surgery.[2] Pamela Anderson's "Tommy" wedding-band tattoo was changed to "Mommy" after the divorce. Halle Berry had a tattoo on her left buttock of her former husband's name, David Justice, outfielder for the Atlanta Braves, covered up with a large flower. Johnny Depp's tattoo from his relationship with Winona Ryder in the early 1990s—"Winona Forever"—has been changed to "Wino Forever." Depp has stated, "You have to look for the humor in these things, you know."[3]

Many tattoo artists are approached by people who want to cover up the scars of their past relationships. These artists replace seemingly permanent mementos with new ones, often for the better. Love also has a way of changing people. Most cover-ups result from breakups. But sometimes, tattoos inspired by an ex, even if there is no name or a partly disguised name, may be covered up by the tattooed person or at the request of a new lover. Jori Lakars of Tatu Tattoo in Chicago recalls one such situation:

> This cover-up was requested by a "walk-in" customer with a limited budget. He wanted to surprise his girlfriend of twelve years with the cover-up because he was planning on proposing to her. She wouldn't marry him yet because his ex-wife's name, "Rose," was still tattooed on his leg. After a short deliberation, we settled on the panther design because I could make it large enough to cover his old tattoo without going over his budget.[4]

When tattoo artists are asked for their opinions on cover-ups and tattooing couples, the full story comes out. Henry Lewis, tattoo artist at Mom's Body Shop in San Francisco, likes tattooing cover-ups because it provides a challenge that requires more problem solving than tattooing on blank skin.[5] Jori Lakars describes tattooing on Valentine's Day as twice the work for the same cost, since customers bring significant others along. When couples get tattooed at the same time, they

often suggest the content and placement of their partner's tattoos, or they are concerned about their significant other feeling pain during the process. When couples come in together, they demonstrate less trust in the tattoo artist than when they come in individually.[6]

Some say love is forever. This may be true, but tattoo artists can vouch for the fact that ink, too, is forever. And many would advise their customers to set some money aside for the day those feelings of infatuation begin to fade, so that it will always be possible to cover up a reminder of Valentine's Day past.

Before   After

Before   After

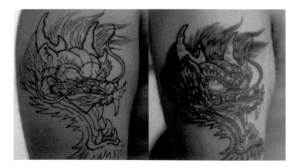

Before   After

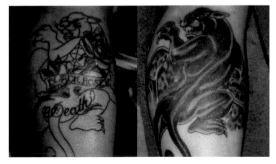

Before   After

Valentine's Day, Wedding Engagements, and Diamonds

Valentine's Day   Rebekah Levine

Valentine's Day is to love as diamonds are to marriage—the day and the jewels honor and decorate the joining of hearts. So it makes sense that the holiday has become one of plighting troths and selling diamonds. With the proliferation of marriage and dating reality shows on television, it is no wonder that the engagement has become a sales pitch at Valentine's Day. As diamond rings get purchased, proffered, and occasionally returned, their history reveals a complexity on par with the mysteries of love. Tiny, easily smuggled, and wildly expensive, the nature of diamonds also leads them to be at times an accessory to crime, from funding civil wars to beefing up terrorists' bank accounts. So the question is, how can this stone steeped in turmoil continue to shine so brightly? What is the real cost of love?

Valentine's Day began, according to one theory, with a February 14 holiday in honor of Juno, the Roman goddess of women and marriage. On the following day, a pagan holiday called the Feast of Lupercalia began. During

this feast, each young man would draw the name of the young woman who would be his sexual partner for the duration of the festival. These holidays seem to have merged into one in the Middle Ages, and St. Valentine was chosen to replace the pagan god Lupercus. Valentine had supposedly secretly married couples in the third century when Emperor Claudius banned the rite, arguing that single men were better soldiers. Valentine was jailed, then beheaded for his efforts.[1]

In the almost two thousand years since, marriage has become an increasingly complicated sacrament, and the diamond ring has become its wily mascot. The ring is, appropriately enough, the only type of jewelry made specifically to fit the wearer. It surrounds a finger, clasping it like a handshake, the oldest way of sealing a deal. Thus the ring symbolizes a contract. Diamonds, able to resist fire and metal, epitomize unyielding power and invincible strength. As the tradition goes, if the properties of the diamond, particularly its indestructibility, are passed to the wearer, then a marriage sealed with a diamond will surely last forever. In these complicated times, however, an engagement ring is available at Rent-a-Center, where rental of a ten-point diamond solitaire set in ten-karat gold costs $5.99 a week.[2] At the end of a year, payments will total $311.48 and ownership of the ring will be complete. It is possible to pay off the rental early at a discounted rate, but if second thoughts arise, the ring can be returned and the couple can walk away from the whole deal.

Enmeshed with the trials and tribulations of love, the diamond itself is steeped in myths that go back centuries, giving it the perfect Jekyll and Hyde facade. For instance, it is said that when the Bolsheviks murdered the tsar's family in Siberia in 1918,

> Several of the assassins were themselves wounded, because bullets bounced off the bodies of the royal family, as if they actually possessed the magical properties mystical Russian royalists traditionally attributed to the family of the tsar. The explanation was more prosaic: The tsar's family had large diamonds sewn into the lining of their clothes, which turned bullets away as if they were rubber and sent them flying back to strike their executioners. Like a girl's best friend.[3]

This special mystique of diamonds feeds easily into the cult of the American wedding, an epic event that has become increasingly large and overpriced and with a significance that gets impressed on young women as early as childhood. Whether promoted by Barbie, Disney, or Hollywood, what is conveyed is that a bride needs the right dress, the right invitations, the proper registry, the trendiest reception hall, the ideal song for the first dance . . . and most important, the perfect ring: the public marker of the groom's worth and perhaps the best and only outward evidence that a girl has found her prince.

Diamonds were rare before the nineteenth-century find of large deposits in southern Africa. The modern history of the cultural and economic power of diamonds starts with the discovery of a few rough diamonds on a farmer's land in South Africa in 1866. Miners from all walks of life traveled to South Africa, each digging to find his own jackpot. As a result, huge numbers of diamonds were dumped on the market at the same time, causing a steep drop in value and severely overextending the diamond market. British imperialist and business magnate Cecil Rhodes recognized the root of these problems, bought out many of the other diamond companies in a £5,338,650 deal (worth more than $200 million today), created the largest diamond company seen to that date, and formed De Beers Consolidated Mines in 1888.[4] He immediately decreased production, giving the diamond some of its value back. Since then, De Beers has mined approximately half the world's gem diamonds and controls two-thirds of the $8 billion market in uncut stones.[5] It still buys most of the world's uncuts from other mining companies and, hoarding them in a style pioneered by Cecil Rhodes, slowly releases stones when the market needs them badly. By rewriting the equation between supply and demand, and tweaking the equation itself, De Beers became one of the most successful cartels of the twentieth century.

In addition to controlling the market, De Beers wanted to sell diamonds to consumers. According to Edward Jay Epstein, author of *The Rise of the Diamond*, in the 1930s and 1940s, De Beers decided that diamonds needed enough sentimental value that they would not be resold by the public. The key was to make the diamond ring a necessity for every engagement. De Beers "hired the N. W. Ayer Advertising Agency [in New York City] to transform the public imagination about the diamond. To do that, the company hired psychologists to burrow into American buying habits . . . 'What the ads really did was concentrate on a combination of emotion and status,' said [Howard] Davis [a N. W. Ayer archivist] . . . 'The idea that they were trying to get across was that if you loved [your fiancee] enough, you're going to spend a months pay on [the diamond ring].'"[6] The campaign became so profitable that De Beers poured a fortune into diamond advertising during World War II[7]— and made a fortune in return. The company declared a 100 percent increase in dividends over 1940 and 1941 and reported that it was spending $500,000 per year on advertising and sales promotion in the United States.[8]

In 1947, a young copywriter at N. W. Ayer, Frances Gerety, created the famous advertising slogan "A diamond is forever." According to advertising lore, "Gerety coined the line after her nightly prayers, when she was awakened by a flash of inspiration. Within three years of creating the 'diamonds are forever' slogan, an estimated 80 percent of wedding engagements in America were consecrated with diamond rings. Gerety herself never wed, but she had wed a concept to diamonds."[9]

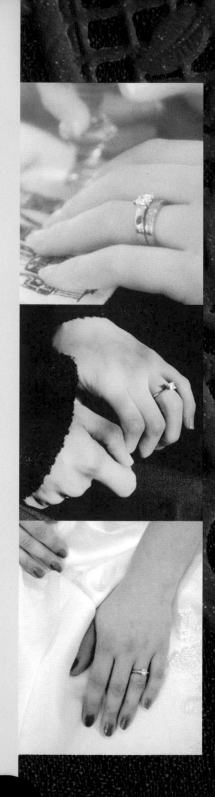

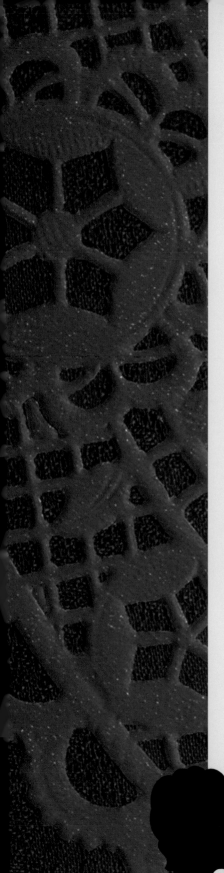

Not satisfied with the usual print and radio advertising, De Beers's agency branched out to get the message to a broad range of Americans. Transforming the consumer's imagination relied heavily on Hollywood and the widespread audience going to the movies during the Depression and World War II. De Beers lobbied directors to include diamond-related scenes in films and worked with N. W. Ayer to get Hollywood stars to wear diamonds for public appearances. One N. W. Ayer memo from the early 1940s strategized, "We spread the word of diamonds worn by [film] stars . . . women who can make the grocer's wife and the mechanic's wife say . . . I wish I had what she has."[10] In *Gentlemen Prefer Blondes*, Marilyn Monroe promotes the idea that the diamonds she receives will outlast the men who give them, and love altogether, giving many women the itch to own their own version of power.

The story of the diamond trade, though, is not solely the usual one of consumers being pumped up by ever more skillful advertising and marketing practices. The realities of the diamond trade in Africa, particularly in Angola, Sierra Leone, and the Congo, are quite literally bloody. The phrases "conflict diamonds" and "blood diamonds" have been adopted to distinguish diamonds brought into the diamond trade from inhumane situations. These diamonds have played a major part in keeping conflict funded in many countries. For example, Angola has been at war with itself since 1956. This war could never have continued for so long had it not been for the rewards of rebels' diamond trafficking.[11] According to an activist group, Fatal Transactions,[12] between 1992 and 1997 some five hundred thousand people have died in this brutal civil war, while tens of thousands more have been injured by land mines.[13]

The business of conflict diamonds also spreads beyond war-torn countries because diamonds are relatively easy to circulate. Before the September 11 attacks, the Al Qaeda terrorist network converted roughly $200 million into conflict diamonds mined by Sierra Leone's Revolutionary United Front.[14] Couriers exchanged about $300,000 in cash for diamonds every week between December 2000 and September 2001,[15] according to European government officials. Of this problem, Alex Yearsley of Global Witness, a group that works to highlight the links between the exploitation of natural resources and human-rights abuses,[16] says, "The ease with which terrorist organizations can use diamonds as a source of funding and money laundering is frightening. They can easily transport them over borders without detection and convert them back into bank notes whenever they need the money."[17]

As news of conflict diamonds began to reach the public in the 1990s, De Beers, spending $170 million on advertising in the year 2000,[18] saw that the image of beauty, purity, and love would be tarnished if the company did not take a stand against the atrocities. It went public in May 2000 to guarantee that none of its diamonds emanated from conflict areas in Africa and that it was in accord with U.N. Resolution 1173, claiming to have withdrawn buying operations from Sierra Leone and Liberia years before.[19] This is a difficult statement to prove, however, since provenance, but not necessarily origin, is required to be declared along with diamond sales.[20] So diamonds originating in these war-torn countries may be smuggled out and sold elsewhere with no mention of origin. But reforms are being implemented. Introduced in October 2001 and passed in March 2002, the Clean Diamonds Trade Act (H.R. 2722) broadens the definition of conflict diamonds. In addition to those used to fund civil wars in Africa, the bill includes diamonds traded by terrorists and by those who use the trade to commit human-rights violations. This bill complements and assists the ongoing Kimberley Process, "an international initiative aimed at breaking the link between legitimate trade in diamonds and conflict diamonds"[21] by empowering the U.S. Customs Service to permit diamond imports only from those countries that have adopted effective controls on the export and import of rough diamonds. New methods of gem identification are currently being developed that will make the "blueprint" of each stone evident and verifiable. The unique characteristics of each diamond would be mapped and put on file for law enforcement in case of troubles in the future. Systems such as these would require the participation of the diamond industry to be successful.[22]

Yet as Valentine's Day continues to make many a hopeful woman hold her breath with anticipation, the diamond's importance as a symbol of love continues. The mystique of the diamond, developed even before De Beers made its slogan a household phrase, has the power to override almost any form of negativity. Diamonds hold a liquidity of value and beauty that is unsurpassed. Old as history and poised to last an eternity, diamonds still embody the ideals of love, loyalty, power, and beauty—and the human tragedies of African diamond mining still remain relatively unknown in the United States. Diamonds can now represent everlasting love in yet another form: LifeGem Memorials of Chicago charges four to twenty-two thousand dollars for a synthetic diamond, made from the carbon you leave behind, that a family member can wear, taking the idea of eternal love a step further.[23]

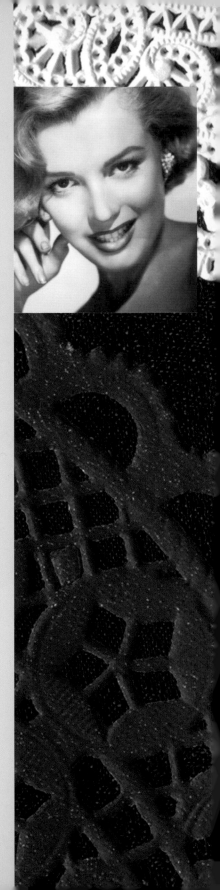

The Patriotism of Spending

Presidents' Day   Melanie Archer

In February 2003, northeastern U.S. retailers braced as a winter storm, now noted as one of the worst in the country's history, headed their way. Ordinarily, the coming of a few feet of snow would not evoke such terror, but the storm was scheduled to hit on one of the biggest sale weekends of the year—Presidents' Day. According to *Washington Post* columnist Art Buchwald, "Presidents' Day is the nearest thing to Christmas stores have. As a matter of fact, there wouldn't be a Christmas holiday season if there wasn't a Presidents' Day to mark down all the goods they didn't sell in December."[1]

Research from ShopperTrak, a company that collates retail sales statistics, shows that, in February 2001, the three-day Presidents' Day period accounted for 13.1 percent of total northeast retail sales for February.[2] In 2003, some $437 million in general merchandise sales was lost to the storm—year-to-year sales slipped nearly 6 percent on Saturday, 20 percent on Sunday, and 55 percent on Monday, the Presidents' Day holiday.[3] Such dismal figures prompted a Macy's representative to state, "I think I'm going to suck gas from the exhaust pipe of my Hummer."[4] Many stores extended their Presidents' Day sales until Tuesday, while others ran their special promotions again the following weekend in an attempt to recoup sales. There was much debate surrounding this second economic observance of the holiday. Has there ever been a Fourth of July sale on the eleventh? But according to a Lord & Taylor's representative, "I'm sure Washington wouldn't care if he knew it would help the economy."[5]

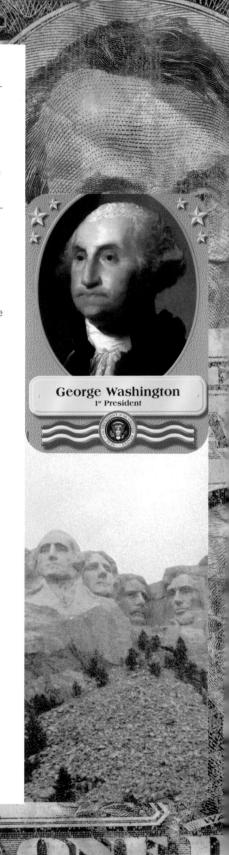

This second celebration of Presidents' Day is oddly reminiscent of Christmas in July—in both cases, a holiday's association with sale items is used to push merchandise, without much attention to the holiday's meaning. It is difficult to think of activities, celebrations, or ceremonies other than shopping that make the third Monday in February stand out from any other day of the year—grade-school colorings of the flag and readings of the Constitution notwithstanding. One interesting take on Presidents' Day argues that its modern observance is financially motivated: "The merchants decided that George Washington's Birthday was the perfect holiday. It was in February, and it was patriotic because it honored the father of our country—so you could take off an extra 15 percent."[6]

Even without the debate over glaringly obvious potential consumerism, the observance of Presidents' Day is a somewhat contentious issue. First, the federal holiday is still legally called Washington's Birthday. George Washington (1732–99) was the first president of the United States and has been hailed as the "indispensable man"[7] and one of the founders of the nation. He was born on February 11, which became February 22 when the British crown and its colonies moved to the Gregorian calendar in 1752.[8] His accomplishments included holding the Continental army together until the British (then in power) decided to relinquish their claim on the United States and presiding over the Constitutional Convention that created the world's oldest written constitution. Furthermore, when he became president, he stepped down as military commander and political leader, thereby disallowing any future Caesar or Napoleon in American politics. Most important, he provided, by character and example, a model of republican citizenship.[9]

Although U.S. citizens began to celebrate his achievements on February 22 even before the end of his presidency, Washington's Birthday did not become a federal holiday until 1879. Then, it was not until 1968 that the debate over the day began. That was the year that Congress passed the Monday holiday law, effective in 1971, moving federal recognition of Washington's Birthday to the third Monday in February.[10] For the sake of efficiency, the birthday of President Abraham Lincoln (1809–65) is celebrated on this day as well.[11]

Lincoln's birthday was paired with Washington's mainly because he was born on February 12—in the same month as the first president. Lincoln's birthday was never an official federal holiday, though by the centennial of his birth in 1909, it was a holiday in eight states.[12] Among Lincoln's celebrated achievements was his delivery of both the Gettysburg Address and a preliminary version of the Emancipation Proclamation. However, the fires he stoked by opposing slavery, along with his prosecution of the Civil War, are often cited as main reasons that his birthday was never federally recognized.[13]

George Washington
1st President

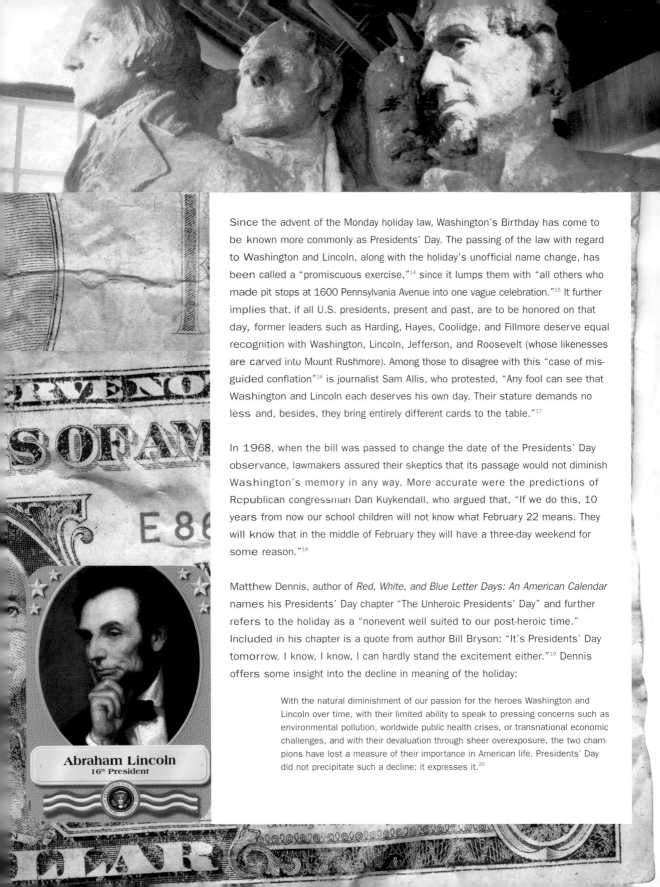

Since the advent of the Monday holiday law, Washington's Birthday has come to be known more commonly as Presidents' Day. The passing of the law with regard to Washington and Lincoln, along with the holiday's unofficial name change, has been called a "promiscuous exercise,"[14] since it lumps them with "all others who made pit stops at 1600 Pennsylvania Avenue into one vague celebration."[15] It further implies that, if all U.S. presidents, present and past, are to be honored on that day, former leaders such as Harding, Hayes, Coolidge, and Fillmore deserve equal recognition with Washington, Lincoln, Jefferson, and Roosevelt (whose likenesses are carved into Mount Rushmore). Among those to disagree with this "case of misguided conflation"[16] is journalist Sam Allis, who protested, "Any fool can see that Washington and Lincoln each deserves his own day. Their stature demands no less and, besides, they bring entirely different cards to the table."[17]

In 1968, when the bill was passed to change the date of the Presidents' Day observance, lawmakers assured their skeptics that its passage would not diminish Washington's memory in any way. More accurate were the predictions of Republican congressman Dan Kuykendall, who argued that, "If we do this, 10 years from now our school children will not know what February 22 means. They will know that in the middle of February they will have a three-day weekend for some reason."[18]

Matthew Dennis, author of *Red, White, and Blue Letter Days: An American Calendar* names his Presidents' Day chapter "The Unheroic Presidents' Day" and further refers to the holiday as a "nonevent well suited to our post-heroic time." Included in his chapter is a quote from author Bill Bryson: "It's Presidents' Day tomorrow. I know, I know, I can hardly stand the excitement either."[19] Dennis offers some insight into the decline in meaning of the holiday:

> With the natural diminishment of our passion for the heroes Washington and Lincoln over time, with their limited ability to speak to pressing concerns such as environmental pollution, worldwide public health crises, or transnational economic challenges, and with their devaluation through sheer overexposure, the two champions have lost a measure of their importance in American life. Presidents' Day did not precipitate such a decline; it expresses it.[20]

Abraham Lincoln
16th President

Much of the overexposure of which Dennis speaks occurs in the U.S. retail industry. Washington's and Lincoln's names and faces are featured by various companies and products, including Lincoln Logs, Lincoln Vehicles, and Washington Mutual. (Their highest circulation, though, is in currency—the one and five dollar bills, the quarter, and the penny.) They have also been featured in numerous ads in every form of media imaginable, for everything from cars to mattresses, vacations to department stores. They have been portrayed in illustrations as golf players, television watchers, vacationers, and businessmen. Mount Rushmore alone has been the subject of innumerable artistic interpretations of its four subjects. The presidents have been shown wearing modern outfits, and their likenesses often promote particular products thanks to crafty comic-strip speech bubbles. Dennis offers an explanation for the frequent use of these images: "Commercialization of famous figures and the holidays that commemorate them in the United States stems logically from the country's contemporary capitalist mode, which is dependent on consumption and commercialized leisure."[21]

Washington and Lincoln are undoubtedly among the United States' most instantly recognizable visages. That they are inextricably linked to patriotism affords consumers the luxury of equating products sporting their names or faces with the performance of civic duty. This idea of "consumption as patriotism,"[22] though, seems to have extended beyond the portrayal of presidents and into the lives of American consumers in general.

This phenomenon experienced a resurgence during the instability of the post–September 11 social and economic climate. On September 20, 2001, President George W. Bush delivered an address before a joint session of Congress to respond to the terrorist attacks. Solemnly he stated: "Americans are asking, what is expected of us?" The president then listed several sentimental suggestions: "Live your lives . . . hug your children . . . uphold the values of America . . . continue to support the victims of this tragedy with your contributions." Yet just before asking for prayers for the victims, their families, those in uniform, and the country, he said: "I ask your continued participation and confidence in the American economy. Terrorists attacked a symbol of American prosperity. They did not touch its source. America is successful because of the hard work and creativity and enterprise of our people. These were the true strengths of our economy before September 11th, and they are our strengths today."[23] In other words—hit the malls. This "consummate evocation of consumption as patriotism" drew numerous comments. Allan Sloan, a journalist from the *New York Times,* interpreted the speech by saying: "In our country's earlier days a president may have called for parades to stoke up patriotic fervor after such an attack, or for the sacrifice of

Presidential Seal

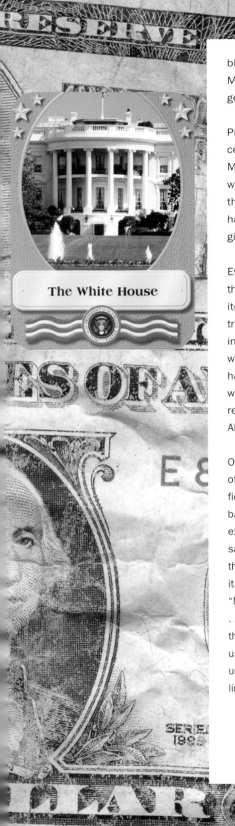
The White House

blood and treasure. But President Bush conflated patriotism with shopping. Maxing out your credit cards at the mall wasn't self-indulgence, it was a way to get back at Osama Bin Laden."[24]

Presidents' Day has been extensively criticized for its devolution from a day of celebration of Washington's and Lincoln's presidential greatness to just another Monday off. Much of this is blamed on the replacement of Washington's Birthday with Presidents' Day. Clyde Haberman, columnist for the *New York Times,* laments this decline: "For 30 years, the days commemorating our two greatest presidents have been kind of squished together into one more Monday holiday designed to give Americans a chance to do what they do best: sleep late and prowl the malls."[25]

Every year, millions of dollars are spent on advertising campaigns that champion the holiday. Cars, along with household goods, are one of the more heavily promoted items for Presidents' Day. In February 2003, Ford ran a television commercial trumpeting a Presidents' Day SUV sale with the usual catch lines—greatest bargains in history, never-before, never-again prices. But the presidents shown in the ad were Lincoln and Jefferson. Glaringly absent was Washington, even though he is half-owner of Presidents' Day, and legally speaking, Jefferson has nothing to do with the holiday. Journalist Bob Levey investigated the faux pas; according to his research, "Three different Ford departments blamed three different ad agencies. All apologized. Some chuckled. One swore that it would never happen again."[26]

Obvious errors aside, the predominant issue with Presidents' Day is not the use of presidents' images for the promotion of goods and services. It is that the sacrifices they made and the trials they endured for the United States seem to take a backseat to a good sale or zero-percent financing. Yet it would be unreasonable to expect that Washington's and Lincoln's birthdays would be celebrated today in the same manner in which they were a hundred years ago. Shopping seems to define the contemporary U.S. lifestyle. Without people spending money, how would a capitalist society survive? The *Harvard Design School Guide to Shopping* notes that "Not only is shopping melting into everything, but everything is melting into shopping . . . shopping has methodically encroached on a widening spectrum of territories so that it is now, arguably, the defining activity of public life . . . few activities unite us as shopping does."[27] If this observation is held as true, it does not seem so unreasonable that Presidents' Day seems to be permanently and inextricably linked to shopping: truth, liberty, and bargains for all.

Making Millions on Girls Gone Wild

Mardi Gras   Courtney S. Perkins

The wildest holiday in the United States is not New Year's Eve, despite its renowned drink-off in anticipation of midnight and beyond. Nor is it St. Patrick's Day, where in Chicago green beer flows as plentifully and in the same hue as its river. Instead the honor goes to the pre-Lenten debauchery in New Orleans known as Mardi Gras. Mardi Gras, which occurs on the day before Ash Wednesday, approximately forty-six days before Easter, is the time and place for drinking without moderation in the French Quarter, stumbling up and down Bourbon and Canal Streets, and doing various deeds, even flashing bare breasts, for Mardi Gras beads. The atmosphere in recent years has lent itself to a video entrepreneur capturing bare-breasted young women on tapes, documenting "girls gone wild."

Mardi Gras had been celebrated for centuries in Europe prior to coming to the United States and is rooted in both Christian and quasi-Christian beliefs. The U.S. supposedly saw its first Mardi Gras observance in 1699, when a French noble-man and his crew of explorers celebrated on an island in the Mississippi River, later named Mardi Gras Island, just downstream from today's New Orleans. This historical claim, however, is hotly debated. Mobile, Alabama, adamantly asserts that it hosted the earliest American Mardi Gras.[1] In fact, the first carnival for which a written description exists is alleged to have taken place in Mobile in 1705.[2] The festivities also took off in other cities—Memphis, St. Louis, and Houston—but in the end New Orleans came to reign over the yearly celebration.[3]

Mardi Gras, literally Fat Tuesday, marks the beginning of Lent. Often less zealously than originally intended, Roman Catholic devotees dedicate the Lenten season to repentance and fasting in preparation for Easter.[4] The European tradition was to eat and drink as much as possible on Fat Tuesday before giving up chosen vices on Ash Wednesday.[5] This ritual finds its roots in a Roman celebration called Saturnalia, which featured vast feasts of food and libation, as well as the selection of a mock monarch to rule over the festivities.[6]

In New Orleans today, the festivities linger for almost two months, a period of public parades and private balls, sponsored by private social clubs known as krewes. The efforts culminate on Fat Tuesday and expire on the stroke of midnight when New Orleans revelers are literally swept off their feet by police and street cleaners —allowed to resurface only in the wee hours of the morning. This Fat Tuesday is the peak not just of the two-month pre-Lenten indulgences but also of a year's worth of preparations:

> There are themes to be selected, proclamations to be read, balls to be planned, orchestras to be hired, stages and platforms to be built, parades to be routed, marching bands to be recruited, guests to be invited, costumes to be bespangled, cakes and ale to be ordered, royalty to be chosen, protocol to be practiced, and rites to be rehearsed.[7]

All of this preparation means money to be spent—lots of it.

Each year New Orleans receives approximately eight million visitors, 95 percent of them said to walk down Bourbon Street. Visitor spending for 2001 amounted to approximately $4.1 billion, of which a surprisingly large portion derived from Mardi Gras tourism.[8] Dr. James McLain, associate professor of economics at Tulane University, has estimated that overall carnival spending for 2000 in greater New Orleans was $1,056,124,885. Out of that billion-dollar sum, preparations, including krewe spending, parade spending, and individual ball and dinner-dance spending, accounted for only approximately $59 million.[9] The bulk of that money, then, consists of visitor spending. Therefore, one quarter of all the money spent by tourists throughout the year is spent during Mardi Gras festivities.

The profits for Fat Tuesday can be considered just that . . . fat. For example, the Mardi Gras revenue for the city government of New Orleans alone in 2000—with expenditures of only $6.2 million, primarily for police overtime—is $21.6 million; this does not include the overall revenues boasted by hotels, bars, and restaurants.[10]

In the end, Mardi Gras is a time for indulgences: food, drink, fodder, and wallet alike. New Orleans natives and local businesses are not the only ones profiting from Mardi Gras. In the larger consumer culture of the United States, the Mardi Gras tradition of bare breasts in exchange for plastic baubles was screaming to be packaged and sold. The crafty entrepreneur who effected this marketing coup was Joe Francis, the thirty-year-old mastermind of the extremely popular video series *Girls Gone Wild*. Since 1997, inspired by the scantily clad muse of Mardi Gras, he has documented young women between eighteen and twenty-five taking off their clothes for the camera. Francis recorded and profited from a tradition of flashing that began in the 1970s.

Francis graduated from the University of Southern California with a dual degree in business and film and television, and always had a particular interest in video. His first venture in an original reality-based series was entitled *Banned from Television*, which compiled images of shark attacks, train wrecks, public executions, and other shocking sequences. He would purchase video footage from amateur cameramen who could not do anything else with the film because of the gore factor.[11] He then marketed these videos with direct-response commercials on late-night television and was marginally successful. It was some amateur footage he received for *Banned*, of drunken college girls at Mardi Gras flashing their breasts for beads, that turned Francis on, both sexually and strategically.[12]

Francis wanted to capitalize on these women and what they had to offer. He himself states that *Girls Gone Wild* materialized as a product of his sexual fantasies: "Girls look really good from age eighteen to twenty-five. It's just a fact that that's the best time for girls. Afterward, things start to happen—bad things."[13] In order to capitalize on this alleged moment of glory, in 1997 Francis began soliciting such film from third-party cameramen. He took less than a month to assemble the footage and bought fifty thousand dollars worth of late-night commercial airtime. The videos did well enough to fund the next production.

Since then, Francis has produced more than eighty different *Girls Gone Wild* videos, ranging in price from $9.99 per cassette or DVD to $29.99 for a set marketed toward the more extreme viewer. In 2002, Francis's company, Mantra Entertainment, sold approximately 4.5 million videos.[14] The *Girls Gone Wild* commercials air over forty thousand times a year all over the United States.[15] According to an inside source, the series provides an estimated hundred-to-one return on its investment and frequently shows up on the list of *Billboard* Top 30 retail sellers.[16] In its first two years of selling tapes, Francis's company earned more than twenty million dollars.[17] As a result of these astronomical sales figures, Francis paired up with Mandalay Entertainment for a fictional film on the *Girls Gone Wild* series.[18] He also enlisted famed rappers such as Snoop Dogg and Eminem to host new video series.

Francis says that many women want to be in these infamous videos. He states, "I think definitely for a girl to be on *Girls Gone Wild* it's a status symbol. It's your 15 seconds of fame."[19] However, not all young women feel as if they have achieved a desired status after appearing in one of Francis's videos, commercials, or Web sites. In fact, since its inception, *Girls Gone Wild*'s parent company Mantra Entertainment has found itself in the legal hot seat more than a few times.

In June 2002, a Louisiana judge dismissed a case filed against the *Girls Gone Wild* producers by three minors who alleged that the producers invaded their privacy by filming them exposing their breasts at Mardi Gras in February 1999 and using their images without permission or compensation. Judge C. Hunter King dismissed the case with the comments:

> An individual, minor or not, that goes down into the French Quarter must be aware of what takes place during Mardi Gras. This is a well-publicized event that I think anyone local, and even those outside Louisiana, would know what to expect . . . They were consenting to the video and/or photographs that were taking place . . . Because when you [expose your body] on Bourbon Street or in a club and you know there is an individual with a video, certainly you must expect that this is going to be shown all over the place.[20]

The minor complainants did not appeal the decision.

In contrast, a Florida State student, Becky Lynn Gritzke, filed an action in Florida in January 2002 alleging invasion of privacy and use of her image or likeness without permission; she sought monetary damages for the videos sold as well as an injunction on any continued video sales with her image.[21] Gritzke appears on a tape, bare breasts in hand, with a wide smile, but despite her jubilant appearance, she claims she did not consent. She was informed of her inclusion by a friend who saw her on a billboard advertising the video series in Italy. Ronald Guttman,

attorney for Francis, said, "What one does in public does not give rise to invasion of privacy claim, because there is no expectation of privacy."[22] As for the lack-of-consent issue, Guttman claimed that a legal exception to consent exists when someone does something newsworthy: "Clearly what she was doing was both newsworthy and of public interest."[23] The *Girls Gone Wild* producers eventually settled with Gritzke for an undisclosed settlement for damages and the agreement to remove her from any future video sales, commercials, and Web sites.

It seems this is a labor of love for Joe Francis, love of money and of women baring all. But despite various legal setbacks, Francis is happy with what he has: two homes, one in Bel Air and one in Tahoe, six cars, two jets, and one helicopter. However, these million-dollar baubles have been put at risk by the recent arrest of Francis and three other employees of Mantra in Panama City, Florida, in early April 2003. Francis was charged with drug trafficking and racketeering related to prostitution after the parents of five underage girls, four seventeen-year-olds and one sixteen-year-old, claimed that Francis solicited the girls to act out nude scenes on camera with the knowledge that they were underage.[24] Allegedly, the girls encountered a *Girls Gone Wild* van and were asked to play nude scenes in a motel for which they would be paid a hundred dollars. After a police search of Francis's cars, various electronic equipment, original footage, and five locations plus his two jets, police discovered videotapes that corroborated the girls' stories.[25] Francis could face up to thirty-five years in jail for the charges.

Hot Cross Buns:
Ash Wednesday Rising

Ash Wednesday **Melanie Archer**

Hot cross buns are average-sized pastries adorned with a crucifix on top, usually priced between four and twenty dollars a dozen. Variations abound. Some buns contain currants or raisins; many are decorated with a cross of icing, others with a cross formed from the dough of the bun itself. The sale of hot cross buns in bakeries is seasonal: seasonal goods boost sales and make it easier for consumers to celebrate holidays with a culinary twist. But there is something special about the buns. They are not merely generic cakes or cookies that can be decorated with colored frosting, iced ghosts, hearts, or Christmas trees to herald different holiday seasons. In fact, hot cross buns derive from the bread that was once eaten by ancient tribes who would sacrifice an ox (called a "boun" by the Saxons, leading to our word "bun") to their gods for a bountiful crop. After the ritual, the tribes would eat cakes marked with the symbol of the ox horns; this custom was later adapted by the leaders of the early Christian church, who interpreted the ox horns as a sign of the cross on which Jesus died.[1]

Hot cross buns may not be the biggest seller in today's bakeries, but they can claim in their entirety to be a representation of Lent—the period initiated by the observance of Ash Wednesday and terminated by Easter. This fact has not been overlooked by the Retailer's Bakery Association, which strives to push baked goods at every opportunity, even during the anti-consumption season of Lent. The RBA Web site's business-program page sports the headline "Increasing bakery profits with seasonal, theme-based items and merchandizing." The site asks: "Looking to boost sales in your ethnically-diverse community? Need extra sales during slower seasons? Welcome to the 7th Paczki system of Sales Campaign." The Paczki system analyzes slower retail bakery periods and strives to find baked items that correspond. RBA says, "This time-tested winner is all about reviving traditions with your customers that translate to extra sales for your bakery."[2]

The layman's translation of that statement as applied to Ash Wednesday might read: "Hear ye, bakers! Sales are mighty slow in March—no Christmas, no Valentine's Day, no Mother's Day, no huge cake-selling holiday, and we need something to fill this retail gap. Maybe we should try to find a traditional seasonal pastry and shape it to suit our financial needs." Enter the feisty and willing hot cross bun, listed for the March to April selling period. It is listed with the Mardi Gras King Cake for December to March, the Polish Paczki for January to March, and the Danish kringle for November to December.[3] RBA goes on to devote a page to the definition, history, and description of the buns, concluding with the offer of a convenient free promotional guide and kit packed with marketing strategies, promotional ideas, formulas, and more.

But RBA is not just in the business of selling hot cross buns; it is in the business of selling an ideal. What the association focuses on is the unsaid depiction of a traditional way of life—a moment of domestic perfection, featuring gleaming, fresh, aromatic buns emerging from the oven surrounded by a halo of heavenly light. It also underlines the importance of maintaining or reviving traditions once held by our ancestors and passing on family moments and values. The buns, at first popular in England,[4] have made their way onto bakers' shelves in the United States. With their crucifix, the buns at one time were the primary edible symbol of Lent and Easter—until the sudden rise of symbolically inexplicable chocolate eggs and marshmallow bunnies.

Hot cross buns are also available around the country at grocery stores' in-house bakeries. Like many other foods, the traditional buns have been modernized to suit the more mature and discerning palettes of today. It seems that keeping up with tradition—however altered the tradition has become—is more important than the meaning behind the tradition. For example, Ash Wednesday marks the beginning of Lent, a period that recalls Jesus' forty days of fasting in the wilderness to redeem the world from its sins. Christians, many of whom attend church on this day to be somberly adorned with ashes, are supposed to abstain from meats and other rich foods. So how do hot cross buns, delicious, sweet, and rich, factor into this equation of restraint? Maybe they were more sober at one time; today, however, they seem oddly incongruous with the Lenten period, especially if the ingredients are taken into consideration.

Hot cross buns' ingredients vary according to the baker. But there is an ever-present threesome: sugar, eggs, and butter. What is so special about these? Well, at one time, these ingredients were forbidden during Lent by Christian doctrine.[5] The key ingredients in early buns were flour, salt, and water—adhering to the idea of epicurean restraint and self-denial. Today, it is safe to say that sugar has effortlessly trumped religious significance, and it comes as no surprise that the recipe has changed over the years into a tasty treat that includes the "sinful" items consumers find more appealing. Today's bun is a yeast-raised item, best made from a bun or coffee-cake dough.

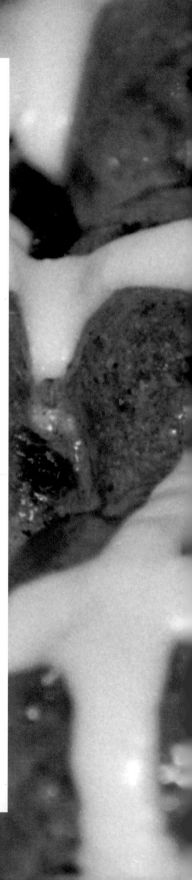

Depending on preference, it can include raisins and diced fruit, or a dried fruit mix, and spices such as nutmeg, cinnamon, clove, and allspice. Once the buns are baked, they are washed with a warm, simple syrup; rolled icing or a fondant glaze is used to form the cross after the buns have cooled.[6]

Baked goods in general enjoy immense popularity in America. They are considered to be impulse buys, which is why bakeries tend to be located at the front of the supermarket, up there with the gum, candy, and magazines. How many innocent people have stopped in their tracks on the way to the detergent or ketchup, assaulted by the delectable smell of fresh-baked something wafting across the aisles? According to *Modern Baking*, fresh bakery products accounted for over $500 million in sales in supermarkets alone for the four-week period ending April 25, 1999; unit sales were over 300 million.[7] Furthermore, a study done by the Food Marketing Institute shows that in-store bakery sales as a percentage of total grocery sales were at about 3.3 percent in 1998—a figure that translates into $13 billion in revenue for sugary baked treats. This figure represents three different categories of production—bake-off, scratch-mix, and thaw-sell. Or in other words—fresh baked goods, boxed goods, and refrigerated and frozen goods. Hot cross buns fall under the umbrella of fresh baked rolls and buns, in-store sales of which topped $117 million during a single four-week period in 1999.[8] With that figure in mind, it is no surprise that the more conventional but less marketable unsweetened version of the hot cross bun can safely be declared extinct.

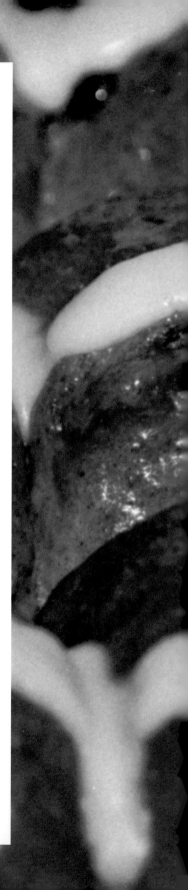

As for the newer, sweet version, hot cross buns are no chocolate chip cookie, but there are indications that they are gaining popularity in the Unites States. An April 2001 food column in the *Rocky Mountain News* in Denver, Colorado, proudly champions the buns, bestowing those of the Rheinlander German Bakery with the honor "Bread of the Week." Columnist John Lehndorff writes, "They are eggy, yeasty treats laced with raisin and candied fruit. Atop each is a thick plus sign of dense, white, shiny frosting. Break open one of the big, soft, yeasty pillows and your nose is tempted by an alluring lightly spiced perfume. Hot cross buns cost a hefty $1.19 each and are worth every penny. Order ahead."[9]

Half a continent away in New York City, Tom Newman is in search of a hot-cross-bun baker. He posted a message on the "What's My Craving?" message board of the food-sleuth Web site Chowhound: "Around Easter, we used to get good fresh hot cross buns at Lafayette Bakers on Bleecker [Street] at Seventh Ave. Alas, they are no longer there, and we are looking for a new source. Does anyone know of any possibilities within Manhattan?"[10] Four enthusiastic replies later, it may be hoped that Newman has found a replacement and once again enjoys the buns around Easter time.

It is sometimes difficult to find hot cross buns outside the Lenten period. But in Chiu Quon Bakery in Chicago's Chinatown, one chilly day in October, I was faced with fifty-five-cent pastries that looked suspiciously like hot cross buns. They were of the same shape and size and were adorned with icing that looked like some sort of impression-istic interpretation of a cross. Was this the real item? I soon learned that those buns, named "custard buns," are available year-round and are commonplace in the Chinese baked-goods market. Thus, what I was looking at was yet another predecessor of hot cross buns, this one dating back to the symbolic bun that was eaten in China to honor specific gods. But I couldn't bring myself to try one—Ash Wednesday, after all, was still six months away.

Hot Cross Buns (makes 24 buns)

1 cup scalded milk	4 cups sifted flour
½ cup butter	¾ teaspoon cinnamon
½ cup sugar	1 cup currants
1 teaspoon salt	1 egg
1 cake compressed yeast	1 tablespoon water
1 egg, well beaten	Icing

Pour the scalded milk over the butter, sugar and salt; cool to lukewarm. Add the crumbled yeast and let rest for 5 minutes. Add the egg, flour, and cinnamon to make a soft dough. Fold in the currants. Let rise in a warm place (80-85°F.) until double in bulk — about 2 hours. Shape into large buns and place an inch apart on a buttered baking sheet. Let rise in a warm place until double in bulk about 1 hour. Brush tops of buns with 1 egg slightly beaten with 1 tablespoon of water. Bake in a preheated oven for 20 minutes at 400°F. When cold decorate top of each bun with a cross, using the following icing:

Place ½ egg white in a small mixing bowl. Using a wooden spoon, beat in as much powdered sugar as the egg white will absorb and add 1 teaspoon of lemon juice gradually as the mixture thickens. Spread at once as mixture hardens quickly.

– House + Garden
May 1956
Ethel M. Kesting

Spending the Green

St. Patrick's Day   Melanie Archer and Raymond Lee

St. Patrick's Day celebrations in the United States do not occur unnoticed. Millions proudly trumpet their Irish heritage; regardless of how far removed that heritage may be, a person runs the risk of being pinched for not wearing green. Leprechauns roam city streets without causing concern, and several rivers and numerous beers are presented in kelly green. According to Frank Jordan Jr., a second generation Irish-American, "I think that Irish Americans celebrate St. Patrick's Day more than the Irish. It's a day of pride. We get a day all to ourselves to celebrate our music and dance and culture and poetry."[1] This March 17 celebration of all things Irish seems far removed from the holy day of obligation that occurs thousands of miles away in Ireland.

St. Patrick, the patron saint of Ireland, was born in Wales around 385 C.E. Then named Maewyn, he was a pagan who, at the age of sixteen, was captured and sold as a slave to a druid in Ireland. During his captivity, he became closer to God, and after six years of hardship, he escaped and traveled to Gaul, where he studied Christianity for twelve years. Memories of the Emerald Isle remained with him, and around 420, convinced that his mission was to convert Irish pagans to Christianity, he returned to Ireland as the country's second bishop.[2]

Patrick (his adopted Christian name) succeeded in converting many pagans and established monasteries, schools, and churches. He retired after a thirty-year mission and died on March 17, 461—the day observed as St. Patrick's Day ever

since.[3] Until the late 1970s, all the pubs in Ireland closed on St. Patrick's Day because, along with Christmas and Good Friday, it was one of three holy holidays on the Irish Catholic calendar.[4]

In the United States, though, early celebrations of St. Patrick's Day, while still honoring St. Patrick, were used by Irish immigrants as a vehicle to show their solidarity and pride. In light of the hostile work and social environments that these immigrants faced, this pride was paramount in the first public observances of the holiday.

Approximately 38.7 million Americans (one in every eight) can trace their ancestry fully or partly to Ireland.[5] Most Irish immigrants came to the United States in the mid-nineteenth century, following the famine that struck their native land in 1845. Irishmen and -women, who had struggled under English rule since the 1500s, were forced to give up their land, were restricted in the practice of their Catholic faith, and were subjected to the increasing use of English rather than Gaelic. By 1861, Ireland had lost almost one-third of its population;[6] between 1820 and 1920, more than 4.4 million people emigrated from Ireland to America.[7]

Sadly, freedom, acceptance, and opportunity did not immediately welcome Irish immigrants to the United States. Americans of British heritage and Protestant faith blatantly showed their hatred of and prejudice toward the Irish. The first immigrants—mainly farmers with limited skills and little education—found it difficult to find employment in America's cities. The few jobs offered to them paid pitifully low wages and were often manual labor in mining or laying railroad track. Thousands died while helping to construct amenities in a country that held them in disdain.

Anti-Irish riots, such as the one in Boston in 1837, served as displays of American society's hostile views toward the Irish.[8] While some settlers suffered in silence, others rebelled. In 1859, Jersey City railroad workers tore up tracks that they themselves had laid to protest withheld pay. More Irish lives were lost when protesters were shot by the police.[9] Increasingly, immigrants' celebration of St. Patrick's Day became a way to demonstrate unity and a chance to turn "the spotlight on the position of the diaspora within their host society."[10] These early festivities were modest—the first publicly held one was a small gathering on March 17, 1737, organized by the Charitable Irish Society of Boston.[11]

Between 1845 and 1856, 2.5 million people left Ireland, most for America.[12] The increase in numbers led to larger public St. Patrick's Day events, which helped to establish Irish immigrants as a legitimate entity in their new homeland but also

led to accusations that the Irish skewed the meaning of St. Patrick's Day to suit specific purposes. By the 1860s, the holiday began to display heavy political messages. Besides its representation of the struggle within America, it was used by "Irish-Americans as a way of focusing attention on the position of the Irish back home, and for Irish nationalists [it also revealed] the ongoing political battle against the British presence in Ireland."[13] Such causes found ideal footing in America, since it was a land that had already struggled to gain independence from the British. Exiled members of the Fenians, along with numerous other political activists, came to America and used St. Patrick's Day parades as a megaphone to voice their beliefs. An article in the *New York Times* in 1872 argued that St. Patrick's Day had become "perverted to the apparent purpose of [the Irishman] displaying his numerical strength, and to manifesting his consciousness of his own power."[14]

Interesting to note is that the first St. Patrick's Day parade was held not in Ireland but in New York City on March 17, 1766, when immigrant Irishmen who had fought in the Revolutionary War introduced the old-world holiday to the U.S.[15] After the War of 1812, local Irish fraternities and charitable societies started to sponsor the parade. In 1851, the Irish 69th Regiment (now the 165th Infantry) became the lead marchers in the parade, and the Ancient Order of Hibernians—a known supporter of Irish nationalist movements—an official parade sponsor.[16] Over the years, the initially small group grew exponentially. In 1867, the parade boasted some twenty thousand marchers; in 1936, forty thousand; and in 1947, eighty thousand. In 1948, national acceptance of and respect for the Irish and St. Patrick's Day rose significantly when U.S. president Harry S. Truman attended the parade in New York. His participation in the event, coupled with his acknowledgment of Irish-American World War II veterans, confirmed "the significance and success of the Irish community in modern America."[17] An even greater victory for the Irish-American community occurred twelve years later when Irish-Catholic-American John F. Kennedy was elected president of the United States.

In spite of society's changed perception of the Irish, political motivations have sprinkled even the most recent of St. Patrick's Day celebrations. In the midst of 2003's concerns over imminent war, President George W. Bush attended Chicago's parade, and New York City's mayor Michael R. Bloomberg participated in Manhattan's event, "[turning] Fifth Avenue into something of a mayoral treadmill, marching up the avenue, then doubling back via his motorcade."[18] He marched the parade route a total of four times: with the Police, Fire, Corrections, and Sanitation Departments. While the crowd's reception was positive, a few people heckled the mayor to protest the city's plan to close several firehouses. Also proclaiming their causes were gay protesters who were barred from marching in the parade under their own banner[19]—perhaps one of the more controversial parade issues today. In recent years, members of the Irish Gay and Lesbian Organization of New York have marched in protest alongside the parade; unable to participate formally, they are nevertheless seen by many.[20]

In 1995, the Supreme Court ruled unanimously in a Boston case that St. Patrick's Day parade sponsors had the right to exclude homosexuals or others, and that the organizers could choose the content of their message.[21] This right to exclude gays is particularly ironic in light of a history in which the parade served to enlighten U.S. citizens on the plight of the oppressed citizens of Ireland and to diminish prejudice and discrimination against Irish-American citizens.

Contemporary celebrations have changed in focus. With Irish-Americans settled comfortably into American society, St. Patrick's Day is no longer needed to make a social or political statement: the "dynamic that demanded Irish Americans be recognized by the wider society within which it lived is now irrelevant."[22] With its original objectives diminishing, St. Patrick's Day appears to have found a new purpose. One of its main roles today is to showcase and celebrate elements of Irish-American culture. Innumerable businesses go green around St. Patrick's Day—many of them bars or restaurants that rely on Irish iconography or traditions to boost sales. The commercial power of the shamrock alone is astounding. (According to commonly held lore, it was once used by St. Patrick to explain the Holy Trinity—the Father, Son, and Holy Spirit.)[23] Restaurants book Irish singers, dancers, and bagpipers, bars advertise specials on beer—green or otherwise—clothing stores and costume parlors offer Irish-themed items ranging from T-shirts to leprechaun costumes, and organizations host Irish lunches, brunches, and

dinners. The Irish Plumber, which serves most of Chicago, receives 50 percent more calls on March 17 than on any other day. Says owner Jack Simonson Jr., who is Irish: "Everyone wants the Irish Plumber in their house on St. Patrick's Day. There's no time for drinking."[24] Irish foods are also popular in March, particularly corned beef and cabbage. For instance, about twenty-five thousand pounds of cabbage are sold around this time of year at Valli Produce in Arlington Heights, Illinois.[25]

Today, it is nearly impossible to find signs of the early discrimination against Irish immigrants. Irish culture has entered the U.S. mainstream, and St. Patrick's Day is loved and celebrated by Americans of varying heritages, races, creeds, and religions. People demand and receive kisses based solely on their Irish heritage, and Irish-themed jokes are told out of affection, not disdain. Celebrities do not hesitate to reveal their Irish heritage—some even rely on it to increase their ratings. A quintessential example is *Late Night with Conan O'Brien*. Hailed as "the Original Irish Jackass,"[26] the funny and irreverent O'Brien frequently jokes about his Irish-American upbringing and residual habits and physique—often adding a gibberish-inspired Irish brogue.

Another way the media profits from St. Patrick's Day is by televising the St. Patrick's Day parades held in most major U.S. cities. In 2003, there were approximately 150,000 marchers in New York's St. Patrick's Day parade,[27] a number that was eclipsed by the estimated two million spectators.[28] While many consider the parade a tradition and attend it to witness and support the showcase of Irish culture, Lisa LaPenna, a parade onlooker from Pennsylvania, stated that she attended the event not knowing anything about it: "They told me it's the world's biggest drink-fest. I didn't know anything about a parade. What do I know, I'm 100 percent Italian."[29] Atlanta's parade, billed as the nation's second largest, usually has about four hundred thousand viewers.[30] While New York's parade organizers exclude floats, vehicles, and corporate signs and banners, this is not the case in most other cities—including Chicago.

In 1994, the larger of Chicago's two St. Patrick's Day parades had more than sixty floats, thirty-two marching bands, forty-eight marching groups, twenty-four special units,[31] and a long list of corporate sponsors. People who wished to partici-pate in the 1994 parade could meet in front of Kincade's, an Irish pub, and pay ten dollars to board a bus that joined the parade at noon. Added by 2003 were a thirty-five-foot-tall leprechaun and a forty-five-foot-long dinosaur at the parade reviewing stand.[32] Chicagoans also celebrate St. Patrick's Day in grand style by dyeing the Chicago River a bright kelly green. Forty-one years of trial and error have seen the perfection of the technique that is carried out by a five-man team on the morning of the parade. In 2003, fifty pounds of dye, costing approximately $1,200, were used in the process, which was accompanied by the Shannon Rovers bagpipe band and viewed by many. According to the Rovers bagpipe major, Bill McTighe, the dyeing has become "an event onto itself." So well known and loved is the river tinting that the crew has been flown to Dublin, Ireland, to color the River Liffey.[33]

The popularity of St. Patrick's Day in the United States has led to recent calls to make it a national holiday. On March 17, 2003, the *Chicago Sun-Times* ran an article on the topic featuring quotes from several celebrities that perhaps reflect some broader views. Sports broadcaster Howie Long joked that he thought the day was already a federal holiday, adding, "I'm from Boston. I thought it was. I didn't know there was a question." More serious were the views of television star Danny Masterson, who explained, "My great-grandfather had to change his name, coming over from Ireland, just to get a job. So I think the country owes us a holiday!" The opinions of talk-show host Jimmy Kimmel reflected the influence of Irish pub culture: "St. Patrick's Day means fun, drinking, eating things that aren't supposed to be green, and more drinking. If that isn't worthy of official recognition, I don't know what is. It beats the hell out of Flag Day."[34]

A major advocate of the official holiday push is Diageo, the company behind the U.S. marketing of Guinness, which has been hailed as St. Patrick's Day's most authentic beer. A 2003 survey conducted by Guinness revealed that 51 percent of Chicagoans older than twenty-one would favor the creation of an official holiday.[35] It is interesting to note that the survey does not include eighteen- to twenty-year-olds, who possess the right to vote but not to buy alcohol. Additionally, the company, through radio ads and bar displays, directed consumers to Guinness.com where they could learn about the campaign and even sign petitions online. Guinness also distributed petitions at pubs and posted information on the Web site for a prize sweepstakes.

The name Guinness is synonymous with Ireland. St. Patrick had a personal brewer named Mescan, whose knowledge and skill were passed through generations. In 1759, Arthur Guinness introduced the then mysterious dark brew,[36] which is now Ireland's number-one beer and a worldwide favorite. Approximately 1.9 billion pints of Guinness are served around the world each year,[37] and an estimated 10 million every day.[38] In March 2002, the brew was the subject of the "Beer of the Week" column in the *Denver Post*. Guinness's virtues were extolled by columnist Dick Kreck, who spoke of the "rich, creamy texture of the beer, which is a mouthful of flavor." He added, "The dark black brew with its lacy head residue clinging to the sides of the glass as it is drained have inspired poetry."[39]

In the early 1990s, many aspects of Irish culture were mainstreamed. The popularity of musicians of Irish heritage—Sinéad O'Connor, U2, and even Riverdance—was enormously influential. With the marketing potential of St. Patrick's Day growing stronger and stronger, Guinness launched heavy ad and promotional campaigns throughout March. One of the more unusual promotions was the Annual Guinness Pub Give-Away, first introduced in 1997 and now retired. The contest gave away a pub in Ireland to the person who could best convey love for Guinness in fifty words or less. There were approximately thirty thousand entrants. The follow-up promotion in New York City, called the Guinness Fleadh (Gaelic for festival), drew a large crowd that was treated to performances by popular Irish musicians including Van Morrison and Elvis Costello.

But Guinness's largest promotion, in terms of crowd participation, occurs in the days leading up to St. Patrick's Day. For this annual event, the Great Guinness Toast, people visit local pubs at a designated time to perform a simultaneous toast across the United States. With over 320,000 participants in 2000 and about 545,000 in 2002, this clever marketing ploy (for who would dare toast with anything but Guinness?) made it indisputable that "Guinness was successfully marketed as 'the drink' for St. Patrick's Day; it has become as much a symbol of celebration as shamrocks, leprechauns, or shillelaghs."[40]

The financial payoff of Guinness's sagacious marketing is evident. By 2000, Ireland was sixth in the world in number of gallons of Guinness imported into the U.S.—a figure that had grown 16.6 percent since the previous year. And among the hundreds of domestic and imported beers available in America, Guinness was ranked thirty-third on a list of the top 115 in 2000.[41] These figures reflect a consistent, targeted marketing approach—an approach that, in 2002, was backed by an $11.5 million advertising budget.[42]

Guinness's figures demonstrate how St. Patrick's Day has been marketed to suit modern American culture, as do more subtle social indicators. According to *Arlington Heights Daily Herald* columnist Diana Dretske, "America put the party in St. Patrick's Day."[43] This day that originally honored Ireland's patron saint in a holy manner and later served as a political platform now is primarily a showcase, a giant party, an excuse to drink oneself into a stupor. Even though Catholic masses are offered on St. Patrick's Day, it is now celebrated as a secular holiday—a transition reminiscent of Christmas, but to a much greater degree. It is difficult to imagine bars open on December 25, and those who overindulge at family gatherings on Christmas Day would likely choose eggnog or mulled wine—not beer.

While the U.S. has adopted (and adapted) Ireland's pub culture, St. Patrick's Day celebrations in Ireland—formerly modest—now incorporate U.S.-inspired elements. Irish essayist and novelist Nuala O'Faolain observed that "Ireland got smart and copied the entertainment values used in American parades. Instead of just a few dozen baton twirlers, now we've got displays, lights and music."[44] In addition to the parade are fireworks, concerts, and festivals. This intermingling of cultures is commonplace in the United States, where no group's traditions have remained unaltered. Evolution is inevitable and often leads to interesting and unique hybrids of tradition. Consumerism continues to be a major factor in U.S. St. Patrick's Day celebrations, a phenomenon that would have seemed unlikely considering the initial hardships of Irish immigrants.

Yet the observance of St. Patrick's Day has persisted for over 250 years. Over time the holiday has thrived and won first the respect and then the affection of many. Its success is no doubt based in part on evolution in an ever-adjusting society, in part on thoughtful marketing ploys, and in part on the infallible luck of the Irish.

GENUINE
4-Leaf Clover
Good Luck

ERIN GO BRAGH

Palms and More

Palm Sunday   Shayla Johnson

palm
1. any of a family (Palmae, the palm family) of mostly tropical or subtropical monocotyledonous trees, shrubs, or vines with usu. a simple stem and a terminal crown of large pinnate or fan-shaped leaves
2. a leaf of the palm as a symbol of victory or rejoicing; *also:* a branch (as of laurel) similarly used
3. a symbol of triumph; *also:* VICTORY, TRIUMPH
4. an addition to a military decoration in the form of a palm frond esp. to indicate a second award of the basic decoration

The word *palm,* although simple and quite common, carries a variety of associations and origins. Its meaning is wide-ranging, colorful, and symbolic of the palm's "outstretched" character. In ancient times, palm branches symbolized victory and triumph, even in celebrations of the military. The Romans used them to reward champions of athletic games. For Jews, carrying palm branches was a common practice during festive occasions. According to biblical texts, when Jesus entered Jerusalem before his last Passover, a multitude including Greeks, Jews, and Pharisees welcomed him, and some took "branches of palms" into their hands. The Christians in Jerusalem would later reenact Christ's triumphant entry into the city. By about the fifth century, the ritual spread to Egypt, then to Syria and Asia Minor. In Constantinople, even branches from such plants as olive and myrtle trees, lilac blossoms, and laurel fronds were blessed and handed out.[1] Naturally, cold weather in certain regions did not permit the growth of palm or olive trees. However, branches—whether willow or palm—were taken home and displayed as a visible symbol of Christ's presence. Hence, Palm Sunday.

This holiday occurs on the Sunday before Easter, and it is celebrated today with similar respect for the palm. The palm also thrives in the home, as more living rooms are adorned with folded and woven palm fronds. They are typically entwined in a crucifix or other icon that signifies salvation, serving as a pledge of protection and blessing. The celebration has come to include crafts projects using palm branches that children can take part in. "People like the idea of spiritual or sacred things in the home," says Sister Cecilia Schmitt, who is considered to be a one-woman crusade after the 1999 publication of her *Palm Weaving: The Story . . . and the Art*.[2] Her goal, she says, is to restore the practice of palm weaving, which is now increasing in popularity. Crafts enthusiasts can order supplies by phone or via the Internet from such places as the In His Name Catholic Store in Raleigh, North Carolina.[3]

Schmitt, a nun and music teacher in St. Cloud, Minnesota, has sold approximately three thousand copies of her self-published book on palm weaving.[4] Her main targets are the thousands of people in Wisconsin who bring home this "prehistoric plant" on Palm Sunday. She says, "Our thrust is 'keep the tradition alive.'" A three-thousand-dollar grant from the Minnesota State Arts Board enabled her to collect patterns of palm crafts and the oral histories behind them. She feels that the "tradition of blending ethnic craftsmanship with patient piety is dying out in today's fast-paced society."[5] She has since published a second book with forty palm-weaving patterns and guide sheets and released a videotape that provides instructions for several dozen designs and for the process of preparing palm leaves.

What is most interesting, according to Sister Schmitt, is that the craft is popular with senior citizens in their seventies, then skips a generation, and is embraced by younger parents in their late twenties and thirties. It stems from a tradition practiced primarily among Italians from Sicily and Poles. In a recent interview, Schmitt recalls that her German-American grandfather would "take some of the palms and bury them in the corners of the various fields as a prayer for God's blessings. Every building would have a cross above the doors where the people walked." Her research found that these outward displays of religion were common among Italians. Many who braid or fold palms are Roman Catholic. However, the *Milwaukee Journal Sentinel* reports that one member of the local Lutheran church has commented on the talented women of her church who practice this craft. She declares, "My mom did it for me, and now my daughter does. So I never did learn."[6] Schmitt attributes the attraction to what she considers a newfound hunger for family-oriented, sacred activities in the home. Although she gets her palms from friends during her frequent visits to Florida, anyone can buy a few hundred twenty-four-inch-long palm strips, which are shipped fresh by online merchants for about twelve dollars per box.[7] Some florists carry them as well.

Upon receiving the palms, it is important to prepare them by "stripping away their stiff ribbing, refrigerating them to keep them fresh and making the dried palms pliable with hot water."[8] The most common palm-weaving design is the Folded Cross:

> Trim a piece of palm and cut to about 10" and cut another to about 5". Fold the longer piece so the ends meet about 2" from the top of the back side. Staple in place. Fold the second piece so the ends are also in the center and place this as a crossbeam on the cross. Staple, sew, or glue the center. If you wish, you can secure the center by wrapping a narrow piece of palm or the tough rib. Press until dry.[9]

There is also the Thumb-Tack Cross, the Folded Aura, the Circular Folded Rose . . . the possibilities are endless. In fact, some people use these patterns with green construction paper rather than palm leaves. At my local Bible-study fellowship in Chicago, youngsters glue twigs to their paper palm cutouts. The twigs complete the stem and complement the green quite well. The results are not fancy or grand but are fun to create and fun to remember. This activity helps the children understand the day and its meaning, even though the pieces are constructed from a stash of everyday school supplies. It seems that the palm not only signifies faith but also helps to tell a story—making it real and alive. It offers a special form, resembling the outstretched hand. This crafty hand spans across many generations, urging all to come, see, and learn.

palm
Middle English, fr. Old English, fr. Latin *palma* palm of the hand, palm tree; fr. the resemblance of the tree's leaves to the outstretched hand; akin to Greek *palame* palm of the hand, Old English *folm*, Old Irish *lám* hand.

The Mainstreaming of Kosher Foods

Ilivia Marin Yudkin

For many years in the U.S., it was primarily during the weeks leading up to Passover that Jews would scan the shelves of their local grocers in search of the newest kosher products. Since the 1980s, though, the demand for kosher products has increased dramatically year-round. According to market studies, kosher foods have attracted the interest of many ethnic and religious denominations including Muslims, Hindus, and Seventh-Day Adventists. Vegetarians and those who are lactose intolerant also consume kosher products. In fact, contrary to common perception, Jewish consumers comprise only 20 percent of the kosher market.[1] IMC Events and Exhibitions has estimated the total number of U.S. Muslims and other non-Jews who buy kosher at three million.[2] The kosher market once associated only with Passover or Orthodox Jews has a growing niche of customers and products; consumers spend approximately $165 billion on kosher products each year, compared to $250 million around 1980.[3]

Passover, the first of the major Jewish festivals mentioned in the Bible, is observed and celebrated by more Jews than any other holiday on the Jewish calendar. Passover celebrates the escape of the Israelites from the Egyptians' "house of bondage,"[4] and it serves as a reminder of the continuing battle for peace and freedom. Jews eat matzo, or unleavened bread, for seven days to commemorate the hasty departure from Egypt, when the Jews "took their dough before it was leavened" (Exodus 12:34). The use of corn, wheat, barley, spelt, rye, and oats is prohibited during the observance of Passover. The Ashkenazi community also excludes rice and beans from the Passover diet.

The B. Manischewitz Company is the most ubiquitous brand in kosher households. "Manischewitz is to kosher brands what Coca-Cola is to general consumers," says Richard A. Bernstein, president and chief executive officer of R.A.B. Holdings.[5] In 1998, R.A.B., a large independent distributor of specialty foods, purchased Manischewitz for $124 million, planning to broaden the traditional Jewish consumer base: "Non-Jews perceive kosher as clean, better, purer, and healthier, and we have a line of products with good brand identity and a favorable consumer perception. What we're trying to do is get more products on mainstream shelves. Rather than have our [products] be kosher food, we want them to be ethnic food."[6]

Manischewitz, the leading manufacturer of Passover foods, was founded in 1881 when Rabbi Dov Behr Manischewitz of Cincinnati, Ohio, opened a small bakery to make Passover matzo for his friends and family. By the end of the century, the demand for Manischewitz matzo was so intense that Manischewitz purchased gas-fired ovens; the business quickly evolved into a prosperous one. A second plant was opened in Jersey City, New Jersey, in 1932, which rapidly enlarged Manischewitz's client base throughout the East Coast. In 1940, Manischewitz produced its first Tam Tam cracker, signaling the company's departure from matzo products. Manischewitz also specializes in baked goods and canned and jarred products such as gefilte fish, chicken soup, and borscht. Under the Manischewitz, Horowitz Margareten, Goodman's, and Season names, the company sells its specialty foods all over the world.[7]

"The fact that a kosher brand has a rich history with kosher and Jewish consumers seems to add value to the brand," says Menachem Lubinsky of MetroMix/IMC. "But unless they adapt to the new realities of the kosher marketplace today, they are doomed to failure."[8] Mainstream brands have invested time and money since the 1990s to advertise that their products also meet the standards of kosher dietary laws. Nabisco, Hershey, Keebler, Maxwell House, Heinz, Post, and Frito Lay are just a few of the companies that have secured kosher certification from the Orthodox Union. Even Pepsi prepares a special batch of two-liter bottles for Passover, replacing corn syrup with sugar. The bottle cap is stamped with an OUP (Orthodox Union Passover) or KP (Kosher for Passover) logo, indicating that the product has been blessed by a rabbi.

For a product to be considered kosher, a rabbi must inspect the factory to insure that the facility meets specific guidelines. For example, the product must not contain a combination of meat and dairy, nor may it include ingredients like pork or shellfish. If animal products are used, the animals must have been executed with minimal pain and suffering. To obtain kosher certification, companies are willing to pay an annual fee of one thousand to forty thousand dollars. Within that year, inspections occur from every day to every quarter. This is a small price to pay to appeal to the growing kosher food market. If a product is falsely advertised or labeled as kosher, the U.S. Food and Drug Administration may enforce a mislabeling penalty under chapter three of the Federal Food, Drug, and Cosmetic Act, which prohibits "forging, counterfeiting, simulating, or falsely representing, or without proper authority using any mark, stamp, tag, label, or other identification device authorized or required by regulations promulgated under the provisions of section 404, or 721." First-time violators may receive a maximum penalty of five hundred dollars and one year in jail.

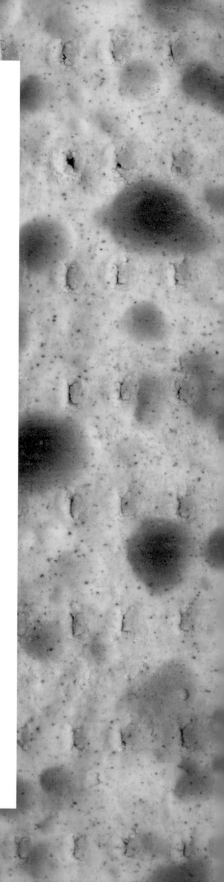

Although Manischewitz monopolized the kosher market for nearly a century, competition has meant a drastic need for the company to pursue advertising and update its brand identity. The old orange-and-green packaging was ambiguous; customers did not know what they were purchasing unless they had tried it before. The packaging also discouraged non-Jews from buying the product—it looked more religious than delicious. The current package, designed by Polan & Waski in 1998, is intended to be more inviting on supermarket shelves to both Jewish and non-Jewish consumers. Although orange and green are used as accents, beige and white are now the dominant colors. A cleaner, more legible typeface was chosen, along with crisp full-color images of the product inside.

Preparing for the Passover seder has become increasingly costly, because only foods meeting the strict dietary laws of Judaism may be consumed. Many Jews do not follow strict kosher laws when preparing a seder, the ritual service and ceremonial dinner for the first night or two of Passover, but nevertheless like to incorporate some kosher elements. A typical family seder for twelve people can cost up to four hundred dollars. Hope Trebilcock, a customer of Kroger's in Louisville, Kentucky, said that she visits the store several times before the seder, spending approximately seventy-five dollars a visit. Most of the staple foods used during the seder can be made from scratch, but these versions are more time-consuming and not necessarily cheaper. A visit to the Passover aisle is part of the Passover tradition. "Knowing that my grandmother purchased the same products fifty years ago makes the experience more special for my family," said Trebilcock.

In 1997, the price of matzo in Florida, which has a large Jewish population, was so high that shoppers reported their complaints to Representative Robert Wexler, a Florida Democrat.[9] Bob Buchner, assistant attorney general, investigated the complaints: "The investigation stems from the fact that it appears that the price for matzo is significantly higher here than in other places. We've heard prices of $12.99 for a five-pound box of matzo in Florida, compared with $4.95 a box in New York."[10] In New York, the city's Department of Consumer Affairs performs a yearly Passover price check to ensure there is no gouging.[11]

Passover's commercialization in the U.S. has had positive effects. Upon request, most airlines now serve kosher food, and certified products are generally available throughout the country. This consumer trend means that an aspect of a minority culture has been embraced—or at least shelved in supermarkets—by the majority culture.

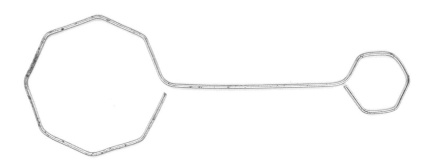

Peeps: A Letter from a Fan

Easter   Jason Warriner

Peeps are the frequently maligned marshmallow treats that flood the candy aisles every spring before Easter and, more recently, on shopping days leading up to Halloween, Christmas, and Valentine's Day. Originally called "little yellow chicks," the handmade candy was purchased along with its then-producer, the Rodda Candy Company, by Just Born in 1953 and over the years has been transformed into an Easter standard.

Just Born has been making candy since 1923, including Mike and Ike, Zours, Hot Tamales, Peeps Jelly Beans, Just Born Jelly Beans, and Teenee Beanee Gourmet Jelly Beans. The company was started by a Russian immigrant, Sam Born (also the inventor of the Born Sucker Machine—a device that inserts sticks into lolli-pops; so important to the world of confectionery manufacturing was the machine that Sam Born was awarded the key to San Francisco).[1] According to Just Born, freshness was of paramount importance to Sam Born, hence the company name, a combination of his own name and the idea of "newness." This idea was carefully illustrated by the company's original logo: a baby on a candy scale. Initially located in Brooklyn, New York, Just Born moved in 1932 to its current location in Pennsyl-vania.[2] After more than fifty years in the business, Just Born had acquired so many different types of candy that the brand name was being diluted. So in the

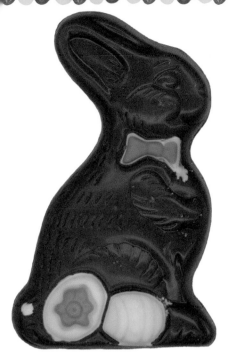

mid-1980s, the company began to focus on the most successful products (including sponsoring a Nascar team).[3] In 1999, Just Born began to advertise on television, one of a number of marketing maneuvers[4] designed to maintain brand identity and to avoid losing the signature product, Peeps, to generic candy land.

You cannot buy one Peep; you must buy at least five. While consumers often find it difficult to buy just one of many candies, Peeps are intense and monotonous—each package contains just a single color and flavor, just sweet marshmallow Peep. Any true lover of Peeps must love marshmallow, because there is nothing else (except for the sugar coating, a few preservatives, and artificial colors). The Peep is an elegantly simple candy by today's standards of motorized lollipops and caramel-nut-crunch bars. It is almost minimalist, functioning in a similar way to that other marshmallow oddity, Circus Peanuts—although Peeps are much more popular.

The Peep may be maligned as much as it is celebrated. Countless Internet sites have cataloged ways to torture Peeps, lasering, burning, boiling, and microwaving them.[5] A popular contest is "Peep jousting." Two Peeps face off inside a micro-wave; a toothpick (serving as a lance) is inserted into each. The microwave causes the Peeps to expand; the Peep that overwhelms the other wins. But why? The Just Born product manager says, "Some people on the Web . . . are doing mean things to Peeps."[6]

Is it the cuteness that causes this violent reaction? Do the lemon yellow chicks and cobalt blue bunnies contain elements of the grotesque that, as Daniel Harris claims in his book *Cute, Quaint, Hungry and Romantic,* define our culture's view of what is and isn't cute?[7] Do these people find Peeps' sad faces sickening rather than sweet? Perhaps: yellow chicks stare longingly through the cellophane packages; slightly down-turned beaks and runny brown eyes make them appear deeply depressed; friends are fused on either side.

But why would that cause someone to turn the deadly beam of a helium laser on a Peep? It could be the synthetic and unreal texture of the marshmallow. Or the rubbery skin of the Peep may confuse some consumers. Is it food or is it rubber? Journalist Kim Severson, in the *San Francisco Chronicle*, quotes Steven Peno: he is fascinated with Peeps because "they're just weird."[8] It is this ambiguity and plasticity that interests me the most. The texture is similar to sandpaper; the flesh, when fresh, has the consistency of a delicate marshmallow.[9] They have a malleability that is inherently fun to play with. As children we are told not to play with our food, but here is one food that begs you to break the rule. Why not throw one in the microwave for fun?

The Just Born company itself suggests that you play with its Peeps. It has more than seventy descriptions of Peeps projects and crafts on its Web site; some edible, some not. It is easy to understand these projects from a business point of view. Just Born claims to have a 98-percent share of marshmallow bunnies and chicks candy sales for Easter.[10] Roula Amire states in *Candy Industry* that Just Born has a 26-percent share of non-chocolate Easter candy sales.[11] This is more than one-quarter of the annual $1.7 billion U.S. Easter candy market. Just Born produced more than half a billion Peeps for spring 2001.[12] According to *CIO* magazine, Just Born sells about 480 million Peeps during Easter and 120 million Peeps during the rest of the year.[13] Is there a maximum number of Peeps that can be consumed by any one individual? Just Born marketers must find new ways to coax consumers to buy more Peeps. The Easter-bonnet Peeps project requires one hundred chicks, so the rate of consumption clearly increases once a consumer takes on a project. While I cannot deny the financial logic, I prefer Peeps project ideas that are an earnest celebration of a unique holiday treat.

As a fan I wanted to express my own creativity with Peeps, designing projects that would begin to reflect the true potential of Peeps as a craft-making material. I contacted Just Born to ask how its craft ideas were developed and whether I could submit concepts of my own. The response:

Dear Mr. Warriner,

Thank you for your recent e-mail. We hope you enjoyed your visit to www.marshmallow-peeps.com. We certainly appreciate your interest in our Marshmallow Peeps craft and recipe ideas. Our product development and marketing teams are always busy working new ideas; and we always enjoy hearing what our valued consumers want.

Again, thank you for taking the time to contact us and be sure to visit Peepsville again soon.

Regards,

~~██████████~~

Just Born™, Inc.
Consumer Relations Department

This sounded encouraging, so my partner and I started working on some ideas for Peeps projects to celebrate the coming of spring. Since many people begin to shop for new beachwear in the spring season, we decided to celebrate the warm weather with Chicks Swimwear. We created a swimsuit made entirely of Peeps. The process involved long hours of sewing the sandpaper-like candies together, first into long strings and then into a marshmallow tapestry. The swimsuit functions as both a flotation device and an emergency snack provider. But does the wearer dive into the water with the Chicks Swimwear? Although the Peeps would surely provide buoyancy for a short time, they would eventually dissolve, and then, well, the wearer would have a new problem. Nevertheless, we were so excited that we sent a photograph of the suit to Just Born.

Unfortunately, the company did not find the swimwear appropriate. Just Born did not say what it was it did not like; the company simply did not respond. Perhaps, we thought, Just Born finds fan modification of its products uncomfortable— especially when humor not necessarily in line with the company's stated values is injected. But there is a long history and culture of modification: to name just a few, low riders, PC game MODs (modified video games created by fans), and most recently, modified versions of Hollywood movies.

George Lucas and his protection of the *Star Wars* franchise is an interesting case study. Lucas stopped the distribution of one fan's modification of *Star Wars, Episode I: The Phantom Menace,* which eliminated from the film the controversial character Jar Jar Binks. But in a conciliatory gesture, Lucasfilm created a contest for fan-created versions of *Star Wars* films, provided that these films did not stray into controversial territory.[14] In this case, the corporation acknowledged the fans' efforts but tried to steer them, using financial and publicity rewards, in an appropriate direction. Just Born, though, does not have a chance. Peeps users, like the ones competing in the yearly Peeps Eating Contest in Sacramento, have left words like "appropriate," "control," and "good taste" far behind. Peeps fans will continue to celebrate their beloved product in endless creative ways—from fabricating Peeps jewelry to adhering Peeps to their nipples.

Business Quarter 2
Spring

Let's Make Whoopee! This Is War

Mary E. Ragsdale

It may have been the dog-food sandwiches that wounded Uncle Frank at an early age. My mother, the oldest of four, was left in charge of the kids while my grandparents were out. It was Aunt Kathy who made the sandwiches, but my mother was the mastermind. She instructed Kathy to use the whole can of Gaines extra-chunky, extra-moist dog food. She spread the toasted whole-wheat bread with mayo and added sliced tomatoes and fresh lettuce. It took my uncle less than three minutes to gobble it down. The youngest brother, Frank was doomed to years of sibling torment. And so he grew to believe that his mission in life was to battle all who rubbed him the wrong way—a project he has continued well into middle age. His favorite day to mark his victims is April Fool's Day. His war cry sings sweet revenge: "Sink or swim kiddies, this is whoopee war." Uncle Frank, or Uncle Fluffy as he is sometimes known, plans his vengeance on a large scale. Every April 1, Uncle Fluffy invests a nice chunk of change into some automatic fart-breathing machine, fountain pen that squirts disappearing ink, stink perfume, or his all-time favorites, the classic whoopee cushion and fake vomit.

Like my perverse Uncle Fluffy, thousands of other April 1 pranksters seek enjoyment by preying on friends and family. Consumers (maybe the real fools) feel the mesmeric lure of the thirsty merchants (probably the biggest pranksters).[1] But is April Fool's Day really a trivial holiday without genuine purpose? Why do we need a rubber chicken or a loud fart explosion to make us snicker and laugh?

April Fool's Day is thought to have originated from the reformation of the Christian calendar, in which the New Year's celebration was switched from April 1 to January 1; or it may have evolved from international celebrations involving the spring equinox, which usually falls on March 19, 20, or 21. In sixteenth-century France, the New Year was celebrated from March 25 through April 1.[2] It was believed that God created humankind on April 1. In 1562, Pope Gregory, under Charles IX of France, introduced a new Christian calendar, moving the New Year to January 1. News of the change was slow to travel; most information was delivered by foot and exchanged by word of mouth. So some people did not know of the calendar conversion and were labeled "fools" and subjected to ridicule and harassing tricks. France continues to celebrate April 1, also observed as "Poisson d'Avril," or "April Fish." Children tape paper fish to each other's backs, and this labels them as fools because the newly hatched fish of April are considered to be easily caught. This holiday tradition spread through Great Britain and Scotland in the eighteenth century and was finally introduced to the American colonies by the English and French.[3]

Jokes and pranks are opportunities to communicate and network through relationships in communities and between individuals. Sigmund Freud has written, "No one can be content with having made a joke for himself alone . . . telling it to someone else produces enjoyment."[4] According to Freud's *Jokes and Their Relation to the Unconscious*, humor is a relaxation of tension and a release from constraint; it produces a psychical energy that results in pleasure. Jokes allow us to evade restrictions and rebel against authority, which is sometimes why adults, more than children, become the culprits of tomfoolery.[5] The "activity, which aims at deriving pleasure from mental processes, whether intellectual or otherwise," awards us the power to laugh.[6] But not everyone is equally capable of forming jokes and materializing pranks, which are associated with intelligence, imagination, and memory: "Only a few people have a plentiful amount of it, and these are distinguished by being spoken of as having wit."[7] Consumer products make jokes accessible to every person, whether they are funny or not. For fewer than five dollars, gags allow anyone to purchase and exhibit the power of humor. Jokes and pranks are most successful when they are easy to understand. Companies and large corporations have capitalized on crude, simple, unchallenging products that can be related to and valued despite barriers such as language, race, culture, nationality, and financial status. Age, sex, and natural bodily functions are often utilized and exaggerated to increase offensiveness and sales.

While cutting edge monkeyshines and shenanigans are relentlessly devised and sold, shoppers continue to purchase novelty pranks that hold certain nostalgia. The two largest wholesalers of pranks and magic are S. S. Adams and Company and Loftus International.

Soren Sorenson "Sam" Adams founded his novelty company in 1906; originally named Cachoo Sneeze Powder Company, it had profits of fifteen thousand dollars in the first year of business and was run solely by Adams himself. Today, the company, based in New Jersey, sells about two hundred different items. Sam Adams patented thirty-seven gadgets out of the roughly seven hundred he invented; the best known include Cachoo Sneezing Powder, the Dribble Glass, the Jumping Snake, and the Joy Buzzer. Adams held that "the whole basic principle of a good joke novelty is that it has to be easy and simple to work."[8] Loftus is America's only manufacturer of rubber chickens. Interviewed by Buck Wolf of ABCNews.com, CEO Gene Rose claimed, "Gag gifts and practical jokes come and go. But the rubber chicken is forever."[9] A leading innovator of the devices he sells, Rose was the first to make chickens out of rubber latex. He has built Loftus International from a small novelty store in Salt Lake City that he opened in 1939 with his father-in-law into a major wholesaler and importer-exporter of spoofs and pranks. Still based in Salt Lake City, Loftus operates from a seventy-thousand-square-foot warehouse with a team of forty-seven employees. Gene Rose and son Jim Rose travel the world to various international trade shows for innovative gizmos. In the business of fart candy, fake dog doo, and stink bombs, Rose maintains that "Gross is good."[10]

Another established celebrity among bad-mannered gags that surface around April Fool's Day is the whoopee cushion. This heavyweight dates back to a time when "fool's bladders" were air-filled balloons made from the bladder of a pig or cow. Jesters would use them as props for their acts. Whoopee resulted from the English word "whoop" or "whoup," which is defined as a natural exclamation.[11]

My family never has enough time to prepare for the yearly battle of wit and wiles. This year, we are plotting something huge against dear, sweet, unsuspecting Uncle Fluffy. It is time to teach him another lesson about family loyalty and trust. My grandmother wants revenge for the eruptive fart powder in her angel food cake, and his siblings, including my mother, want blood for a hoax involving grape jelly and water balloons. Laughter is a genuine expression of the emotions.

The Consumption of Cinco de Mayo in the United States

Cinco de Mayo   **Courtney S. Perkins**

There are currently 37 million Latinos in the United States, accounting for approximately 13 percent of the population; they now outnumber African-Americans as the largest and fastest-growing minority in the country.[1] Latinos' buying power is estimated at $580 billion per year, with an upward growth of 12 percent annually. These statistics mean that, by 2010, Latinos will likely have over $900 billion to spend per year, which will make them a powerful portion of the market courted by big businesses.[2]

In some major markets, many Spanish television shows, especially news broadcasts, garner a larger viewing audience than those on major networks. Ironically, however, direct marketing to Latinos has been virtually untapped. Only three percent of current advertising dollars is spent marketing directly to the Latino population.[3] But this is changing. Latino buying power has forced corporations to recognize the audience as one worth marketing to, and as a result, large business deals are being made in an effort to control the segment. For example, in 2003, Univision Communications, a Spanish broadcasting giant, sealed a $3.5 billion deal with Hispanic Broadcasting Corporation, the largest Latino radio network, giving Univision control of the over $2 billion per year in advertising proceeds gained by this group. Also in 2002, NBC purchased Telemundo, the number two Spanish network, for $2.7 billion.[4] These major business deals signal the very recent change in strategies of marketing to the Latino community and are indicative of a trend to come.

The growth of Cinco de Mayo demonstrates (for both Latinos and non-Latinos) the consumer power of Latino culture in the U.S.—with a potential only starting to be recognized. Cinco de Mayo, falling directly after Easter and just before the summer season, has proven to be a lucrative holiday, and advertisers and businesses have taken to marketing it to the non-Latino population. Lisa Navarette, spokeswoman for the National Council of La Raza, a Hispanic advocacy group, says that Cinco de Mayo is the "cool new holiday."[5] Not only is Cinco de Mayo fashionable, but it means big money to businesses in the pre-summer season. The difference between what Americans spend at the checkout counter during a normal summer week and one "branded" with a holiday can be as much as $500 million, according to Paris Gogos, a vice president of Efficient Market Services, a Deerfield, Illinois–based supermarket research group.[6]

Started by Chicano activists attempting to develop a holiday celebrating pride among Mexican-Americans, the celebration of Cinco de Mayo in the United States began in the 1960s.[7] The holiday marks a battle that took place in the town of Puebla, Mexico, in which a small Mexican army, led by General Ignacio Zaragoza, defeated six thousand French troops sent by Napoleon III to conquer Mexico.[8] Some argue that if it were not for this victory, Napoleon would have gone on to invade the U.S. and join forces with the South.[9] Allen Brown-Gort, associate director of the Institute for Latino Studies at Notre Dame University, reports, "It grew in popularity here partly because the general who led the victory was a Texan. Also, it's the first spring celebration, and Cinco is easier to say than Diez y Seis de Septiembre [September 16], which is Mexican Independence Day."[10] Many Americans today, however, mistakenly refer to Cinco de Mayo as Mexican Independence Day. September 16, which falls during Hispanic Heritage Month, is the actual day of Mexican independence from Spain.[11] In Mexico, these two holidays are referred to as the Fiestas Patrias (Patriotic Festivals).[12] While Mexican Independence Day remains a significant celebration in Mexico, Cinco de Mayo is considered much less important.

In the U.S., however, the small Mexican holiday has been transformed into a beer-drinking, margarita-gulping good time, served with a little guacamole on the side. U.S. consumers annually spend upward of one billion dollars during Cinco de Mayo weekend.[13] More than five hundred cities across the United States have official Cinco de Mayo celebrations. Los Angeles, for example, sponsors Fiesta Broadway, a festival to kick off the week of Cinco de Mayo partying, which attracts over 500,000 visitors every year, along with over 130 sponsors.[14] Thousands of celebrants attend the annual Cinco de Mayo parade in Chicago's South Side neighborhood of Pilsen.[15] In St. Paul, Minnesota, the Cinco de Mayo festival is one of the city's largest. It attracts more than 75,000 visitors in a state with a Latino population of less than 150,000.[16]

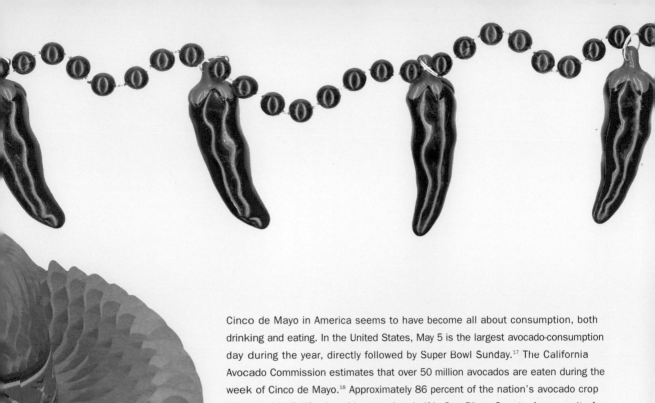

Cinco de Mayo in America seems to have become all about consumption, both drinking and eating. In the United States, May 5 is the largest avocado-consumption day during the year, directly followed by Super Bowl Sunday.[17] The California Avocado Commission estimates that over 50 million avocados are eaten during the week of Cinco de Mayo.[18] Approximately 86 percent of the nation's avocado crop is located in California, with more than half in San Diego County. As a result of the boom during Cinco de Mayo season, as well as Super Bowl marketing, the avocado business boasted $358 million in sales for its 2001–2 season.[19]

David Ayon, a researcher of ethnic spending trends for the Center for the Study of Los Angeles at Loyola Marymount University, stated of Cinco de Mayo, "It's food-driven, it's calendar-driven. Mostly, it's beer-driven."[20] Mexico's top-selling beer, Corona, spends an estimated $5 million during the Cinco de Mayo season on television, radio, print, and outdoor advertising and other promotions, out of approximately $40 million for the entire year.[21] During the two-week span of Cinco de Mayo advertising, it is estimated that Corona will sell approximately 100 million bottles of beer. Since the early 1990s, Corona beer, branded as a fad upon its market debut in Texas and California in the 1970s, has shown steady growth of between 10 and 40 percent.[22] Although Corona had a number of relatively slow years, the last one occurring in 1991 with sales of only 950,000 barrels, the nation's recent switch to lighter beers and higher consumption of Mexican food, along with Corona's segmented marketing, has pushed the beer toward improved sales. By 1999, Corona saw sales amounting to an estimated 4.9 million barrels. Corona is now the tenth best-selling beer in the United States and has opened the door for competitors, such as Tequiza, to market their products.[23] In fact, "According to Latinos and Latinas for Health Justice, the top three domestic brewers in the U.S. spent a combined $37.7 million in 1998 on Hispanic advertising."[24]

In response to Cinco de Mayo in the United States, Guillermo Hernandez, at the time the director of UCLA's Chicano Studies Research Center, stated, "[The holiday has] become a commercial event that's totally devoid of its political meaning. It's just another excuse to party."[25] Such criticisms are not isolated, and it seems that in the past few years their rumblings have become louder and more disdainful. In 1997, Cinco de Mayo con Orgullo (Cinco de Mayo with Pride) promoted alcohol-free Cinco de Mayo celebrations in Los Angeles, San Diego, the San Francisco Bay area, many cities in Texas, and Chicago. The coalition aims to promote the idea that "our culture is not for sale." However, Jose Pares, the director of communications for Grupo Modelo, Mexico's largest brewer and the producer of Corona, stated, "I think there is nothing wrong with having a Mexican drink to celebrate the day. It is the individual's choice to drink, not ours."[26]

But some disturbing statistics have been released in two reports by the Center on Alcohol Marketing and Youth (CAMY) at Georgetown University. The reports state that young people in general, and young Latinos in particular, are exposed to more alcohol advertising than adults. In 2001, it was calculated that youths saw 21 percent more magazine advertisements for alcohol than adults did.[27] Furthermore,

Latino youths see 32 percent more alcohol advertising than youths of other cultures:[28] "Major alcohol companies spent $23.6 million in 2002 on commercials that targeted 12 of the 15 TV programs most popular with Latino youth."[29] With 41 percent of the Latino population under 21, these are potentially dangerous statistics.

Crossing the border from Mexico to the United States, Cinco de Mayo has gained significance and importance. Some may, and many in fact do, argue that the holiday is being exploited by the consumer-driven culture of the U.S. to sell beer, tequila, and snack foods—items generally altogether irrelevant to the holiday. However, at Cinco de Mayo celebrations, be they parades or festivals, the viewer, whether Latino or not, is compelled to recognize and celebrate Mexican-Americans and their presence in U.S. culture. The view may be littered with giant, inflated beer bottles wearing sombreros and scantily clad women holding tequila bottles, but an equally strong message is the pride and strength of the culture of Mexican-Americans. On May 5, a non-Latino American citizen may not know that the day honors the fighting spirit of Mexican troops in a small battle against the French in Puebla, but he or she will assuredly be able to identify the holiday with Mexico and Mexican-Americans. So the marketing of alcohol and avocados has helped inform all citizens not just what is being sold on that day but also that it is a day to celebrate Mexican culture. Furthermore, commercial sponsors often partially or fully fund the parades and festivals that honor the day, the history, and the Mexican culture. So in the end, a delicate and often problematic balance is established between honoring a tradition and making millions off of it—two things that, in the U.S., may not be able to exist independently.

Sentiment, Guilt, and Profit

Mother's Day   Jennifer Getz

Mother's Day is perhaps one of the best examples of a celebration that can create as much stress as sentiment. Idealized images of motherhood, annually cast in floral-scented greeting cards and glossy advertisements, perpetuate a facade of perfection for child and mother alike, making Mother's Day emotionally hard to celebrate or not to celebrate.

Mother's Day belongs in a special category of "obligation holidays." Consumers feel pressure to participate in some aspect of the formula for celebrating the holiday—phone call, flowers, candy, dinner out, card. In 2002, Mother's Day annual card sales totaled $136 million and flower and plant sales accounted for over one-quarter of all holiday flora sales. Ninety-eight percent of all Americans celebrate Mother's Day.

For many, Mother's Day, like other family-focused holidays, is a relaxing day filled with hugs, cheer, and good company. For others, though, reports one commentator, "the tender images touted by Madison Avenue and the television networks generate feelings of sadness, loneliness, shame, guilt, or anger. These media-generated images of feel-good families can underscore the disparity between the relationships people have with their parents and the relationships they wish they had."[1]

"We put too much pressure on ourselves to have a good time [during holidays], to make it really special, to make everybody happy," says Richard O'Connor, a therapist in New York and Connecticut.[2] However, painful childhood memories may linger just beyond the radar screen, only to surface during special occasions such as Mother's Day, provoking renewed conflicts or bittersweet feelings.[3]

Children are not the only family members experiencing feelings other than sentiment on Mother's Day. For mothers critical of their own mothering skills, the day heightens these emotions. Mothers have traditionally shouldered the responsibility of molding their children's character. And often society looks to the mother as the reason for failure in a family or with a child. The mother becomes the scapegoat. "If mothers work and the kids have problems, blame mom for being selfish," says one newspaper. "If mothers stay at home and their family goes on welfare, blame her for setting a bad example. It goes with the job."[4] Mother's Day can be a self-reflexive, -scrutinizing, or -repressive experience for mothers. Eileen Brown from the *Chicago Sun-Times* writes:

> Breakfast aside I loathe Mother's Day . . . Being a mother is not my thing, so I hate being feted for the role . . . Don't get me wrong. I love my son. Passionately. Completely. We all have expectations of what a good mother is. Unfortunately, what comes to mind for me is Donna Reed. For the record, I am no Donna Reed. Of course, I'm not without maternal attributes. I keep my son's secrets—to the grave. I laugh at his dumb jokes. And I make a mean grilled cheese sandwich . . . Still, Mother's Day is a mixed bag for me. I feel like a fraud. Instead of concentrating on my good points as a mother, I brood about deficiencies—the cookies I didn't bake, the sand castles I didn't make.[5]

The guilt associated with celebrating Mother's Day is as complex as the relationship between mother and child. Gift giving can invoke the stress of fulfilling expectations, or of living up to embellished family memories, as well as feelings of inadequacy and indebtedness. Gift giving is an honorable gesture but also a way to make up for lost time, poor communication skills, and emotional distance.

Mothers are known as the family organizers, family caretakers, and queens of family rituals, so it is no surprise that mothers began the act of gift giving for all occasions. The tradition of purchasing commodities or services to create a sense of celebration was originated by mothers at the turn of the twentieth century when manufactured gifts were considered novel in comparison to handmade items. In families and social circles, bestowed commodities quickly appropriated the sentimental value of handmade gifts, creating a sense of group identity and social status. "Women became the major purchasers of gifts. In joining ritual with consumer culture, women shoppers used the goods they bought as a means of strengthening family solidarity," notes an observer.[6]

Today, with the purchasing power of the modern woman combined with the diversity of commodities available, gift giving has reached new levels. It has become so specialized that it is now almost an art in itself, aided by gift stores, such as Hallmark Stores, online shopping, discount stores, and malls: "'There is so much hype out in stores, I think so many people think they have to go out and spend a lot of money,' said Peggy Post, an etiquette author and great granddaughter-in-law of the etiquette queen, Emily Post. 'But what it really boils down to is a tradition and terrific sentiment.'"[7]

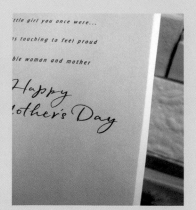

Lately, though, we have all spent a lot on Mother's Day. The National Retail Federation's 2002 survey estimated that shoppers spent ninety-seven dollars per household on Mother's Day. Mother's Day is the second most popular holiday of the year (Valentine's Day ranks number one) to purchase flowers, and FTD.com pulls in 30 percent of its annual revenues the week leading up to the holiday. A total of $19 billion is spent on flowers every year on Mother's Day. That holiday-driven increase requires more than the usual support. Michael Soenen, the president and chief executive officer of the Downers Grove, Illinois–based FTD.com, stated that the company plans a year in advance for the increase in business. Server capability is expanded four to five times, and fewer Web pages are available, in hopes of minimizing slow downloads. FTD.com employs about 200 employees year-round but hires an additional 115 part-time employees to handle additional customer support. Amazingly, even with the dot-com crumble, FTD.com has reported quarterly profits since September 2000. Revenues for the 2001 fiscal year, ending in June, totaled $130 million, second in the Internet floral industry to the $442.2 million earned by 1-800-Flowers.com.[8]

Buying cards with prewritten messages and double-clicking on floral arrangements and gift baskets is not too difficult a task every year. But the many who called (AT&T estimates that 122 million long-distance Mother's Day calls are placed annually)[9] after mom went to bed, or mailed a card *on* Mother's Day, may be wondering—who started this?

In 1868, Anna Jarvis organized a committee to sponsor a Mother's Friendship Day, aiming to reunite families separated during the Civil War. Her daughter, Anna Reeves Jarvis, mourned her mother's loss in 1905 and decided to organize an official day to observe all mothers. On May 10, 1908, the second Sunday in May, churches in Grafton, West Virginia, and Philadelphia, Pennsylvania, held services to honor mothers. However, this was not an official observance. Jarvis had to win over a few constitutional pettifoggers who were not going to let Mother's Day slip in so easily.

But Jarvis continued to elicit support, and in 1914, President Woodrow Wilson finally proclaimed Mother's Day an official holiday. Interestingly, as the holiday gathered momentum, popularity bred commercialization, which upset Jarvis. Enraged by festivals celebrating what was meant to be a day of somber observance, Jarvis, the daughter of a minister, attempted to squash her own accomplishment by filing a lawsuit to stop a 1923 Mother's Day festival, and she was arrested for protesting the celebration of her own creation. Jarvis was quoted as saying, "This is not what I intended." Angered by the sale of white carnations, the symbol Jarvis originated to honor her mother, she said, "I wanted it to be a day of sentiment, not profit!"[10]

Furthermore, Jarvis appealed to sons and daughters to stop buying flowers for mothers and was reported as saying, "[Greeting cards are] a poor excuse for the letter you are too lazy to write." She also declared "charlatans, bandits, pirates, racketeers, kidnappers, and other termites, [ruined] with their greed one of the finest, noblest, truest movements and celebrations known." The commercial industries, upset by her perspective, ceased crediting Jarvis and became dismissive toward her plight. But the publicity caused by the debacle between Jarvis and the commercial industries that stood to profit from Mother's Day created the best advertising ever—and it was free.[11] Also, Anna Jarvis was not a mother herself. In 1948, right before her death at a sanatorium in West Chester, Pennsylvania, she reported that she regretted ever starting the holiday. Ironically, the room where she spent the last years of her life was filled with flowers and cards from all over the world every Mother's Day.

Some blame the greeting-card industry for creating holidays or making holidays commercial nirvana rather than simple unassuming observances. "We have never created a holiday," asserts Deirdre Parkes, spokesperson for Hallmark.[12] But with millions of dollars spent on advertising, Hallmark certainly reminds consumers of the annual obligation. A $30 million campaign from ad agency Leo Burnett uses "They'll never forget you remembered" as a call to action, since "Mother's Day is an occasion where you want to reach out and connect," says Kylie Watson-Wheeler, Hallmark's director of advertising. "This is not an occasion where you can just e-mail or fax."[13] For this third-largest card-sending holiday in the U.S., with 75 percent of all Mother's Day cards sold in the week before the holiday,[14] Hallmark offered 2,463 faces for Mother's Day in all its card lines in 2002: Expressions from Hallmark, Ambassador, Fresh Ink, Warm Wishes, Mahogany, Hallmark en Español, and the regular Hallmark brand.

The greeting-card industry may not have created Mother's Day, but it continues to redefine the holiday. In 1999, Hallmark tried to stretch the holiday to even more consumers as it encompassed women's empowerment in its messages. One card read: "To those who comfort with a mother's hand, we thank you. To those who encourage with a mother's praise, we applaud you. To those who love with a mother's heart, we honor you. Not just on Mother's Day . . . always."[15] Lending the celebration to all womanhood, not just to mothers, was a result of extensive research on Hallmark's part. American Greetings, the second-largest company in the greeting-card industry, banks on the modern family by offering cards for "single mothers, stepmothers, foster mothers, caregivers, guardians [and expecting mothers]." A senior writer and editor for American Greetings notes that the perception of step-mothers has changed significantly: "Ten or 15 years ago, there was a reluctance to use the word 'stepmother' on a card because of the negative, fairy-tale connotations."

But with one-third of American families including a stepparent, the card industry celebrates the niche. Hallmark offers cards to meet not only stepfamily relationships but also cards for "ex-in-laws, dads-as-moms, dad's wife, and friends who are 'like family.'"[16]

Research done by Hallmark in 1999 predicts that "men will be searching for their place in society, women will be heading in new directions and all of us will be influenced by other cultures."[17] This sensitivity to a range of parents' roles exposes Mother's Day observers to niche-marketing pitches. Still, the tensions between obligation and love, spending and intimacy, will, no doubt, remain a constant.

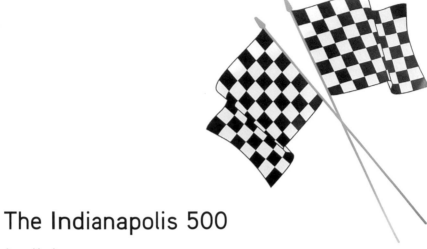

The Indianapolis 500

Memorial Day   Anne Hankey

What do tailgates, princesses, and beer-guzzling race fans have in common? This is the recipe for an Indiana-style Memorial Day. Patriotic contemplation is expendable, as long as no one forgets the words to "Back Home Again in Indiana."

Growing up in Indianapolis, I have always dreaded the month of May, when the entire city turns black and white in anticipation of the Indianapolis 500. Traffic is terrible, restaurants are impossible, and the penetrating smell of gasoline fills the air. This great shift culminates on Memorial Day, the end of spring and the commemoration of American military losses. But aside from one rendition of taps at the race and the display of American flags, how much do we think about our lost soldiers? Do we instead just look at Memorial Day as a three-day weekend?

There are several theories about the conception of Memorial Day, originally called Decoration Day. According to historians, Southern women began decorating the graves of the Civil War dead in May 1865.[1] Southern legend says that Mrs. Charles J. Williams, a Confederate widow, asked that a holiday "be handed down through time as a religious custom of the South to wreathe the graves of our martyred dead with flowers."[2] The springtime tradition of memorial decoration was consequently adopted throughout the South, although no specific date was assigned. The practice spread to the North when Union wives toured Southern battlefields and carried the idea home.

Two Northerners also claimed responsibility for the creation of Memorial Day. On May 5, 1865, Northern abolitionist James Redpath gathered a group of freed African-American children to decorate the graves of Union soldiers in Charlestown, South Carolina.[3] Waterloo, New York, pharmacist Henry C. Welles also asserted ownership of Decoration Day. Welles claimed that he proposed the grave-decoration idea in 1865 and then brought it up to his local government representative, General John B. Murray.[4] It was not until 1966 that Lyndon Johnson settled the debate and declared Waterloo the birthplace of Memorial Day.[5]

On May 5, 1868, General John Logan, the commander of the Grand Army of the Republic, decreed General Order No. 11, and Memorial Day was born:

> The 30th of May, 1868, is designated for the purpose of strewing with flowers or otherwise decorating the graves of comrades who died in defense of their country during the late rebellion, and whose bodies now lie in almost every city, village, and hamlet church-yard in the land.[6]

Although grave decoration was rooted in the South, Southerners viewed the May 30 celebration as a "Yankee holiday" and consequently continued to observe their own Decoration Day. And many Northerners did not want to allow the South to partake. In fact, in 1869, Union soldiers patrolled Confederate graves to prevent them from being decorated. This divide did not faze Logan, who asked Congress on June 22, 1868, to make Memorial Day a national "commemoration of the gallant heroes who have [sacrificed] their lives in defense of the Republic." This bill was defeated in 1876; Congress, like the country, was divided. To facilitate the end of Reconstruction, Union troops were removed from the South in 1877. Americans began to forget the immediacy of war and civil strife, and the holiday consequently shifted to become ambiguously patriotic.[7]

As the country unified and developed economically, leisure activities became part of the daily regime. Many Americans spent their weekends playing sports and relaxing, both of which crept into holiday observances. In 1888, President Grover Cleveland "allegedly went fishing on Memorial Day, which did not help him in his unsuccessful bid for reelection that year." The Grand Army of the Republic condemned this activity by stating their disapproval of "indulgences in public sports, pastimes, and all amusements on Memorial Day."[8] But the damage had been done; Americans began looking for leisure activities to fill this late spring celebration.

Starting in 1911, Memorial Day became the traditional date of the Indianapolis 500, America's oldest automobile race. According to Indianapolis Motor Speedway track historian Donald Davidson, Memorial Day was selected for attendance reasons. At the turn of the century, local farmers would hay their fields in mid-May. Since the hay needed to sit for a brief period, farmers had a number of free days right around May 30. Thus the race planners allowed for maximum local attendance. As the years progressed, the Indy 500 became the staple leisure event for a midwestern late spring. The race was always held on Memorial Day proper, unless the holiday fell on a Sunday, in which case the race was moved to the Saturday or Monday. In keeping with the military flavor of the date, the Indiana National Guard provided race security until 1948, when the track created its own security force.[9]

The 500 Festival, a not-for-profit group, was organized in 1957 and charged with creating civic events during the month of May. The festival brings together a board of thirty-five community leaders, a full-time staff of sixteen, and approximately two thousand volunteers. The first 500 Festival included a parade, ball, and square dance. Since its creation the events have expanded to include a 13.1-mile mini-marathon and health exposition, AT&T Wireless 5K race, mayor's breakfast, Volunteer Recognition Day, Pole Day, Qualification Day, Rookie Day, Kids Day,

Bump Day, Community Day, Honor Student Recognition Day, Carburetion Day, Memorial Service, 500 Festival parade, and the race itself. In 2002, four hundred thousand people participated in festival events.[10]

The most important part of the 500 Festival is the parade. Originally, the parade was held the evening before the race, but in 1973 it was scheduled for a Saturday—two days before the race. After three days of rain, the race was moved to a Thursday, breaking the May 30 tradition. Race fans liked the extended celebration, the parade was officially moved to the week before the race, and the actual race was moved to a Sunday. This coincided with the National Monday Holiday Act of 1968, which moved many federal holidays, including Memorial Day, to Mondays, which therefore made Memorial Day a three-day weekend.[11] In Indiana, Indy 500 scheduling essentially took over the entire month of May. Memorial Day was no longer important as a holiday and instead, at least in Indiana, became part of the Motor Speedway hoopla.[12] Ironically, Memorial Day became an official federal holiday in 1971.[13]

In an effort to honor the root of the holiday, the first grand marshals of the parade were all members of the armed forces. Later, civic celebrities such as Walter Cronkite (1966), Gerald Ford (1979), David Hasselhoff (1984), Dan Quayle (1990), Larry Bird (1993), and Garfield (1996) took over the role.[14] Further removing the military stamp on the day was the creation of the Festival Princesses, a court of local teenagers who exemplify solid American virtues. According to festival organizers, princesses need to have exceptional poise and appearance, excellent interpersonal communication skills, a strong desire to serve others through community service, maturity and responsibility, academic achievement, patience and flexibility, a great sense of humor, and a high energy level.[15] After they are crowned, these girls serve as modern-day memorial decorations, adorning the parade floats and the pages of the city newspaper.

On January 19, 1999, Bill S189 asked the Senate to move Memorial Day back to a specific date, May 30, instead of using a changing day, the last Monday in May.[16] Senators believed that a set date would make the holiday seem more valid and less like time off from work. A December 2000 resolution called "National Moment of Remembrance" also had this goal in mind. At 3:00 in the afternoon, in each time zone, Americans are asked to "voluntarily and informally observe in their own way a moment of remembrance and respect, pausing from whatever they are doing for a moment of silence or listening to 'Taps.'"[17]

Perhaps May 30 is just too beautiful a late spring day to mourn American soldiers killed in battle. Maybe the princesses and the beer cannot make us remember what we seem to have forgotten. Or possibly we just do not feel guilty for our lost commemorative holiday because we still have Veterans Day. Whatever the reason, many Americans would agree that Memorial Day weekend is a time for hamburgers, beer, and checkered race flags.

At the Indy 500, silent commemoration is far from the minds of attendees. The Indianapolis Motor Speedway "is the single largest sporting facility in the world with more than 250,000 permanent seats."[18] The seats are reserved months before the race. For those who cannot secure tickets, television plays a key role in delivering loud engine noises to the American people: the "2000 Indianapolis 500 placed first among televised motorsport events and generated a record $102.4 million in sponsorship exposure."[19] To ensure that Indianapolis residents attend the race instead of watching from their air-conditioned homes, though, race coverage is blacked out throughout the city. The televised version is run later in the evening, well after the winner has drunk a ceremonial glass of milk and been interviewed by sportscasters and news reporters.

According to a January 15, 2000, article in *Sports Business Journal*, the Indianapolis 500 was the "largest producer of economic gains in 2000 among all annual major sporting events in the United States."[20] Professor Mark Rosentraub, dean of the Levin College of Business at Cleveland State University, found that the Indianapolis 500 creates an economic impact of $336.6 million annually ($100 million more than NASCAR's Daytona 500, second on the list): the "Indy 500 is responsible for almost 50% of the Indianapolis Motor Speedway's $727 million annual impact on the central Indiana economy."[21] In comparison, the thirty-fourth Super Bowl brought Atlanta $215 million. Rosentraub stated, "While the public sector does incur expenses on the day of the race . . . the State of Indiana receives more than $25 million and local governments nearly $10 million each year. This is in addition to

the $1.5 million the Indianapolis Motor Speedway Corporation pays annually in property taxes." The statistics in this report include only out-of-town guests, who make up approximately two-thirds of the total race crowd.[22]

In Indianapolis, this holiday has generated not only a sporting event but an entire town. Indianapolis Motor Speedway founder Carl Fisher encouraged suburban development around the speedway because he wanted an "attractive residential area to complement the industrial sites emerging from the cornfields near the track."[23] In 1926, the community of Speedway became a town recognized by the state of Indiana. Speedway also boasts the largest strip mall in Indiana, which generates approximately $85 million in annual sales. Although completely surrounded by metropolitan Indianapolis, Speedway has its own town hall, police department, fire department, and school system. The high-school mascot? The "Sparkplug."

The Ties That Bind

Father's Day   Loren Stephens

In contemporary times, a holiday promoted by an organized industry may not seem so shocking. In fact, corporate promotion has come to be expected, with expressions such as "Hallmark holiday" entering mainstream discussion. In the early 1900s, however, the concept was met with great skepticism and mistrust. Initially created as one daughter's way of paying tribute to her own father, Father's Day became a household celebration only through the advertising efforts of the mens-wear industry. Not entirely an altruistic day of honor, not entirely a marketing ploy— Father's Day falls somewhere in between.

The official history of Father's Day begins with Sonora Smart Dodd of Spokane, Washington. Sonora Dodd was one of six children raised by her father, Civil War veteran William Jackson Smart, after his wife died in childbirth. In 1909, at the age of twenty-seven, Dodd conceived of the celebration of a father's day, reportedly while listening to a Mother's Day sermon. She wanted to create a celebration that would pay tribute to her own father as well as honor all fathers. She took her idea to the Spokane Ministerial Association and the local YMCA, both of which supported her proposal, and the first Father's Day was celebrated in Spokane on June 19, 1910.

With Father's Day's ninety-plus-year history, why is it that mom still gets perfume on her holiday and dad only a paperweight? Father's Day is commonly considered a commercial afterthought to Mother's Day (founded in 1908) by the general public and many fatherhood scholars alike.[1] After all, it was second to become an official holiday, it falls second on the calendar, and it is consistently second in sales and the number of long-distance phone calls. According to AT&T, more long-distance phone calls are placed on Mother's Day than on any other day of the year, with Christmas Day coming in second and Father's Day a distant third.[2] The International Mass Retail Association reported that, in 1999, Americans spent an average of seventy-five dollars on Mother's Day, nearly twice the forty dollars they spent on Father's Day the previous year. And according to Hallmark, Americans give approximately 144 million cards for Mother's Day every year, but fewer than 90 million for Father's Day.[3] These Mother's Day/Father's Day discrepancies go back to the very beginnings of both holidays.

Anna Jarvis organized the first Mother's Day services in 1908; only six years later, Congress voted to make it a national holiday. Not so for Sonora Dodd's Father's Day. It was not until 1972—fifty-eight years after President Woodrow Wilson proclaimed Mother's Day and sixty-two years after Father's Day was first officially celebrated—that Congress finally passed a bill in favor of Father's Day.[4] Dads do come in first in one category, although perhaps not one to brag about. According to AT&T Worldwide Intelligent Network, Father's Day generates more collect calls than any other day of the year, taking the "father as provider" role to a new level.[5]

The anemic interest in Father's Day could never be blamed on a lack of public awareness or exposure. In fact, this holiday of lower sales is actually the one that was historically the most heavily advertised. Unlike the founder of Mother's Day, who opposed all commercial gain associated with the holiday, Sonora Dodd did not mind people using Father's Day for profit. In fact, she sought out merchants for their support from the start. She asked local store owners to display cards publicizing the observance and urged them to prepare windows featuring Father's Day gifts. Father's Day in Spokane was produced as much in stores and through advertisements as through churches and the YMCA.[6] Anna Jarvis sneered at all the activity surrounding Father's Day, seeing the whole observance as a poorly disguised plot of "some necktie, tobacco, whiskey, and lottery promoters." With "millions of dollars to back its promotion," it was, Jarvis believed, "an absolute failure as to sentiment or uplift."[7] Despite Dodd's embrace of publicity, common feeling seemed to side with Jarvis. There was not a single article published in the *New York Times* on Father's Day between 1915 and 1923, but there were twenty-eight published on Mother's Day.[8]

In the first years of observance, promotional sidebars in department-store advertisements hailed the new event and described the homage due to father for his love and fortitude. Similarly, in 1910, a Father's Day window at Spokane's Graham

and Co. borrowed heavily from the display conventions of other civic holidays: it featured George Washington as the Father of His Country, a silk American flag, and the placard "Remember Father," all of which highlighted a number of holiday gift items. To these sentimental and patriotic portrayals were shortly added more straightforward advertising slogans, such as "Give Dad a Tie," "He Needs Hosiery," or "Father's Day Tie Special."[9]

Throughout the 1920s, the promotion of Father's Day was generally scattered, with each trade organizing its own small-scale campaigns. Then, in the 1930s, some members of the business community decided to pool their resources and work together. In 1932, the *New York Times* reported that "a group of business and advertising men headed by the president of the Retail Clothiers' and Furnishing Association of New York, Inc. had chosen a slogan, 'Show Dad You Remember,' around which to frame their Father's Day campaign."[10] The Associated Men's Wear Retailers of New York City took an increasing lead in promoting the holiday, hoping to give existing Father's Day advertising national direction and coordination. The group had its own Father's Day Council, which had the forthright slogan "Give Dad Something to Wear," and it was already working on getting the holiday "decreed" a state and national observance. At its heart, this group hoped to turn the celebration into "a Second Christmas," at least so far as "the sale of men's wear gifts" was concerned. Sales for Father's Day in 1935 were brisk, and in 1937, the Father's Day Council estimated that more than a million dollars was spent for Father's Day advertising in magazines and newspapers.[11]

The Father's Day Council also recognized that observance of the holiday was still "spotty"; according to one survey, only one in six fathers in 1937 had been duly honored "with socks, ties, suspenders, pipes, and other gifts." The group realized that it would take more work to make the holiday a success and, in that same year, expanded the Father's Day Council into a larger group with a broader reach, the

National Council for the Promotion of Father's Day. The aim of the group was to boost sales through increasing demand for gifts, and to do this it needed to get Father's Day accepted, as one council member said, as "a real day . . . firmly established in the minds of everyone."[12] The man behind the National Council for the Promotion of Father's Day was advertising executive Alvin Austin. Austin's concept was to develop Father's Day into a national holiday through public-affairs programming based on a civic-oriented campaign. The breakthrough that Alvin Austin brought to the concept of promoting Father's Day was the public downplaying of commercial gain.[13]

In 1937, the "volume of national and local newspaper advertising devoted to Father's Day doubled and was the largest on record,"[14] and by 1939, the Father's Day Council and its allies in the business community had managed to convince growing numbers of public officials and private organizations to throw their support behind Father's Day. The governors of New York, Minnesota, New Mexico, New Jersey, Florida, Wyoming, Maryland, Virginia, Utah, Kentucky, Michigan, Ohio, and Texas reportedly gave their approval. So did the boards of the Rotary, Kiwanis, Lions, Exchange, and other men's organizations. Sales were 20 percent higher than they were in 1938.[15]

In 1940, the *Times* reported that "advertising of Father's Day gifts by retailers reached a new record." In 1941, Father's Day sales were up 22 percent over the previous year, and 1942 saw yet another 20 percent jump. Financially, the Father's Day movement was the strongest it had ever been. The years 1941 and 1942 were also a time when Father's Day was immediately and deliberately tied to the war effort. The 1941 slogan chosen by the Father's Day Council was "Salute Dad the American Way," and in 1942, the slogan was "Father—The Defender of the Home."[16] In 1949, Alvin Austin announced that what was most important about Father's Day was its "sentimental and spiritual character." The group's slogan was appropriately retailored: "Remember Father, Molder of Our Children's Future— For a Safe World Tomorrow Teach Democracy Today." Following this 1949 campaign with its loaded slogan, the council delighted in an estimated $106 million in holiday sales volume.[17]

Sonora Smart Dodd remained involved in some way with the Father's Day Council throughout her life. While she declined to become the spokesperson for any one line of Father's Day goods, she happily endorsed the various "gifts for father" campaigns of the Father's Day Council. When asked about the commercialism of Father's Day in 1972, six years before her death at the age of ninety-six, she responded, "Oh, I like it, I love it. I love seeing fathers get gifts. Besides all the cards, advertising and special promotions have done one major thing—focused attention on observance of the day." Even three years later, speaking from a convalescent home she was hortatory: "Father's Day is best celebrated by showering the fathers with gifts on his special day." By then, the Father's Day Council estimated the holiday to be worth more than $1 billion in retail sales.[18]

By the mid-1980s, the Father's Day Council was convinced that the group had achieved its dream: "Father's Day has transcended a day of celebration into a 'season' of three weeks, has become a 'Second Christmas' for all of the men's gift-oriented industries."[19] At the turn of the twenty-first century, Father's Day retains an important economic impact for retailers. "There is not much else to drive retail sales in the summer, except clothing," says National Retail Federation spokesman Scott Krugman. "Having spending days like Father's Day, where people are purchasing things other than clothing, like electronics or home improvement items, gives a much-needed boost to retailers until we hit the start of school."[20]

With such a long consumer history, why do dad's gifts still seem inferior to mom's? In 1927, a writer for the Spokane, Washington, *Spokesman-Review* observed, "What Mother's Day is to the florists, Father's Day is to the necktie trust."[21] From the beginning, Father's Day gifts were regarded as a joke: "Observers often found it funny how people bought up gaudy ties or bad cigars or pasteboard greetings for Dad. (It was funny, too, how fathers had to feign appreciation for these things and actually wear, smoke, or display them.) That such holiday merchandise could be moved was part of the wonder of American enterprise and salesmanship."[22] At no other time of year are work clothes and razors elevated to the lofty status of gift. In 1995, 78 million electric razors were sold; 15 percent of those were sold for Father's Day.[23] Socks, shirts, ties, and shavers are dad's gifts.[24]

Some of the awkwardness surrounding Father's Day gift giving stems from traditional male roles. Both Father's Day and Mother's Day are holidays celebrated with expressions of affection, and while mothers are seen as emotional caregivers, fathers are labeled protectors and providers. The fact that Americans tend to shy away from sentiment when it comes to their fathers is one explanation for the ten million ties handed out every Father's Day.[25] "There is a sacredness associated with mothers that is not accorded to fathers," says Ralph LaRossa, professor of sociology at Georgia State. "While one could make a convincing argument that fathers should be celebrated for being the defenders of the home and the primary economic provider, these holidays emphasize the domestic sphere, and Mom is still much more of an integral part of that sphere."[26] According to Allen Jones, a professor of family studies at Miami University, "Fathers today are sort of relief pitchers. When mom needs a break that's when dad is likely to step in. It's almost like a second-rate holiday for that reason."[27] A second-rate holiday with second-rate gifts. And "those 'gag gifts' associated with Father's Day reflect the profound ambivalence that our culture feels about emotional connections to fathers," says Scott Coltrane, a sociologist at the University of California at Riverside.[28] It is dad's historically established role of breadwinner that stereotypes his position as unemotional and therefore makes Father's Day gifts a source of particular irony. Dad was the one who, in the end, would have to pay for all those gadgets and trinkets.[29]

Some of the discrepancies between Father's Day and Mother's Day also have to do with ever-changing family dynamics. Roughly half of all first marriages end in divorce; the rate is even higher, nearly two-thirds, for remarriages. As many as two out of three children spend some time in a single-parent household before reaching age eighteen. Most children stay with their mothers; maternal custody remains at nearly 90 percent. After divorce, non-custodial fathers lose much of their power over their children. They also lose their relationship with their spouse, which often connected them to and facilitated their relationship with their children in the first place.[30] Even adult children of divorced parents live, on average, twice as close to their mothers as to their fathers.[31] Additionally, it is becoming more common for children to grow up without ever knowing their biological fathers. This also helps to explain the significantly lower sales figures associated with Father's Day celebrations.

As more households have become two-income, parents' roles have evolved. Fathers are no longer the sole providers; mothers are no longer the only ones responsible for childcare. As men take more active roles in their children's lives, Father's Day may move up in the holiday pantheon.[32] A National Retail Federation survey from 2002 showed that consumers planned to spend an average of $95 per household on Father's Day that year—a big jump from $52.30 in 2001. According to Gerald Celente, director of the Trends Research Institute, the shifting role of fathers in today's society is one reason for the increase in Father's Day–related spending. He points out that today's dads are more involved with raising their children than were fathers in the 1950s.[33]

As father-child relationships change, so too do the variety of Father's Day gifts. Hallmark features fewer dads befuddled by diaper changes and more straight-faced sentiment. Spas are recommending pampering dads with manicures or facials.[34] Even though neckties and tools may be traditional Father's Day gifts, technology and entertainment products are becoming increasingly popular for today's dads. According to a study done by the International Mass Retail Association, entertainment products such as CDs, books, videos, and DVDs ranked as some of the top items planned for Father's Day in 2002.[35] Sure beats a tie covered with airplanes.

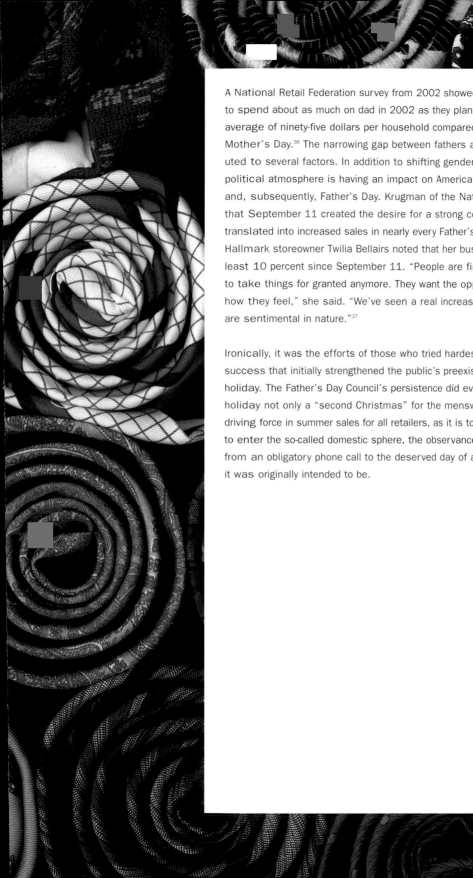

A National Retail Federation survey from 2002 showed that consumers planned to spend about as much on dad in 2002 as they planned to spend on mom—an average of ninety-five dollars per household compared to ninety-seven dollars for Mother's Day.[36] The narrowing gap between fathers and mothers can be attributed to several factors. In addition to shifting gender roles, the current unstable political atmosphere is having an impact on America's attitudes toward family and, subsequently, Father's Day. Krugman of the National Retail Federation said that September 11 created the desire for a strong connection with family that translated into increased sales in nearly every Father's Day gift category in 2002. Hallmark storeowner Twilia Bellairs noted that her business has increased by at least 10 percent since September 11. "People are finding that they don't want to take things for granted anymore. They want the opportunity to tell loved ones how they feel," she said. "We've seen a real increase in Father's Day cards that are sentimental in nature."[37]

Ironically, it was the efforts of those who tried hardest to make Father's Day a success that initially strengthened the public's preexisting skepticism toward the holiday. The Father's Day Council's persistence did eventually pay off, making the holiday not only a "second Christmas" for the menswear industry but also the driving force in summer sales for all retailers, as it is today. As more men continue to enter the so-called domestic sphere, the observance of Father's Day may evolve from an obligatory phone call to the deserved day of appreciation and honor that it was originally intended to be.

A Family Tree

Paula GGGM

GGGF

George GGGF

Georgette GGGM

Charles GGGF

Bethany GGGM

Fred GGGM

Sidney GGGF

Carla GGM

Margaret GGGM

Molly GGM

Henry GGF

Jude GGF

Kenneth

Charlie GF

Charlie GF

Caroline GM

M. GM

Kay GM

GF.

Julia M.

David

M. Janet

The Making of a Holiday

Maud Lavin

Since I am a stepparent, I decided to exercise my rights as a citizen and try to create a commemorative day through Congress to be called Stepparents' Day. No date has been settled on, but June 21 has been suggested; it comes after Mother's Day and Father's Day but is still in the vicinity. I contacted Yul Edwards in the Washington, D.C., office of Representative Danny Davis, Democrat of Illinois, and he formalized my proposal. Subsequently, staffer Caleb Gilchrist has suggested that I raise individual and organizational (from religious and child-welfare organizations, for example) support for the day. With this support, the bill could garner cosponsors.

107TH CONGRESS
2D SESSION H. RES.
Recognizing the contributions of stepparents to the lives of their stepchildren.
IN THE HOUSE OF REPRESENTATIVES
Mr. **DAVIS** of Illinois submitted the following resolution . . .
RESOLUTION
Recognizing the contributions of stepparents to the lives of their stepchildren. Whereas given the high rates of divorce and remarriage a significant number of children are raised by stepparents in addition to their biological parents; Whereas stepparents love, nurture, and care for their stepchildren; Whereas stepparents are essential to motivating, guiding, and supporting their stepchildren; Whereas on Mother's Day or Father's Day, children with stepparents can feel stress and divided loyalties; Whereas having a day specifically for honoring stepparents would help children with stepparents express their appreciation for a stepparent; and Whereas both the stepchild and the stepparent deserve this celebration of their familial relationship: Now, therefore, be it Resolved, That the House of Representatives recognizes the contributions of stepparents to the lives of their stepchildren.

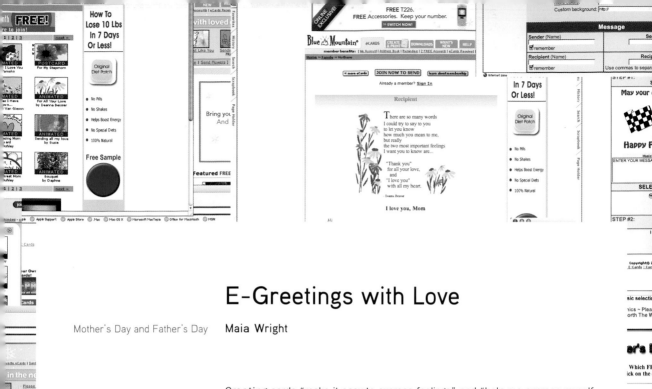

E-Greetings with Love

Mother's Day and Father's Day   Maia Wright

Greeting cards "make it easy to express feelings" and "help me express myself
better than I can alone."
—Greeting Card Association[1]

People look to Hallmark to help them say what they may not know how to say
on their own . . . The relationships we have with our friends and families are the
most important part of our lives. Hallmark is privileged to be trusted with those
relationships.
—Paul Barker, senior vice president of creative product development, Hallmark[2]

It's like you're having words put in your mouth, and if they're not just right, it
doesn't sound like you . . . And it's never just right—unless *you* wrote the copy
for that card!
—Dan Chrzanowski, illustrator for American Greetings[3]

Mother's Day is a holiday based not on religious observance or historical commemoration but on burned French toast served in bed, flowers, and cards, all with the
same message. It is a day based on "Thank you for everything. I love you." Since
it is a holiday expressly set aside for communicating, Mother's Day has been a
greeting-card darling since its inception in 1908 and currently ranks third in seasonal card sales, behind Christmas and Valentine's Day. Father's Day, founded in
1910 (also through the grassroots efforts of a devoted daughter), follows Mother's
Day not only in the calendar but in greeting-card popularity.

When it comes to saying "I love you, Mom and Dad," Americans overwhelmingly turn to our Cyrano de Bergeracs in the greeting-card industry, primarily the giants: Hallmark (founded in 1910) and American Greetings (founded in 1906). In 2001, the Greeting Card Association reported sales of roughly 140 million Mother's Day cards and 87.5 million Father's Day cards.[4] According to an industry homily, those purchases depend on how well the card speaks for the consumer: "It's the design that attracts, but it's the verse that sells."[5] What is it about sharing personal and intimate emotions that causes buyers to run to the anonymity of the greeting-card aisle?

Whatever the psychological mechanisms at work, this phenomenon does not show any sign of fading. The paper-greeting-card industry reported a 20 percent growth in retail sales from 1993 to 2002,[6] and on Mother's Day 2001, nearly 3.5 million children and spouses sought out prepackaged eloquence in the form of electronic greeting cards at the three major e-card sites (Bluemountain.com, American-greetings.com, and Hallmark.com).[7] What *is* changing is not the search for words of familial love but the communication of those words.

In May 2002 (just a week before Mother's Day), the Nielsen/NetRatings research group released a study that reported, "Sending and receiving e-mail was the dominant online activity in 12 countries over the past six months . . . at least 75% of households with Internet access participated in e-mail."[8] According to a 2002 study by the Centre for Urban and Community Studies at the University of Toronto, "The Internet has blended into the rhythms of every day life . . . it is used for a wide variety of purposes, such as surfing for information, playing online games, and chatting."[9] The organization is also conducting extensive research on a place it calls Netville, an experimental mid-price housing development near Toronto that is equipped with high-speed direct Internet access. The researchers found a community of "glocalized" citizens: people involved in both local and long-distance relationships. Rather than isolating people, the Internet became a way to keep in touch with friends and family near and far, close or casual. In fact, in comparison with their non-wired counterparts, the residents of Netville knew more of their neighbors' names, had more face-to-face contact with neighbors, and maintained more long-distance contact with far-flung friends and relatives.[10]

These days, we are all living in Netville. The Internet has become a pervasive way of life; for most, it is mainly about e-mail. A new communicative organ has been born, and new generations who grow up in an increasingly wired world are more adept at using it. Little wonder that a small, family-owned greeting-card company with no business plan to speak of became an industry giant simply by launching a Web site offering free electronic greeting cards.

Blue Mountain Arts dates back to 1971, when the husband-and-wife team of Susan and Stephen Polis Schutz decided to start a line of home-grown greeting cards. Susan wrote poetry and Stephen painted watercolors. They filled a gap that the major greeting-card corporations had overlooked—cards that would help people express non-seasonal love and affection, what Susan called "relationship oriented emotions."[11] In other words, they were making Mother's and Father's Day cards for every day of the year.

In 1992, when the Schutzes' son Jared left Boulder, Colorado, for Princeton University, the family relied on e-mail to keep in touch. After graduating in 1996, Jared started Bluemountain.com with a simple ambition: to "offer a service that would be fun and would help build our brand of printed cards."[12] But it took off. The greeting-card industry's service to the American public—supplying the words and images to articulate and illustrate emotions—was now translated into bits and bytes. In two and a half years, Bluemountain.com took over the tenth position on Media Metrix's list of most-visited Web sites, besting big names like Time Warner, Amazon.com, and eBay, with 12 million visitors in February 1999.[13]

The e-card revolution was groundbreaking in several ways. First, there was the business model. Ink-and-paper greeting-card corporations had built a billion-dollar business by fulfilling the need for prescribed emotions ($7.5 billion according to the Greeting Card Association's 2002 industry report).[14] But then came the dot-com explosion. Internet start-up companies operated on economies of scale and focused on the amount of traffic, instead of the number of dollars, they could generate. In *Emotion Marketing: The Hallmark Way of Winning Customers for Life,* Hallmark's marketing strategists identify the Internet as a source of enormous potential market growth. The authors point out that "marketers haven't yet leveraged emotion on the Internet" and state that "online consumers yearn for a brand to speak to them as individuals."[15] With a bank of computers and some innovative programming by Stephen Schutz, Bluemountain.com was capable of offering its users a choice of two thousand electronic greeting cards—all for free. "We have no need for capital right now," Jared Schutz said in 1999. "But we're keeping our options open."[16] On October 25 of that same year, attesting to the value of Bluemountain.com's popularity among the online population, Excite@Home purchased the e-card company for $780 million.[17] The site has since been passed on to American Greetings Corporation, which purchased it for $35 million in September 2001 and now asks users to pay a subscription fee.[18] The Schutz family business ethic of free emotion and free e-cards had fallen back on tried-and-true capitalism.

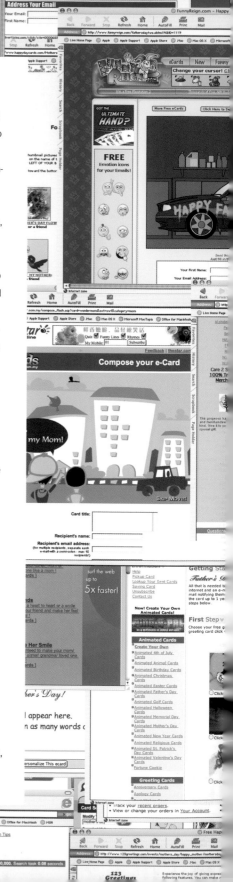

But the Bluemountain.com venture was pushing other revolutionary buttons as well—in fact, they were getting consumers to push buttons. The sender of the card became the copywriter and sometimes also the art director. People who had spent hours searching through drugstore racks for that perfect greeting card, who would never dream of designing that card themselves, were suddenly coming up with their own words. The familiarity of the computer-screen format made the transition a smooth one. One Hallmark writer comments, "People aren't comfortable with their power of writing. They feel they can't say it right."[19] But the card-buying public *is* comfortable with the power of writing—writing e-mail, writing in chat rooms, writing in Web forms.

The potential for a customer to tailor his or her own card to the specific relationship between sender and recipient has freed up card design, especially for Mother's and Father's Day cards. Dan Chrzanowski, an illustrator who has worked at American Greetings for more than thirty years, laments the limitations of illustrating this genre of cards: "They're pretty much in the same category. If I go to work tomorrow, and someone says 'pick a card,' I would not pick those holidays. I'm just not interested."[20] For Father's Day, he says, the acceptable image is a solitary male figure, usually seen from the back and rendered as generically as possible. "Think of yourself walking up to a rack," he explains. "You know your father is balding and gray-haired. This figure has a full head of hair. That will hurt sales. That's what we are told, through the corporate culture." Here is where e-cards offer room for artistic creativity. Father's Day cards at Bluemountain.com include interactive cards that serve up a full menu of facial features, hair (or lack of it), wardrobe, and accessories.

The interactive aspect of e-cards has still not been fully explored. Most Bluemountain.com cards have a uniform look—a visual approach Jared Schutz admits is "mushy."[21] John Sullivan of Hallmark.com predicted, in a 2001 interview with the *New York Times,* "A year from now . . . with so many broadband users coming on, those cards will look like the old Pong game."[22] In even less generous terms, a critic for *Newsweek* summed up Blue Mountain's e-card line: "Looks like a 6-year-old's art project."[23] So there is some room for improvement. The current design process starts and ends at the computer; an illustrator sends a digital file to an art director, who selects a musical score and integrates a program that makes certain card features customizable.[24] As an illustrator for the paper-card division of American Greetings, Chrzanowski does not come into much contact with the creatives in the Americangreetings.com wing. Occasionally, a few adventurous Web artists will visit his studio, which has intaglio and offset printing, ceramics, and letterpress capabilities: "They're just glad to work in any media

where they can get their hands dirty." He supports more emphasis on interactivity: "They should explore that. That's a valid way to go."[25]

As for his own plans for Mother's and Father's Day, Chrzanowski will not be browsing the racks for a mass-printed greeting card for his own family. "I don't like most of them—I don't." Instead, he will create a personal painting for his wife and attach it to a bouquet—"but it's not a traditional card that you buy and sign and put in the mail." And what is he expecting from his children on Father's Day? "A blank card with a wonderful piece of art on the front from the latest show they saw— like a Matisse or a Picasso image. And it would be addressed to me, and have the sentiments that they want inside."

In its 2002 report on the future of the industry, the Greeting Card Association predicts, "Not only are computers bringing people closer together, they are also getting people back into the habit of correspondence by writing. In fact, e-mail and electronic greetings are complementing paper greeting cards, not replacing them."[26] Either way, there is hope that more people will be writing the words of their cards themselves, so that the sentiments on the inside of the card will match those from inside the sender.

Icons, Activism, and the Cachet of Pride

Gay Pride Day   Gerald Posley

Gay Pride Day is celebrated every year on the last Sunday in June to commemo-rate the anniversary of the Stonewall Riots of 1969, which are widely perceived as the start of the gay liberation movement in the United States. The celebration of Gay Pride has gone from a simple protest march in June 1970 to a major parade of products, pitches, and icons clamoring for a moment in the spotlight and for the attention of dollars. In the process of enhancing the visibility of gays and gay issues, consumerism has turned a political movement into a lucrative niche mar-ket—but to what end? Does the hyperactive consumption of gayness compromise the integrity of the movement or serve to push it into the wider consciousness? Is gayness too simply rendered in its iconic representations of a diverse community? Has consumerism been beneficial to the gay community? What is the next step in this marriage of consumerism and activism? How can this dynamic best facilitate understanding, enlightenment, and empowerment?

On Friday, June 27, 1969, police raided the Stonewall Inn, a private club at 53 Christopher Street in Greenwich Village. They served a warrant allowing them to confiscate liquor and expel some two hundred patrons from the bar. Though Stonewall had been in operation for two years, the police department suddenly claimed knowledge that the inn was serving liquor without a license,[1] and for this violation, the bar was to be closed. Such raids on gay bars were routine occurrences that exploited homosexuals and lined the pockets of corrupt police officers.[2]

Although there were only a few policemen on hand for the initial confrontation, a crowd gathered in Sheridan Square across from the Stonewall. Spectators were cheering the patrons who were being escorted onto the street. The mood was surreal as the queens waved and blew kisses to the crowd.[3] Gay street youth, a faction often overlooked in the history of that night's riot, provided much of the uprising's heat. These young gay men, often homeless, turned tricks as a means of survival. As the conflict escalated and taunts became airborne debris, this group was front and center along with the drag queens.[4] The gays began spewing money, compacts, lipstick tubes, bobby pins, curlers, and eventually rocks and a parking meter. Clearly overwhelmed, the policemen fell back inside the bar to regroup and call for backup. Forty-five minutes later, the tactical force arrived. The scrap lasted from about midnight until about 2:00 in the morning. Official reports listed four injuries and thirteen arrests. The crowd reached a volume of about four hundred.[5]

More significant than the first night of rioting, which was a spontaneous reaction that grew out of a sense of repeated and long-term abuse, were the second and third nights. The rioters' return on the subsequent evenings turned a police raid into a political protest, which Craig Rodwell called "a public assertion of real anger by gay people that was just electric."[6] Also different on the second night was the self-empowerment infusing the crowd. Gays and lesbians had realized that they could stand up to oppression together and fight. The tactical force was once again called to Sheridan Square at 2:15 in the morning after the Charles Street station house was unable to control the crowd.[7] Pride took root those nights in the Village and brought resistance into fruition. A new wave of gay liberation had begun.

In 1970, thousands of gays and lesbians participated in the first Gay Pride Day Parade—essentially a protest march starting in Greenwich Village and ending in Central Park. The participants came from all over the Northeast to protest laws that declared homosexual acts between consenting adults illegal and to voice concerns over social conditions that made it impossible for them to show affection for one another in public, rent apartments, and hold jobs. They gathered in Sheridan Square and marched up the Avenue of the Americas to hold a "gay in" in the park. "We're probably the most harassed and persecuted minority group in history, but we'll never have the freedom and civil rights we deserve unless we stop hiding in closets and in the shelter of anonymity," said twenty-nine-year-old Michael Browne, founder of the Gay Liberation Front, an activist homosexual organization.[8] The march garnered the attention of hundreds, some taking pictures, others seemingly startled, but there was little open animosity, and some even applauded. Homosexuals had found their strength.

In the years since the Stonewall Riots and that first Gay Pride Day Parade, "gay" has become more and more radically visible, shedding stigmatization and defining its own identity. The pursuit of civil liberties through activism has served to politicize movies, art, fashion, popular music, commercial advertising, theater, and pornography. More and more Americans have become sensitive to the ongoing struggle of gays and lesbians to claim equal rights, including the rights to love and live happy, fulfilled lives with dignity and respect. The passions and talents of gays and lesbians have left an indelible impression on American culture and informed a revolution that will reach deep into the future. Visibility has helped to lift stigmatization and fear, and it is becoming clear that people have more things in common than not. At the same time that gayness is becoming more mainstream, how can the spirit of the movement be preserved and inequities within the gay community be addressed? How much of this responsibility should be in the hands of consumerist interests involved in Gay Pride Day? How can integrity be maintained?

As I thought about these questions, three answers were inspired by the unexpected arrival of an invitation: 1. Show up. 2. Speak out. 3. Be counted. On April 14, 2003, Zipatoni, an advertising agency based in Saint Louis, with offices in Chicago, held a focus group on beer advertisements targeted to gays. The invitation read, "Is anyone out there really doing it right? Join us for happy hour (drinks and eats) as we discuss marketing to the gay community."

Zipatoni convened a group of ten gay men, ranging in age from twenty-two to thirty-six, from diverse ethnic and professional backgrounds, for ninety minutes of meet, eat, drink, and participate in a videotaped question-and-answer session. The topic was social drinking habits, and as we soon discovered, the project in

development was the 2004 Gay Pride campaign for Miller Lite beer. The ads we viewed and discussed were for placement inside gay bars and were diverse in their approaches to Gay Pride. While the "spiritual" ones did not exclude the body beautiful, it did not feel like their primary focus. The look was pleasantly sensual with poignant and powerful tag lines and starred flying or floating figures swathed in the rainbow flag. Other ads solicited groans of displeasure. These tended toward a beer-in-one-hand, sex-in-the-other approach with tag lines like "More than friends" or "See where the night goes." The good taste of the group and the receptiveness of Zipatoni were pleasant surprises, especially given some past print ads aimed at the gay community.

The kitschy and humorous ads featured some reworked Tom of Finland drawings from the late 1980s. The funniest featured men in leather jackets and tight jeans holding bottles of Miller Lite; the image used was one of Tom's milder works, but amply present were his over-buffed body parts rising up like impossibly molded loaves of bread. The headline, "Bottoms Up," was a spin on a 1966 gay pulp novel of the same title by Ned Winslow. As we looked over the ads, one of the designers quipped, "We just threw in the Tom of Finland stuff to make Miller nervous."

It is noteworthy that an artist like Tom of Finland would even be considered for such a mainstream product. This move reflects not only a shift in the level of awareness of gay buying power but also the radical alteration in work environments since the time of the Stonewall riots. Discrimination then was a much stronger force, one that kept people closeted, especially at work.[9] Several of the designers working on the Miller Lite campaign were openly gay, as was the target market and thus the focus group. Miller may be exploiting an opportunity by aligning itself with the Gay Pride celebration, but then again, homosexuals are no longer invisible socially, politically, or economically. The people involved in this project, especially the gay ones, have a deeper connection and commitment to its outcome and, because of this vested interest, could well create communication that reflects more positively on the gay community.

Who in 1969 would have thought that thirty-four years later mainstream companies like Starbucks would be making strides to foster more gay-, lesbian-, bisexual-, and transgender-friendly work environments?[10] According to the Human Rights Campaign's "State of the Workplace 2002" report, between 2000 and 2002 there was a 50 percent increase in the number of companies nationwide that offer domestic-partner benefits.[11] The number of Fortune 500 companies with nondiscrimination policies that include sexual orientation reached 311 in 2002, and the number of Fortune 500 companies offering domestic-partner benefits grew to 189.[12] As change sweeps through the corporate infrastructure, should there be a concern about what is motivating it?

Fortune 500 companies are picking up on the power of the gay dollar and wooing gay consumers. Advertising in the gay media is one of the fastest-growing niches in publishing, with a 20 percent increase in 1998. With the exception of black media, ad revenue in other niches had only single-digit gains. Advertising dollars in the gay press more than doubled in the years between 1994 and 1998, from $53 million to $120 million.[13] Gay Pride events mirror this growth trend with dramatically increased levels of corporate sponsorship. In 1988, the Los Angeles Gay Pride event attracted only one corporate sponsor, Anheuser-Busch. By 1998, corporate sponsorship of the event topped one million dollars.[14] Whether it is good will or just good business, corporations are rejoining the parade that they all but abandoned during the height of the AIDS crisis in the mid-1980s. Two major components contribute to this dynamic: the disposable income of gays and the failure of protests against corporations that acknowledge gays. The latter has sent the message to corporations that they can market to the gay community without fear of backlash and has led to advertising directed at gays in the mainstream media as well.[15]

A shift occurred in advertising in the late 1990s. More and more mainstream ads became openly gay to a degree greater than previously seen even in gay publications. In 1994, Ikea made history with the first prime-time television ads featuring a gay male couple shopping for furniture.[16] A Diesel Jeans ad featuring real-life couple Bob and Rod Paris-Jackson passionately kissing in front of a military vessel full of cheering sailors ran in *Details* magazine in May 1995. Levi Strauss ran a series of ads on MTV featuring teenagers speaking about their lives. A gay teen describes the moment when he inadvertently outed himself to his father.[17] What is most significant is that these ads were featured in mainstream venues.

The gay influence is everywhere, and the hard line between gay and straight is softening. Today, young straight men mimic the fashion profile of gay men of the 1970s with tattoos, piercings, and hyper-masculine drag. The affectation of "bling bling" in hip-hop culture as well as the preoccupation with painted fingernails among young straight men in the Goth and alternative-music scenes echoes drag-queen costumes and grooming. What was once taboo is now everyday. These elements of visual culture are an indication that much progress has been made. This progress is due in part to the synthesis of commercialism and activism and its effect on the people it has touched. Gay Pride is on parade, not just on the last Sunday in June but in the integrated fabric of daily life. With activism, creativity, and passion, gay and lesbian people have transformed themselves from violated, fragmented individuals into a cohesive movement seeking liberty in the pursuit of happiness.

Among the many icons of the movement is the rainbow flag, created by Gilbert Baker in 1978 to embody the potential of the gay community. The eight colors of the original flag were for a time reduced to six, due to limitations of commercial reproduction, but 2003 saw the return of the lost colors. The stripes are pink (restored, sexuality), red (life), orange (healing), yellow (the sun), green (nature), blue (art), violet (the spirit), and turquoise (restored, harmony).[18]

Gay Mart, a retail shop specializing in gay-themed merchandise, was opened by Shelly Rosenbaum in Chicago in 1993. Items in the store range from the erotic and political to the silly and whimsical. He explains why he opened the store: "I saw a need to provide specific goods for and about people in this community. Years ago there were no places that collected all of these products together in one place to sell to gay and lesbian people."[19] The business began its operation in a 500-square-foot space and expanded to 1,200 square feet to accommodate the growing volume of products. Rosenbaum notes that in the 1980s the neighborhood was rather seedy: "There was prostitution and drugs, but it has really come up, due mostly to the gay-owned businesses in the diverse neighborhood. We as a community made this what it is today." He describes his customer base as being about 80 percent gay and notes that "the rainbow flag and anything adorned with it" are his most popular items "hands down." Rosenbaum says that June, Gay Pride month, is outranked in sales only by December and Christmas.[20]

Even the world of toys is coming out in pride. Totem International has created three thirteen-inch, eleven-pound, molded-vinyl effigies to manhood: Billy, "the world's first out and proud gay doll"; Carlos, "the world's first out and proud boyfriend"; and Tyson, "the world's first out and proud best friend."[21] One-of-a-kind Billys were featured in a charity exhibition and auction, "Billy Opens His

Closet for LIFEbeat: The Music Industry Fights Aids," at the New Museum of Contemporary Art in New York on June 2, 1998. The Billys were dressed by international fashion designers including Calvin Klein, Gianni Versace, and Jean Paul Gaultier. Other corporate brand names included Levi Strauss, Fila, Stüssy, and Diesel; gay fashion icons represented were Tom of Finland and Raymond Dragon. The dolls were auctioned by Christie's. Sales reached $60,000; the event, which raised a total of $425,000, was covered internationally.[22]

"Fierce ruling diva" RuPaul became the first drag queen in history to represent a major cosmetics company when in 1994 MAC Cosmetics declared him the first face of MAC and launched the "Who is the MAC girl?" campaign.[23] The visual presentation was over the top, with RuPaul dressed in an extreme corset outfit and posing to spell out the words "Viva Glam," a line of lipsticks developed by MAC. The proceeds of all Viva Glam lipsticks go to the MAC AIDS Fund.[24] An out and proud gay black man, in stiletto heels no less, as the beauty icon for women shopping for lipstick: it does not get more mainstream or more consumerist than this. Mainstream consumerism notwithstanding, activism remains important to the Viva Glam story and to the public presence of gays and lesbians.

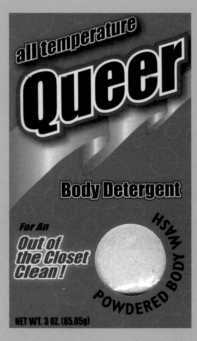

all temperature
Queer
Body Detergent

For An
Out of the Closet Clean !

POWDERED BODY WASH

NET WT. 3 OZ. (85.05g)

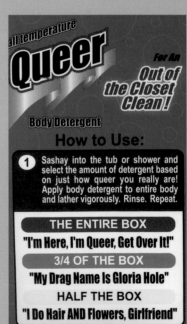

all temperature
Queer

For An
Out of the Closet Clean !

Body Detergent

How to Use:

1. Sashay into the tub or shower and select the amount of detergent based on just how queer you really are! Apply body detergent to entire body and lather vigorously. Rinse. Repeat.

THE ENTIRE BOX
"I'm Here, I'm Queer, Get Over It!"

3/4 OF THE BOX
"My Drag Name Is Gloria Hole"

HALF THE BOX
"I Do Hair AND Flowers, Girlfriend"

Business Quarter 3
Summer

The Nation's Glamour:
Fireworks on the Fourth

Independence Day   Zhivka Valiavicharska

Whether we are fifth-generation Americans or illegal aliens smuggled across the border, once we are on U.S. land, we all celebrate the Fourth. Independence Day, the most national of American holidays, is a day of incorporation and assimilation, not of exclusion.[1] For example, on July 4, Chicago's Humboldt Park—a neighborhood densely populated by Mexicans and Puerto Ricans—turns into one of the most festive, loud places in the city with ethnic food and music accompanying hamburgers, chilled cans of beer, and improvised fireworks displays.

A manifestation of American democracy, pluralism, and freedom, the Fourth of July was once celebrated with organized parades, political speeches, and public reenactments of the signing of the Declaration of Independence. Today it is more concentrated around barbeque grills and fireworks spectacles. While the generous picnic spread remains an expression of family celebration, states and municipalities spend millions of dollars on more and more sensational, staggeringly large-scale fireworks performances. The content of such events is ideologically programmed to arouse optimism and excitement in the hearts of people from diverse ethnicities, races, and social categories in order to provide a common positive experience and to create the emotional content of a national community. In this respect, Matthew Dennis notes in his *Red, White, and Blue Letter Days* that fireworks "seldom connect spectators to their historical past or call matters of civic importance to their collective attention."[2] Only the famous quote by John Adams, who signed the Declaration of Independence as a member of the Continental Congress, remains central to present-day commemorations of the historic Independence Day: "[The Declaration of Independence] ought to be solemnized with pomp and parade, with shows, games, sports, guns, bells, bonfires, and illuminations, from one end of this continent to the other, from this time forward forevermore."[3]

Every collective history can be repressive and exclusionary as well as a ground for a common identity, and the historical circumstances around American Independence Day are not an exception. July 4, 1776, was the date when the Continental Congress—a committee formed two years earlier to represent the concerns of the American colonies to the British Empire—adopted the final draft of the so-called Declaration of Independence. Today, the American nation is comprised of people with divergent pasts and cultures, and this is why the celebration of its beginning need not be a day of remembering specific historic events but rather a day of forgetting different pasts.[4]

Thus devoid of any political or historical content, fireworks have become a positive emotional expression of nationalism, a spiritual embodiment of Americanness, an abstract celebration of democracy and pluralism. The visual power of fireworks, along with their political "neutrality," is a cultural push that contributes to the flood of immigrants converging continuously into a single national community. Today, fireworks have become an emblem of American values to the extent that it is difficult to use them for other events without invoking nationalist sentiments. Everyone expects a spectacle provided by their local governments on the Fourth, and each year cities have to come up with a more and more glamorous show. In 2000, New York's annual Macy's extravaganza, produced by Grucci, spread not only over the East River but also over the Hudson River and several other locations to make hundreds of thousands of people look toward the sky. Sixty thousand shells of gunpowder (two thousand per minute) were launched into the dark sky on that day from three buildings and twelve barges around Manhattan.[5] The "oohhhing" and "aahhhing" was loud and expansive.

For those who prefer to spend the holiday in someone's backyard, the homemade fireworks display is an inevitable part of the festivities. And this is where patriotism meets consumerism in contemporary American culture. The American Pyrotechnics Association reports, "due to increased pride and patriotism of Americans," consumer fireworks usage has almost tripled since the 1990s, from 67.6 million pounds of gunpowder to 161.6 million pounds in 2001.[6] Yet reliable statistics are hard to come by for a number of reasons. It is no secret that there is a black market for fireworks—from homemade firecrackers to illegal distribution networks—so much so that the illicit goods comprise a considerable part of the business. In this sense, it is safe to assume that consumption is actually much larger than the official number. For safety reasons, state governments attempt to keep the production, sale, and consumption of fireworks under legal control through a variety of laws. Personal, unauthorized use of gunpowder is restricted to "consumer" fireworks virtually everywhere in the U.S. and completely banned in eight states.[7] Yet many are tempted to break the law for the sake of national celebration.

And law enforcement is often quietly complicit in the illegal use of explosives on the Fourth of July. Weeks before that day, dedicated fireworks lovers who live in states where the use of the festive explosives is prohibited drive for hours to load their cars with splashy shells, snakes, dancing butterflies, helicopters, satellites, sparkling jets, and parachutes landing with whistles and spins. Local and corporate distributors line up their seasonal retail booths along state borders. Illinois residents drive to Indiana to buy loud amusements; residents of Memphis do not even have to leave the city area, because the Mississippi/Tennessee border cuts right through the suburbs of Memphis.

In recent years, the U.S. fireworks industry has grown enormously, while fireworks companies have come to rely almost exclusively on American Independence Day pride to prosper. For example, each year the national corporation Zambelli produces more than 3,500 megashows, half for "fireworks season," when over one million shells burst into the air;[8] the cost of Grucci's best-known "state-of-the-art" shows can reach one hundred thousand dollars for thirty minutes.[9] Other companies have gone global, using cheaper labor in developing and underdeveloped countries to produce the sparkly goods. The irony of the "Made in China" tag on the majority of fireworks and American flags currently purchased in stores—both products are undeniable manifestations of national identity—is rich. In 2001, for example, the fireworks import business totaled $128.9 million, with China providing $121.6 million (about 95 percent).[10] Another striking statistic is the staggering growth in the import of American flags immediately after September 11—from $1.1 million in 2000 to $51.7 million at the end of 2001. More than half of the flags (worth $29.7 million) were supplied by China, due to an unevenly developing global economy.[11] In the Chinese province Jiangxi, for example, fireworks production is a dominant industry responsible for the survival of millions; nevertheless, the unsafe conditions of thousands of private workshops and factories throughout the region expose workers to the risk of serious injury or death. Such facts are reminders that, in an increasingly globalizing world, national celebrations of holidays like the Fourth of July are no longer simply national events—they affect, culturally as well as economically, distant parts of the rest of the world.

Man, I Feel Like a Woman

Southern Decadence   Loren Stephens

If John Waters were asked to organize Mardi Gras, it would look a lot like Southern Decadence. It is a celebration that prompts bar and restaurant owners to post signs requesting of their patrons "No public urination, no sex in public, no public nudity, and no bottles in the street." "Go cups" are acceptable, and the definition of nudity is open to debate. It is the kind of all-out, over-the-top (with little on the bottom) celebration that only New Orleans could host.

Southern Decadence began in September 1972 in a New Orleans home affection-ately dubbed "Belle Reve" in homage to Blanche DuBois's plantation in *A Streetcar Named Desire*. A group of gay and straight college friends living in Belle Reve threw a private farewell party for fellow resident Michael Evers and encouraged attendees to dress as their favorite "decadent southern" character.[1] The friends continued to meet annually, and the event has grown and gathered followers ever since, evolving into one of the largest and most outrageous gay celebrations in the South.

The celebration is held on the traditional Labor Day weekend with an added two days of partying. The largest single event of the holiday is the Southern Decadence parade. Each parade has a theme, which is kept a secret until that morning, causing much anxiety among participants wishing to conjure up costume ideas. The themes are chosen annually by the appointed grand marshal (or mar-shals) and generally spoof and play off drag queens and other gay stereotypes.[2] Past themes have included 2003's "Carnaval Decadence," 2002's "Fairy Tails," 2001's "Ménage a Trois," and 2000's "Taboo x 2: The Forbidden Pleasures Tour," complete with theme song "Man! I Feel Like a Woman!" The grand marshal chooses the parade route, which changes annually, and leads marchers through the French Quarter. The parade, however, is only part of the weekend's festivities. Along with numerous street closures and crowds spilling out of bars throughout the French Quarter, local clubs host shows including Harrah's "Mr. Louisiana Leather" contest, the Bourbon Pub's infamous "Big Dick" contest, the Oz's "Calendar Boy" contest, and Good Friends Bar's "Miss High Hair" contest, along with sev-eral drag shows, parties, and concerts.

The celebration has grown to approximately one hundred thousand participants,[3] tourists and locals alike, who bring an estimated $80 million into the local economy. Gay-friendly bar sales are so high during Southern Decadence that it has earned a reputation as the "gay Mardi Gras." According to Kyle Scafide, former editor of the gay and lesbian paper *Impact*, "Bar owners weigh success by the amount of booze they sell, and lots of bars sold more during Decadence . . . than they sold during Mardi Gras. A lot actually ran out of alcohol, and for a bar on Bourbon Street to run out of alcohol is unimaginable."[4] A survey conducted by *Ambush* magazine among fifty local concerns after the 2002 holiday found that, in most cases, business was up between 10 and 37 percent from 2001. Hotels also reap the benefits of Southern Decadence, noting full bookings for the weekend months in advance. This high demand allows several hotels to require three- or even five-night minimum stays, a practice primarily reserved for the Mardi Gras weekend.[5]

The holiday's success is largely due to the marketing efforts of the New Orleans gay, lesbian, bisexual, and transgender (GLBT) business community along with *Ambush* magazine, the self-proclaimed "campiest and most popular GLBT guide in the region." *Ambush* is headquartered on Bourbon Street in New Orleans and is distributed across the Gulf South. The magazine advertises local businesses, and according to its publisher, Rip Naquin-Delain, it saw a 30 percent increase in advertising in 2002 from gay-friendly businesses in New Orleans looking to attract the Decadence crowd.[6] *Ambush* also runs the Web sites ambushmag.com, ambushonline.com, and southerndecadence.com, offering news and information about the event to the gay community around the country throughout the year. Southerndecadence.com reported a record 156,000 visitors in the week prior to Southern Decadence 2002[7] and has produced enough of an impact to prompt Absolut Vodka and Harrah's Casino to sign extensive sponsorship agreements with the Web site,[8] even causing Harrah's to proclaim "We'll treat you like a Queen."

Recognition of the gay and lesbian market by such mainstream companies as Harrah's and the New Orleans Tourism Marketing Corporation is indicative of a greater acceptance of gays and lesbians as desirable consumers. This recognition could simply mean that the almighty dollar continues to trump social prejudices; but whatever the motive, the result is an increased awareness and perhaps even a higher tolerance. The growing acceptance of Southern Decadence is visible not only in the form of sponsorships and advertising but also in the facilitation of the celebration by the city of New Orleans. In 2002, the New Orleans Police Department, which authorizes all holiday-related street closures, began working closely with businesses and community groups involved with Southern Decadence, adding extra patrols on the streets and even assigning officers to serve as liaisons to the gay community specifically for the event.[9]

Southern Decadence has no official organizer, therefore all costs of the event are paid for by *Ambush* magazine and the GLBT business community.[10] Those expenses are becoming an increasingly difficult burden for small businesses as the event grows larger. According to Lou "Lucille" Bernard, whose bar, Lucille's Golden Lantern, is the official starting point for the annual parade,

> We're having to foot the bill for parade permits, police officers, and street closures and that wouldn't be a problem if we were a bunch of major business owners. Here you have a group of mostly small bar owners, *Ambush* magazine and a couple of other supporters trying to foot the bill for Decadence, when the whole city benefits from the large number of tourist dollars that are being brought into the city. It's just ridiculous, when you think about it.[11]

The responsibility of cost is also a point of contention since the holiday weekend gives life to what would otherwise be a slow tourism season in the oppressive September heat.

In addition to helping the local economy, some of the proceeds from the special events and appearances of Southern Decadence are donated to a local charity of the parade's grand marshal's choice. Past charities have included Locks of Love, an organization that creates wigs for cancer patients, and Food for Friends and the William Fanning Foundation, both New Orleans–based programs that help area residents with HIV and AIDS.

As the event gets larger and continues to require more planning and organization, some fear it may lose its informal spontaneity and spirit. With numbers potentially exceeding one hundred thousand and the New Orleans Police Department assisting in crowd control, along with rising prices and the possible formalization of events, it is likely that some of Southern Decadence's esoteric kitsch status may wane. But then, popularity always comes at a price.

Back to School: Crafting Young Consumers

Labor Day Debra Riley Parr

Even for those schools that begin their academic year in August, Labor Day, more than a day to celebrate workers, remains the official end of summer and the beginning of the academic year. As children head back to school, Labor Day also marks the yearly back-to-school sales. Returning to school is no longer a matter of buying pencils, pens, and a new backpack; students and parents now must hunt down an array of expensive electronic necessities, not to mention the latest designer kid's clothes and footwear. It is a ritual of preparation repeated each year, forging strong—if unintended—connections between a holiday, commerce, and expectations for the coming year.

The academic calendar is organized around the holidays that begin right after Labor Day. American public schools time vacations to coincide with holidays like Christmas, Hanukkah, and New Year's Day. Only a few holidays merit the suspension of classes during the ten-month school calendar—Thanksgiving is probably the most nationally important among them. It is, however, *during* school that the seasonal progression of holidays structures the visual culture and flow of time, especially for young students. It is during school that a critical time offers the opportunity to imprint children with the expectations of holiday celebration, shaping desires that continue long past the elementary school experience.

In centuries past, holiday celebrations punctuated the daily round of work with moments of relief; since the mid-nineteenth century, holidays have provided a significant amount of the fuel for retail production. It is no secret that U.S. economists read the retail reports of sales during the Christmas season as a key indicator of market health. Why is the economy so tied into the business of holidays? My theory is that the experiences of elementary school activities, especially visual ones, organized around holidays provide at least a partial answer to this question. Such activities create not only a demand for the production of holiday stuff but a generation and more who have been required, however willingly, to produce, however simply, St. Patrick's Day shamrocks, turkey placemats, and Easter baskets. The production of holiday-themed projects in school may seem academically insignificant, but socially it offers an enormous collective visual experience and expectation.

In my memories of the early 1960s at Sherburne Elementary School in New Hampshire, first-grade reading and math lessons pale in comparison to Valentine's Day cards and Christmas decorations made with a minimal number of simple materials. Many colleagues and friends share similar memories, acknowledging that the fun but seemingly small-time school activities involving cotton balls, glitter, and rounded scissors might be more important than they had realized in shaping attitudes toward and expectations of holiday culture. Who could have predicted that six to ten years of cutting out pumpkin shapes every Halloween could be a useful way of conditioning a whole generation to be extremely eager, if unconscious, consumers (and amateur producers) of the visual culture of holiday celebrations?

The elementary school practice of giving holidays a kind of privileged exemption from the alienating effects of other academic moments, or giving the illusion of free creative activity in schools where there is no real budget for art classes, creates a message-sending and production-molding force. Harvard University's Gutman Library houses a great deal of documentation of historic curricular material on holiday activities, which were seen as a way to build an understanding of culture and aesthetic experience in children. Kathleen Thompson writes in *School Arts* magazine that she tries to get children to imagine what a Christmas tree by Jackson Pollock might look like, or to convince them that "Van Gogh's *Starry Night* could light up a holiday tree better than any commercial string of bulbs."[1] Clearly Thompson wants to give her holiday projects an art historical twist. Nowhere, however, have I discovered direct acknowledgment that more humble holiday projects might also be conditioning consumers, creating desires and demands tied to holiday goods.

The business of holidays is not just about the commercialization of holidays. It is tied to desires and expectations developed in those pink-construction-paper bunnies, those glittery snowflakes, those feathery turkey sculptures. Martha Stewart Living Omnimedia (MSLO) shows how school holiday activities and the business of holidays intersect. Stewart, with her acute business sense, has obviously figured

out that holidays loom large in the American imagination, and that this seasonal recurrence also produces a highly marketable (and never depleted) spectacle in the world of commerce. With her kits and clip art and recipes, Martha Stewart's successful business strategy seems similar to the elementary school curriculum of the latter half of the twentieth century; MSLO's television and radio shows, magazines, and Web site tie into the same round of holiday celebrations and often feature craft projects very similar to those children make in school. Easter brings the dyeing of eggs; Memorial Day and the Fourth of July, tiny patriotic flags in homemade cupcakes; Halloween, ghoulish costumes and bewitching paper cats to put in the window. In Stewart's instructions (her mother was a teacher), these activities are seamlessly sutured to products available from the MSLO Web site and catalogs. By miming the way fun activities of holiday culture are situated within the "real" work of school—wedged between math and social studies—Martha Stewart embeds holiday craft projects into the work of housekeeping, cooking, and gardening.

Even during some of her company's most trying financial moments of 2002 and 2003, when the U.S. government conducted investigations into Stewart's personal stock trading, holiday products and projects helped her stay afloat even while earnings were down for the first time since the company went public in 1999.[2] In the last quarter of 2002, the television revenue of MSLO "fell to $6.4 million from $9.6 million the previous year, a decline mainly attributed to the canceling of Ms. Stewart's network holiday special."[3] In the spring of 2003, however, Stewart told a reporter for the *New York Times* that the introduction of "a holiday collection of ornaments and other decorations sold at Kmart had generated 'sales of nearly $100 million.'"[4] The demand for the new Martha Stewart Everyday holiday line might have been even bigger had Kmart not filed for bankruptcy protection and closed some of its stores.[5] It is not simply that her company creates a demand for holiday stuff, though that may be true now that it is so successful. It is more that Stewart satisfies (and extends) demands her customers began learning and experiencing back in school.

MSLO holiday projects (and products) respond to a deeply imprinted desire, but one that hardly seems important—certainly not as important as all the other socialization and training that happens at school. And perhaps this is the brilliance of the MSLO emphasis on holidays: it taps into memories and meanings formed in grade schools throughout America and capitalizes on the repetitive round of events, iconography, color, shapes, sounds, and smells associated with school holiday celebrations. While Martha Stewart cleverly and consistently reprises the collective American childhood experiences of holiday activities in public elementary schools, her corporate success at the same time makes manifest the latent effects of such shared activities.

If cultural critic Guy Debord in the 1960s defined "spectacle" as the accumulation of capital until it becomes an image, the early-twenty-first century is experiencing this spectacularization with a vengeance.[6] But there also seems to be a concurrent reversal or undertow to this formula: now it is the accumulation of images that becomes capital. Piling up images of holidays is especially profitable, as Martha Stewart's success shows. When Stewart creates a continuous spectacle around the progression of holidays, the corporate desire to manufacture a world where habits of consumption merge fluidly with the activities of everyday life seems to have been splendidly fulfilled.

Simultaneously and on several fronts, Stewart creates month-long images—in "omnimedia"—of traditional holidays: one can watch and/or listen to Turkey 101, read directions for creating turkey-motif place cards in *Martha Stewart Living*, download clip art for them from marthastewart.com, get ideas for Thanksgiving side dishes from *Everyday Food, from the Kitchens of Martha Stewart Living*, and order a turkey serving platter from Martha by Mail (now Martha Stewart: The Catalog for Living). For Valentine's Day, the company makes available a similar onslaught of options, including kits to assist in making "handmade" Valentines. In 2003, Martha Stewart published a free pamphlet called *Good Things for the Holidays,* which included simple instructions for Valentine's Day boxes, Mother's Day breakfast, Father's Day gifts, Fourth of July votives, pumpkin vases, and jingle-bell wreaths. For the Valentine's boxes—for all the craft projects—tiny photographs show the tools and materials needed to finish the project. In their simplicity, they are redolent of the past. The graphic design of the small booklet is not an inchoate remembrance of the holidays; its specificity of details recalls school activities.

Kids continue to make such holiday projects, as evidenced by the work of a third-grade class in Derry, New Hampshire, led by teaching assistant Janet Hickey. She reports that teachers still emphasize holiday celebrations throughout the school year—if only as a break from more academic lessons.[7] In Freeport, Maine, however, third-grade teacher Terry Lincoln says that none of the teachers in her school organizes the social-studies curriculum around traditional holidays like Easter or Christmas. Instead they create projects celebrating more institutionally important dates, such as the hundredth day of school.[8] *School Arts* magazine asked, as far back as 1958, whether "holiday themes should be used frequently or infrequently, or be entirely eliminated from elementary art programs."[9] The debate over holiday art projects in elementary art programs notwithstanding, most schools still punctuate the school calendar with traditional holiday activities, with new ones like Kwanzaa occasionally added to reflect respect for diversity. Holidays still rule at school, as they obviously continue to do in stores and other public places. Holiday impact on retail economics is ever more pervasive and fine-tuned, and with the relentless business of holidays driving the economy, holiday visual culture is everywhere and on the minds of businesspeople every day. That world where consumption and everyday activities merge, splendidly activated as it is in the world evoked by Martha Stewart's spectacle of holiday projects and products, begins in elementary school after Labor Day.

The Workingman's Holiday

Labor Day   John-Paul Avila

Held on the first Monday of September, Labor Day commemorates the dedication and achievements of American workers. The movement to create a holiday started on Tuesday, September 5, 1882, in New York City, with planned demonstrations and picnics for workers. The day was marked by a parade down Broadway of organized workers carrying signs calling for equality in wages and hours. Twelve years later, Congress made it a federal holiday. Although it is not clear who is responsible for the first Labor Day celebration, the honor has been divided between two individuals: Peter J. McGuire and Matthew Maguire.[1]

Peter McGuire was the general secretary for the Brotherhood of Carpenters and Joiners of America. He was known for leading the movement for the eight-hour workday as well as organizing unions and strikes in New York in the late nineteenth century that included over one hundred thousand workers.[2] Later serving as the vice president of the AFL (American Federation of Labor), McGuire sought the distinction of being the person responsible for Labor Day. Actually, he played "a less instrumental role, but he did attend the Central Labor Union's meetings about the demonstration, sat on the reviewing stand for the procession, and was one of the featured speakers at the picnic."[3]

Matthew Maguire, a member of the International Association of Machinists, is said to have proposed the idea and, along with Robert Blissert, to have been a key organizer of the first Labor Day demonstration while Maguire was secretary of the Central Labor Union in New York. It was with the help of this organization that Labor Day began and spread to other cities in the country.[4]

Regardless of the founder, the holiday is like no other in America. According to Samuel Gompers (1850–1924), founder and longtime president of the American Federation of Labor, "All other holidays are in a more or less degree connected with conflicts, and battles and man's prowess over man, of strife and discord for greed and power, of glories achieved by one nation over another. Labor Day . . . is devoted to no man, living or dead, to no sect, race, or nation."[5]

Nowadays, Labor Day symbolically marks the end of summer with the last picnics of the year and beach and resort closings, regardless of the fact that the fall equinox is still weeks away. The holiday also features sales offered by the retail industry, which employs 22.8 million people and produces $3 trillion in sales. Ironically, for retail workers, Labor Day is now business as usual—a day of work.

Business Quarter 4
Fall

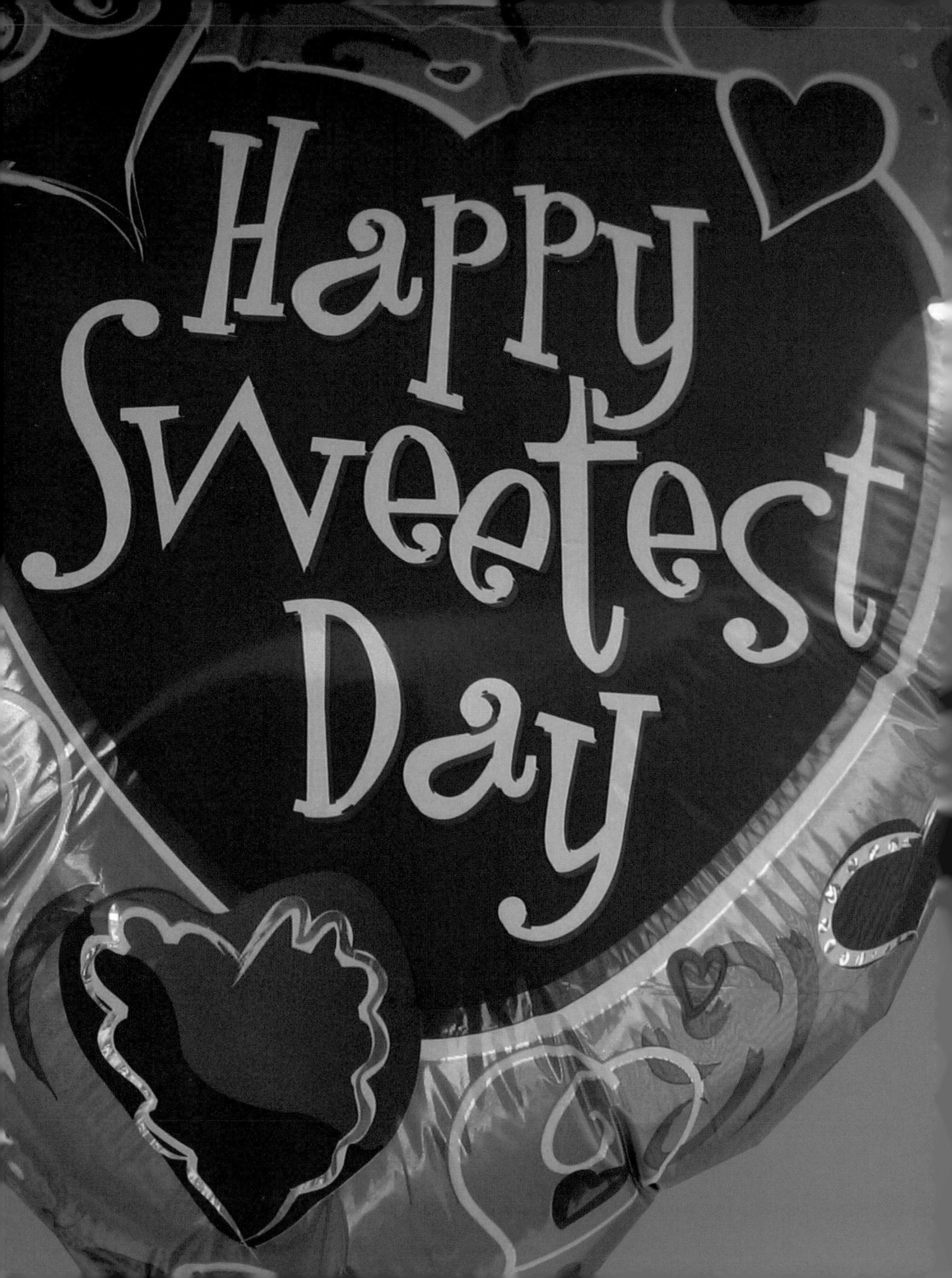
Happy Sweetest Day

Fiscal Flop or Secret Success?

Sweetest Day   D. Denenge Akpem

While caught up in the blur of Halloween's costume-making, apple-dipping, and treat-buying, many people do not give a thought to the third Saturday in October. Still, Sweetest Day, the "little holiday that could," has been celebrated to greater or lesser degree since its creation by candyman Herbert Birch Kingston in 1922. It has been the focus of national marketing efforts since the 1960s, when Hallmark first began making greeting cards specifically for the day. Sweetest Day is a kind of bastard Valentine's Day, remembered with flowers and candy, but it originated in a different form. Many people assume that it is another "Hallmark holiday," conveniently created to gobble up consumer dollars, but in reality, Sweetest Day did not begin with the greeting-card giant or with a religious celebration or historic battle. In the 1920s, Kingston started a Cleveland tradition of visiting orphans and the infirm and giving gifts and candy on Sweetest Day. The idea was adopted in other cities and towns in the Midwest and soon became a publicly acknowledged holiday. Cleveland, Ohio; Detroit, Michigan; and Buffalo, New York, top the list of cities in which Sweetest Day is most heartily celebrated—if it is celebrated at all.

But could this seemingly innocent day have been waging the goodwill-or-profit fight since its early days? Consider the following: Theda Bara, demonizing of women, vamps, vampires, sex symbols, silent movies, publicly marketed film stars, fantasy, and escape. All of these play a part in Sweetest Day's early history. In 1922, silent-movie star Theda Bara paid a visit to Cleveland, Ohio, to celebrate Sweetest Day. In 1915, Bara rose to prominence as one of the earliest nationally famous

actresses with *A Fool There Was,* and after this success, she continued her rise through the 1920s and 1930s. This exotic temptress and screen siren was famed for her black-lined lips and ruthless onscreen attitude, which did to men what men often did to women: "took them for everything they had and dumped them."[1] Her characters were aggressive and self-assured; these women chose love instead of waiting for love to choose them. Bara's actions spoke loudly of woman in control, as vamp, vixen, and fantasy image. But in 1919, she incurred public outrage for a film in which she played a beloved Irishwoman, Kathleen Mavourneen, in the movie of the same name. The combination of anti-Semitism, protests by Irish and Catholics, backlash against her scandalous public image, and her insistence on more varied roles contributed to a fall in popularity.[2] The uproar from her appearance as Mavourneen included stink bombs in theaters, public demonstrations, and death threats to her and Fox producers. The film ran only for a couple of days,[3] and Bara left acting after marrying in 1921, returning for only two films in the 1920s.

In 1922, Bara reappeared—this time to utilize Sweetest Day's goodwill to boost her own public image. She gave candy to people entering theaters to see her movies as well as to ten thousand Cleveland hospital patients. She was not alone in her philanthropic efforts. Star Ann Pennington also gave candy on Sweetest Day to over two thousand newspaper boys in Cleveland in recognition of their public service. Meshing philanthropy with publicity as shrewdly as ever, the Cincinnati-born Bara gave the people what they wanted.

By promoting a holiday such as this, Bara connected her bad-girl, sex-symbol image with wholesomeness, tradition, and basic goodness. Perhaps even today, Sweetest Day has the faintest tinge of the vixen. Just prior to the holiday in 1996, several romance novelists responded to a request by the *Chicago Sun-Times* for "some epicurean delights to tame the palate of your savage beast" for the newspaper's

special "Sweetest Day Seductions" recipes.[4] Readers learned that Emilie Richards, who is the author of forty-eight "lusty novels" and lives outside Cleveland, prepares steaming fish creole for her sweetheart on the holiday.

Today, *Kettle Talk*, the newsletter of Retail Confectioners International, encourages active promotion of Sweetest Day with the statement "Remember, the joy of living is the joy of giving, and Sweetest Day gives you the opportunity of spreading happiness through the customers you serve!" It also suggests that confectioners "be prepared to explain Sweetest Day and to make suggestions regarding appropriate gifts, keeping in mind that the possibilities are limitless."[5] The focus has moved from charity to romance, from sweets to the sweetheart. A list of products marketed for Sweetest Day, products that seem to veer a little (or a lot) from the holiday's humble origins, includes Kama Sutra Sensual Oils, sexy board games for lovers, and Krispy Kreme stock certificates (for him). One Chicago resident explains that she celebrates Sweetest Day only if she is involved in a serious relationship; then she will focus on non-commercial acts of love, like hot baths and a home-cooked meal. A resident of Ann Arbor, Michigan, exclaims, "I've never even heard of it." In an unscientific survey I performed—interviewing ten people in downtown Chicago on Sweetest Day 2002—half of the participants claimed to have no idea the holiday was that particular day. Four out of these five had never even heard of the holiday. Of the other half, one was on hold on the telephone with his sweetie at the moment I inquired and seemed genuinely shocked at the suggestion that anyone could ever forget the day. He was an anomaly; the rest just shrugged and expressed little more interest than "Oh, yeah, I heard it was Sweetest Day." An ongoing poll at RomanceStruck.com asks, "Do you celebrate Sweetest Day?" Of the 242 respondents, 47 percent answered yes and 53 percent answered no. This survey, also rather unscientific, still reflects the reality that the population is rather evenly divided on the Sweetest Day issue: first on whether they know about it; second on whether they celebrate it.

YOU'RE SWEET BOUQUET
10/26/02

Apathy or annoyance with a seemingly corporate holiday comes up over and over again in response to the little holiday that could. On his Web site, zug.com, comic writer John Hargrave has shared his comments on Sweetest Day at least twice: "Since writing ['Sweetest Day, My Ass'] on the senseless, made-up holiday of Sweetest Day in 1996, I have become a worldwide clearinghouse for Sweetest Day information." He goes on to describe a ten-year fight with the holiday. Others have referred to it as "bogus," "a pointless holiday," and a "bullcrap piece of corporate propaganda."[6] At the same time, a Web search for Sweetest Day brings up a dizzying array of sweet-themed e-cards and products whose only connection to this holiday seems to be the word *sweet*. While gift giving remains true to the original Sweetest Day, the items pushed are a retread of Valentine's products transformed by advertising lingo or by the manufacturer's category of what will be marketed. Sweetest Day has become, like many other holidays, a marketing opportunity that confectioners, florists, and even Krispy Kreme Doughnuts stock managers are happy to exploit.[7]

Goodwill and philanthropy may have inspired Sweetest Day, but from the beginning people were willing to capitalize on it. Yet the holiday cannot boast of the cash-cow status granted to Valentine's Day or Halloween.[8] A 1999 American Floral Endowment Research article, "Floral Gift Market," speaks of the need to boost "friend/acquaintance" sales in the floral market—hence the Sweetest Day push.[9] Celebrations are centralized in the midwestern United States, but even for Malley's Chocolates of Cleveland, Ohio, positioned in the heart of Sweetest Day history and territory, sales for Valentine's Day are 35 percent higher than for Sweetest Day. Two million Sweetest Day cards are exchanged annually, compared with one billion for Valentine's Day.[10] From a fiscal point of view, Sweetest Day teeters precariously on the border of a financial flop. Money

is made—but it's no Valentine's Day. What was once a day to remember the less fortunate has become a generic version of the most popular day of love; the real story of its inception has been lost in the glut of consumer culture. Could it be that Sweetest Day's relative commercial failure represents its true success as a holiday? Maybe Sweetest Day's greatest strength lies in its adaptability, in its filling any need, in its ability to sell anything to anyone— always under the auspices of goodwill.

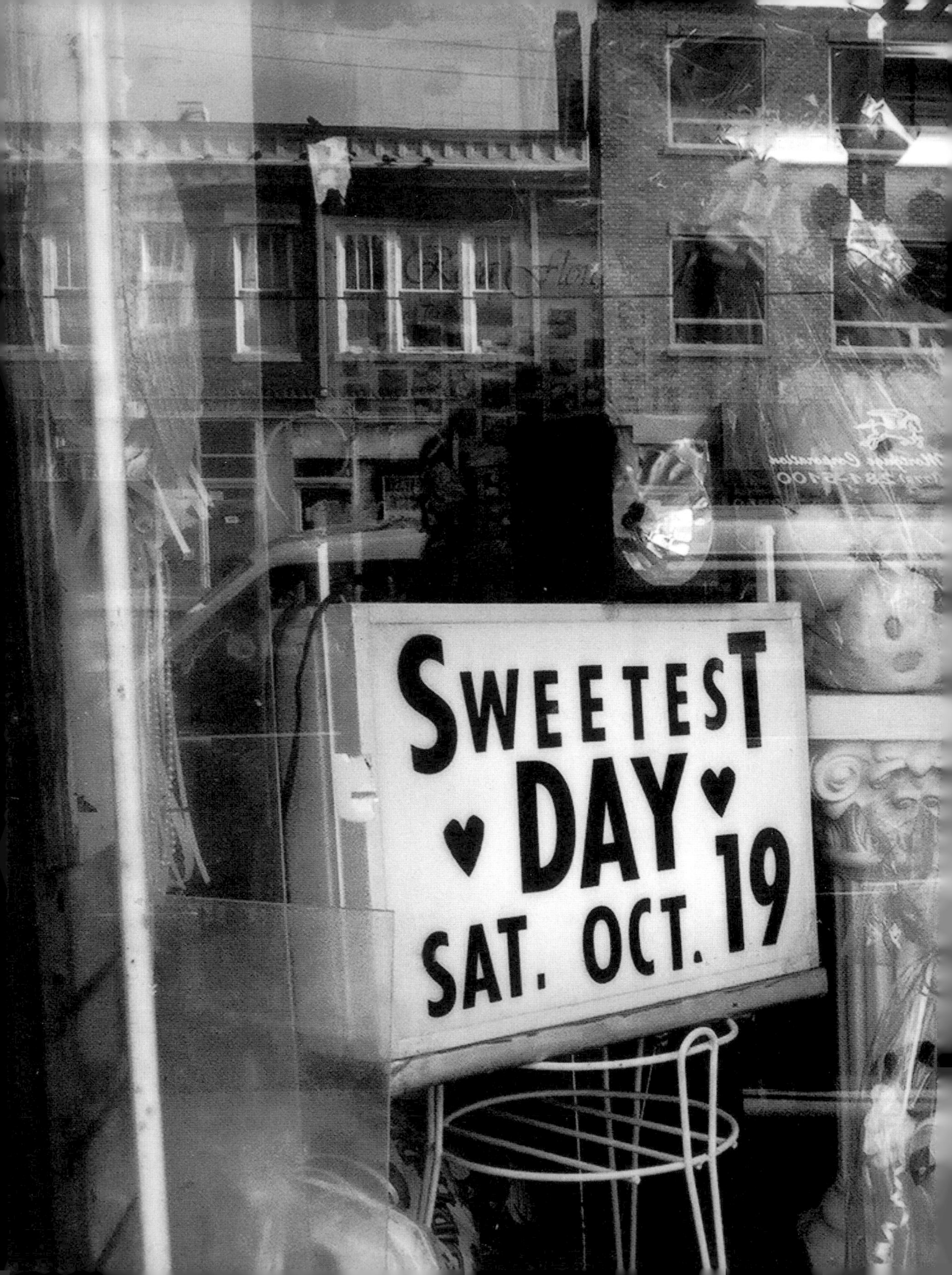
SWEETEST
DAY
SAT. OCT. 19

Devil's Night in Detroit

Rebecca Mazzei

We used to call Devil's Night "the Superbowl of Fires." We would go on a run and there'd be a crowd of people there waiting for us—people who drove in from the suburbs, flew in from overseas, television crews from CNN . . . We would get out of the truck and people would be cheering us on and patting us on the back, and we would say, "Get the hell out of the way!" They'd look at us and you could see the excitement on their faces. They'd stop us, wanting interviews, offering us four or five hundred dollars for a hat or one of our axes . . . and back at the fire-house—if we ever did get back to the house—there'd be tailgating parties out front with hibachis going.
—Firefighter, Squad 3, Detroit Fire Department[1]

Many Detroit community members and city officials have tried to figure out why Detroit has suffered from extreme acts of arson on October 30, otherwise known as Devil's Night. The night before Halloween has become a holiday that is so per-vasive that a majority of the locals have no idea that the celebration is specific to Detroit. Some people believe the criminal activity on Devil's Night is related to political rebellion; others say it is just kids pulling pranks that have gone too far. Some say it has everything to do with the riots of 1967; others believe the two phenomena are unrelated. In fact, all of these truths play a small part in the making of the holiday. Devil's Night is just one example of how a community—any commu-nity in America—builds something from nothing, in order to monogram its spirit, and molds it into a definitive tradition.

Bill Eisner has spent forty years photographing Detroit's fires for Detroit's Fire Department Squad 3. According to Eisner, Devil's Night began in the early 1970s with amateur pranks. Kids would pull down fire-alarm boxes on street corners. After the city caught on, the fire department was ordered to remove the boxes, and that is when teenagers started setting fires. In the late 1970s, most of the fires were small rubble and dumpster fires. Then people began lighting up garages and larger abandoned houses. According to "Tale of the Tape," the Detroit Fire Department's official book of service records, the early 1980s marked the first years of really bad activity on Devil's Night. In 1984, firefighters logged a three-day period of nearly 800 fires; on October 30 alone, they tallied 297 incidents of arson in the city.[2] Lieutenant Larry Gassel, a twenty-five-year veteran of the Detroit Fire Department, recalls, "We'd grab pops and subs in the morning and never bother to come back to the station. We'd know about fires before they came over on the radio because you could see smoke mounds. So we'd go on our first call and just wait at that place for the next one. We'd be out at 4 p.m. and get in at 8 a.m. You could smell the whole city burning."[3] Firefighter Herb Mulford explains that it was difficult to drive by two or three fires while on the way to another one. One year during the 1980s, Eisner took photographs of three buildings in a row that burned themselves to the ground because there were no firefighters left in the city to put out the flames. One Squad 3 firefighter explains, "Normally, for a three-dwelling fire you'd have forty guys. We had one engine and four guys." There just was not enough manpower to cover the burning city. Eisner recalls, "I was photographing a vacant two-story house on fire there, and there were no fire companies coming, so eventually the adjacent house caught on fire and the owner had to get the neighbors to help him remove possessions from his house, and then a third home caught on fire. An engine pulled up half an hour later. By then the guy had lost everything. But it made the front page."[4] It did not help that Mayor Coleman Young (in office from 1978 to 1993) was closing fire squads during the busiest period, stating that there was no manpower, no money, and no hiring.

Devil's Night took hold in Detroit for a variety of sociological reasons; the most prominent are related to the automobile industry, the racially motivated riots of 1967, and what was known as "Hurricane H.U.D." Helen Irving worked as an appointee in Coleman Young's office and as the director of the Municipal Parking Department. Irving explains that she believes "the whole thing was tied up with the lack of mass transportation in the city. Blacks and whites were recruited from the South to work at the auto plants downtown. In the late 1950s and early 1960s, a lot of the corporations closed down or moved out to the suburbs. The auto industry really tried to prevent mass transport because they wanted everyone to drive cars. Any funds the Department of Transportation would get went into building highways."[5] With no transportation system to get them to their jobs,

many Detroiters followed the companies and moved north. By the time of the riots in 1967, a good number of the auto companies were already gone. After the riots demolished the city, remaining citizens began to feel unsafe, and thus, the city experienced what is known as "white flight." The city government installed H.U.D. (Department of Housing and Urban Development) programs to try to help people finance homes downtown. They qualified people for low-interest homes whether or not they could afford the mortgages. Helen Irving states, "Neighborhoods were being vacated, but the city can't just go in and get rid of a home. They can board it up, but in order to demolish it there's a certain legal process that the city has to go through, which can take a while, so hundreds of homes that were abandoned fell into disrepair." With the majority of prosperous Detroit residents raising families in the suburbs, H.U.D. homes became decrepit buildings, often havens for criminal activity within the impoverished communities. Citizens began setting fire to the abandoned houses as a form of Robin Hood community activism. "They were sick of looking at them," firefighter Eric Jurmo explains. "I understand that these people are trying to prove a point to the city, but these people don't understand that squatters live in these homes with kerosene heaters. Abandoned houses are not abandoned."[6]

A small number of fires on Devil's Night are related to insurance fraud, but that also depends on what is considered a crime. In 1979, the city told residents of Poletown, an east-side Detroit neighborhood, that they had to move out: a square mile of neighborhood homes was being replaced by an industrial plant.[7] That year, according to the fire department's "Tale of the Tape," service runs went up 300 percent because people were collecting on insurance before they were kicked out of their homes.[8] The end of October is also a common time for businesses to set fires: they collect on insurance if the business is performing poorly.[9]

One Detroit firefighter explains that arson in Detroit is also used as a source of entertainment:

> Instead of going to the movies for seven dollars, for twenty, you can light up a house across the street from you and watch it burn for three hours. They were burning the whole neighborhood down. Then people would see it televised on the news and get all excited about it. Arson is a relatively anonymous crime that goes unpunished because you usually don't catch anybody doing it. So why not? There's excitement to it because it's so overwhelming, houses are alive with fire. It's talking to you, saying come get me.[10]

Box 42 fire buffs can testify to a fascination with fire—one that is more helpful than harmful. Box 42 has been a state-recognized group since April 1942. The group holds monthly meetings at fire stations in the Detroit area, prints a monthly newsletter, and has established a Web site (which includes a live audio stream of

Detroit Fire Department radio) in order to detail the miraculous and mundane goings-on of local department activities, everything from rescue-service news to reports on fire-department vehicle repairs. On Devil's Night, the members take their own cars, each equipped with a short-wave radio, and restlessly wait to follow the fire department on calls.[11] Dan Jasina is editor of the newsletter, secretary, and treasurer of the group. He explains the group's purpose: "Today, Box 42 exists mainly as a group of enthusiasts who share an interest in anything fire related; from historical photographs, station house journals, badges, patches and insignia to building scale models of fire apparatus, fire and apparatus buffing and monitoring public safety radio communications."[12] Even members of the fire department admit that Box 42 buffs take their hobby so seriously that sometimes officials use their records to scope out developing patterns.[13]

It did not take long for some savvy people in the city to realize that Detroit was getting international media coverage three days out of the year; in just a few years, they recognized that they should bank on it. By the late 1980s, Devil's Night patches and hats were sold in advance of the holiday, and several versions of Devil's Night T-shirts were available for purchase at an arson event. Meanwhile, one firefighter recalls, "Guys on the rig were transferring out of the department because they couldn't take it."[14]

While firefighters were dealing with smoke inhalation, booby traps, and rocks thrown from crowds, citizens were profiting from the chaos—following the rigs to sell fifteen-dollar shirts on the scene. By 1989, the T-shirts featured several different designs, taking stabs at the allegedly corrupt Coleman Young administration. One shirt featured Young's head with a cartoon bubble holding the mayor's infamous words "Devil's Night is finally under control" with a background of raging basement fires. Another featured Young with the title "Liar Liar Pants on Fire." Yet another shirt featured a corrupt mathematical equation—"4,376 + 3,298 = 42 fires"—to show how Young masked real figures.

While local citizens have been earning money from arson, the government of Detroit has declared October 30 an emergency situation. In 2002, the Detroit Fire Department spent a large portion of a $523,230 Federal Emergency Management Agency grant to prevent the holiday. According to a *Detroit Free Press* article published on Devil's Night, Detroit executive fire commissioner Tyrone Scott unveiled a $480,000 fire truck on October 29. The fire department used $190,000 of the grant to purchase four hundred breathing masks, and $15,000 on confined-space equipment such as pulleys and harnesses.[15] That same year, the city also purchased accoutrements for volunteers and their vehicles in preparation for the evening's events. Detroit's southeast-side Butzel Family Center served as one of several "Angel's

Night 2002" volunteer outposts temporarily stationed in the area. In a three-hour period at that location alone, more than one hundred boxes of orange capes, flashlights, and emergency flashers for cars were distributed to community members.[16] But Devil's Night prevention is also an opportunity for political promotion: Commissioner Scott explained at a news-media event on October 29 that the fire department's recent and extreme expenditure "ties in with Mayor Kilpatrick's [elected in 2002] commitment for the safety of all residents, shareholders, and businesses."[17]

Through the late 1990s and into the new millennium, people had begun setting fires a good two weeks before Devil's Night, in order to extend the holiday. But in 2002, the fire department noted that criminal activity on Devil's Night itself, including arson, was actually slower than on a normal day in the city because of the Devil's Night vigil, a three-day anti-arson campaign that puts city officials and community volunteers on the streets to report any criminal activity. The service, which started in 1986 under Mayor Young's office, was renamed and formalized as Angel's Night under the Archer administration (Dennis Archer was Detroit's mayor from 1994 to 2001). The *Detroit Free Press* reports that in 1994, Archer had 3,500 people signed up to help. By 2001, his last year in office, the mayor had employed more than 32,000 volunteers and reduced the number of arson-related incidents to 157.[18]

New Orleans has Mardi Gras and New York has the Macy's Thanksgiving Day Parade, but Detroit, it seems, may be losing Devil's Night. However, fire remains a visual icon that represents Detroit—its desperation, destruction, revolution, and undying plea for resurrection. Fire is also symbolic of the passion that is all-consuming for a lot of Detroiters. At its best, it is a catharsis, an exorcism, a passion to start over. At its worst, it is a dangerous and pathetic passion in a cultural vacuum of kids, artists, annoyed community members, and drug addicts who cannot see past the empty environment that was left after the government and corporations promised prosperity and then disappeared. No matter its moniker, no matter its perhaps temporary dormancy, Devil's Night exists in Detroit. Formed complexly and perplexingly by hysteria, imagination, anger, malaise, originality, and depression, as well as good and bad intentions, it persists as a definitive tradition.

Halloween and the Business
of Witchcraft

Halloween   Maud Lavin

"I'll know when my job as a public witch is done and it's time for me to go into
retirement—when the media calls me on Mother's Day instead of Halloween,"
comments Phyllis Curott, Wiccan spiritual leader, lawyer, and author of *Book of
Shadows and Witch Crafting*. "Still, I'm a pragmatist. I'd rather have media time
at Halloween than no media time. There's a reason my publisher releases my
books in the fall—there's that Halloween table in the bookstores."[1] Witches
are moving into the mainstream, flying not on broomsticks but on the back of the
publishing industry. Jenie Carlin, a spokesperson for Borders, reports that Wicca
is the chain's fastest growing subsection in metaphysics; sales in 2002 rose by
25 to 30 percent over those in 2001.[2] Llewellyn Worldwide, a St. Paul, Minnesota,
publishing house where about half the books are devoted to the craft, has seen a
surge in Wiccan book sales since the late 1990s. Best-selling books there have
won high numbers of readers: Scott Cunningham's *Wicca: A Guide for the Solitary
Practitioner* (1990) sold over 507,000 copies as of 2002, and Silver RavenWolf's
Teen Witch (1998) over 167,250. Books are integral to the practice of witchcraft, avers Lynne Menturweck, Llewellyn's art director: "They are used by
teachers, referenced in discussion groups, and laid open in rituals. They are
indispensable vehicles for supplying the tools and formats to build their own
traditions."[3] Cultural critic Debra Parr affirms that since there is no primary
received tradition in the contemporary Wicca movement, books are key for
forming a common ground.[4]

The Halloween Tarot

Six of Pumpkins

The Empress

©1998USGAMES

The growth in interest in witchcraft, particularly among women in their teens and twenties, can be attributed in part to media events such as the cult success of the movie *The Craft* (1996) and the popularity of the television show *Sabrina, the Teenage Witch*, which have updated a history of witch heroines and villainesses from the *Wizard of Oz*'s Glinda the Good and Wicked Witch of the West to *Bewitched*'s Samantha. Today's television and movie stars with magical talents—whether Sabrina or Buffy or Harry Potter—tend to be teenagers and even preteens with powers that threaten to exceed their ability to control them. As these youths perform magic, they face temptations and explore their own positive potential. Magic also helps the protagonists deal with good and evil forces outside the self. Magic serves as an analogy for the growth of self, and teenagers serve as an analogy for the drama of maturation. These are appropriate witches for an age that believes that internal growth is necessary for worldly survival.

Earlier media witches likewise reflected the times that imagined them. The *Wizard of Oz*'s opposing witches were stereotypes that fit the culture of the Depression (the film was shot in 1939)—Glinda was maternal and round (plumpness at that time signified prosperity), the Wicked Witch was thin and lived at ease in a castle while those under her command toiled. Glinda stood for creation; the Wicked Witch for destruction. In *Bewitched*, Elizabeth Montgomery's Samantha had to curb her powers—at her mortal husband's request—in order for her marriage to succeed. This attempt at wifely demureness was very 1964, the year the first episode, "I, Darrin, Take This Witch Samantha," was filmed. But Samantha's magic was irrepressible, and one early episode even had her successfully lobbying Darrin and his advertising firm to use an image of a glamorous witch in a campaign instead of an ugly one. Shape-shifting in her different contexts, the media witch appears as a mysterious, intelligent, and often unpredictable and sexy symbol of women (and sometimes men) and power. She also functions today as an advertisement for the more diverse and more personal Wicca movement.

Primarily, though, Wicca has grown to a practice of an estimated four million people in the U.S. because of its spiritual and political appeal.[5] Wicca has become a hybrid religion combining spirituality, feminism, and environmentalism with seductive older images of bell, book, and candle. Ever evolving, Wicca draws from a variety of folk traditions of magic and healing (and is a kissing cousin to aromatherapy). Wicca borrows, too, from eccentric historical rituals of Masons and Victorians, long-lived shamanistic practices like drumming and dancing, divination, and pantheism. According to an Internet survey in 2000 by the Covenant of the Goddess, the U.S.'s largest witch organization, 71 percent of responding witches were female and 65 percent were between the ages of eighteen and

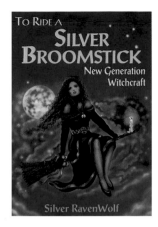

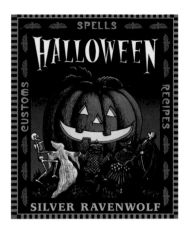

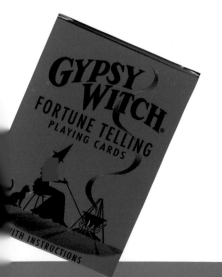

thirty-nine.[6] For some witches, the spiritual side of Wicca parallels that of hatha yoga, and practitioners such as Curott use breathing and meditation exercises in rituals that honor imminent divinity in the self, others, and nature.

Most important for the publishing industry, Wicca is decentralized and nonhierarchical, so neophytes wanting to start witchcraft need books. There has been such a boom in Wiccan books since the late 1990s that competition for the buyer is now keen. "There must be over a hundred Wicca 101 books out there," comments Lisa Braun, publicity manager for Llewellyn.[7] A specialized press, Llewellyn Publications was founded in St. Paul in 1901 by astrologer Llewellyn George, who published such popular books as *The Llewellyn Moon Sign and Gardening Book* (1906). The press grew in the 1960s to offer a wide variety of New Age titles, and in the 1990s it broadened again to incorporate self-help and mind-spirit books. Since the late 1990s, more mainstream publishers such as Random House have also offered Wiccan titles as part of the increased production of New Age or mind-body-spirit books in what has become a crowded field.

How can readers choose? Covers matter, and so design figures large in the competition for readers. It also serves as a field where old and new witch stereotypes battle. Michael Windsor, cover designer of Curott's *Witch Crafting*, says, "You have to get past all the preconceived ideas of what a witch is. When you say 'witch' most people immediately conjure up the Wicked Witch from the *Wizard of Oz*—green skin, warts, pointed hat. Wiccans are not haggard old crones who turn little children into frogs. I tried to show that Wicca is a very warm, rich, and natural religion."[8] Windsor's cover combines green imagery (the flowers of healing herbs echinacea, yarrow, and goldenseal) with Celtic ornamentation for a sensual texture. Other covers work harder to normalize witchcraft. *Teen Witch* (cover design by

Anne Marie Garrison, cover art by Patrick Faricy), a controversial book due to its pitch to underage readers, shows five wholesome teenagers, four girls and a boy, with standard midriff-baring or jeans-wearing outfits, discreetly decorated with pentacles, a yin-yang symbol, and moon and stars. Perhaps too self-conscious about mainstreaming, many Wiccan book-cover designers tend to rely on dark colors and overused symbols like cauldrons. In contrast, one extremely effective Gen-Y-targeted cover graces Fiona Horne's 2000 *Witch: A Magickal Journey* (cover design by Sylvia Kwan). Horne is an Australian witch and former singer for DEF FX. She is centered carefully atop a circle of stones, naked except for a black shawl, long blond hair, and black toenail polish. The back cover shows her in a tube top with her snake familiar, and inside photographs reveal her "skyclad," the Wiccan word for naked. Horne is a model witch, she writes like an inheritor of the grrrl movement, and her Green Witch label includes her own charm-laden cosmetics. Intimately involved in the cover designs for her books, Horne represents the Gen-Y designer witch, self-enchanted and crafted.

Some covers appear cartoon-like and almost desperate to produce a new, positive, and normalized image of a witch. The cover of RavenWolf's *To Ride a Silver Broomstick: New Generation Witchcraft* illustrates a twentysomething witch with long curly tresses in an off-the-shoulder gown sitting sidesaddle on her broomstick in a cloudy night sky—it is a retro bodice-ripper romance cover. In contrast, covers using photographs of witches, like Curott's memoir *Book of Shadows*, which shows her dancing, white-robed, with members of her circle, seem braver and more engaging. Braver because those photographed are outing themselves—coming out of the broom closet, as it is called—and there is risk involved: prejudices dating as far back as medieval Europe's murderous Witch Craze pogroms and Salem's 1693 witch trials and killings still exist today, though in less violent forms.[9] Witchcraft was illegal in England as recently as 1952. It is still common for witch authors to use pen names to protect their identities. In addition to proselytizing and profit, then, Wicca needs books to spread religious information and tolerance.

The leading popularizer of witchcraft at Halloween is Silver RavenWolf, mother of four, resident of a small town in Pennsylvania, and best-selling author of down-home witchcraft books. In her *Halloween: Customs, Recipes, Spells* (1999), she traces the evolution of Halloween from pagan Celtic practice to Christian appropriation as All Saint's Eve to rowdy Mischief Night to candy-coated, consumerist U.S. celebration, a guise that dates from the early twentieth century and is still growing today. She relates witchcraft to folk traditions and advocates homemade treats for trick-or-treaters and apple-divination parties. Llewellyn, her publisher, does a media push for tolerance at Halloween, distributing free copies of Scott Cunningham's *The*

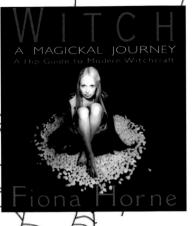

Truth About Witchcraft Today (1992)—the cover shows witches as "normal"—and a black-on-orange fact sheet assuring readers that witches do not worship Satan (or even believe in him) or perform harmful acts.

For the book industry, Halloween is a good opportunity to sell Wicca books. For Wicca, Halloween is a chance to promote religious tolerance. Some witches, though, will not participate in the public holiday since Halloween, or Samhain, its Celtic name, is a Greater Sabbat and the Wiccan New Year. One of the eight Sabbats of the year (the others include ancient holidays based on nature—summer solstice and harvest times, for instance), Samhain is a solemn time to honor the dead, a time of divination and prophecy, of reviewing the past and looking to the future. For Wiccans, it is the time of the year when the veil between living and dead is at its thinnest.

Halloween is also a time of little-girl trick-or-treaters dressing up as witches in black robes, pointed hats, and green, craggy masks. This warty witch garb follows a tradition of costuming as a way to turn ancient fears into carnival and also to embody those fears. Now that an evolution of this witch stereotype is underway, however, it is a good time to explore desirable new images. They should not be too sweet, that is, should not simply turn the Wicked Witch into Glinda. To do the representation of the witch justice in Wiccan terms would be to transform it into a range of images that show feminine power as complex, as having a shadow side (which Wicca explores, often using Jungian terminology) as well as a healing one, a Dionysian side as well as a nurturing one. Images should keep lust and aggression as part of the witch's spiritual power. Witches need wildness, not sugar.

Cultural critic Diane Purkiss notes in her book *The Witch in History* (1996), "The dark sister of the charming herbalist with the well-scrubbed pine table and the bunches of herbs drying in the rafters is for us nothing but a mass of bygone prejudices, a marker which divides us from the benighted and bigoted past into which we have abjected so much of our worst selves." She warns, "In laying hold of the witch, in making her our own, we have also lost her, or perhaps lost what she once was for her original owners."[10] Not quite. Fiona Horne writes, "The energy of an orgasm can be the most powerful fuel to help propel a spell along to fruition; in fact, virtually all power raising in a Circle is based on the buildup/release/wind-down pattern of an orgasm"; she is retaining the life-affirming and also taboo thread of witch mythology.[11] Her familiar is a snake, a python, which connotes primitive fears and transformative powers; she calls it Lulu and treats it like a pet, which connotes playfulness and power trumping fear.

On a personal note, I was once a witch in fiction; my familiar was a groundhog. When I was small, my father made up a long-running bedtime story for me, "The Witch and the Groundhog." The witch was a little girl with long, messy hair and a stomach that stuck out some. I knew she was me, even if my father did not spell it out. I pictured her looking like a cross between myself and Eloise (whose story-book abode was the Plaza and whose disheveled looks, or casual elegance, I very much admired). The witch's best friend was a groundhog who tunneled along with her and kept up a lively conversation. Together they had quite a few adventures.

In contemporary times, it turns out that while Wicca has been enjoying a boom in growth, so has Halloween, which is now widely celebrated by adults as well as children. Wiccan books are not the only items that fly off the shelves in the autumn. The Halloween retail season culminates on All Hallow's Eve, October 31, but it starts the day after Labor Day and is a boon for manufacturers of candy, masks, costumes, and plastic gravestones. Much of the holiday's consumerist growth has been in the 1990s. The National Retail Federation estimates that Halloween spending on goods from candy to home decorations in 2000 was $6.8 billion, up from $2.5 billion in 1996.[12] The International Mass Retail Association reported that consumers spent approximately sixty-one dollars a person preparing for Halloween in 2001, up dramatically from forty-three in 2000 and thirty-six in 1999.[13] What exactly are consumers spending their money on? Of that $6.8 billion spent in 2000, the NRF approximates $2 billion on candy and $1.5 billion on costumes and has found that "Americans have also made Halloween the second-largest opportunity for home decoration behind Christmas, with Halloween sales of home decorations at $659 million in 1999, up 53 percent from 1998."[14] It is a good bet that in those costumes and home decorations the old-fashioned silhouette of the pointed-hat-wearing, broomstick-straddling witch figures large.

How might this new, expanded Halloween support new images of witches? Phyllis Curott states that she does not care if people convert to Wicca, but she feels that it is urgent that Wiccan values of honoring female wisdom and treasuring the earth as sacred enter the mainstream. But the questions of what images promote these messages and whether such images are likely to intersect the current modes of celebrating Halloween on a national scale remain open. Curott understands adults participating more fully in what was a children's holiday as revealing a healthy hunger for play, and she can see a connection between that potential and the creative and ecstatic impulse honored by Wicca.[15] Play, then, and costuming can be imagined as a hopeful intersection of visions of social transformation as well as actions of just plain goofiness.[16]

What would the new witch costume look like? A playful witch. A powerful witch. A spiritual witch. A wild witch. When will little girls, as well as adult women, take on her image? Maybe each one will be different. You'll recognize her, though, when she knocks on your door, all of four feet high, with a certain look in her eyes, and says, "Trick or treat. Blessed be."

Beyond Baklava:
The Consumption of Muslim Culture

Ramadan   Amir Berbic

According to *Skylife* magazine, "Of all Turkey's deliciously sweet confections, the most famous is baklava."[1] A dessert made by sandwiching an assortment of nuts between thin layers of pastry, baklava was once a special treat for Ottoman warriors during Ramadan, the holy month in the Islamic calendar, but has become so widely popular that it is to be found and eaten in about one fifth of the world's countries, from India and Pakistan to the Arabian Peninsula to the Balkans.

As a designer for a Bosnian community magazine in Chicago, I was once asked to create a cover that addressed the celebration of the Muslim holiday Eid al-Fitr, observed at the end of Ramadan. That year, the holiday occurred at the peak of the Christmas season, and it was a good opportunity to showcase issues regarding its celebration in America. I placed a colorful diamond-shaped object (the traditional

form of baklava) in a nest of Christmas lights, attempting to parody the conflicted position in which American Muslims find themselves. The overlaps and differences between the East and the West are reflected in the ways Islamic holidays are celebrated and commercialized here. Overwhelmed by the other holidays in American mass culture, such as Christmas, Thanksgiving, and the Fourth of July, Islamic festivities might be suspected not to be characterized by commercialization. However, with a growing Muslim population in the U.S. and its assimilation into American culture, it is evident that Muslim holidays, too, have become a fertile ground for business.

Ramadan is one of the most important holidays in Islamic tradition. The ninth month of the lunar calendar, Ramadan is the time of revelation from God of the divine books. According to Islamic belief, the Torah was revealed to Moses in the first week of Ramadan; the psalms of David in the second; and the Bible in the third. The first revelation of the Koran came to prophet Mohammad in the fourth week of the month. During Ramadan, Muslims are supposed to undergo intense mental, emotional, and physical discipline in order to stimulate reflection on human imperfection and dependence on God, to focus on spiritual goals and values, and to identify with and respond to the less fortunate. Those of an appropriate age (generally recognized to be past puberty and not too elderly or infirm) are expected to refrain from food, drink, tobacco, and sexual relations every day, from the first morning light to the setting of the sun, during this month. Muslims are also expected to follow strict ethical codes during this time, being careful to be honest, thoughtful, and sensitive to the needs of others and to abstain from foul language and untruthful words. The lunar calendar followed by Muslims moves Ramadan throughout the solar year. Some years, the days of fast can be unusually long; in a thirty-year cycle, one will eventually coincide with the longest day of the year. Under such circumstances fasting can be an occasion of severe mental and physical strain.

At dusk, the fast is broken with a light meal, known as Iftar. Many go to the mosque for the evening prayer, which is followed by special prayers recited only during this month. The end of Ramadan is marked by a three-day festivity known as Eid al-Fitr. Muslims put on their best attire and head to the mosque early in the morning. A congregation prayer in large crowds is followed by visiting, feasting, and celebration among family and friends.

"There is a common human tendency to associate fasting with feasting," says Sufi cuisine cookbook writer Kathleen Seidel in her online cookbook "Serving the Guest: Food for Remembrance." "Both are marked alterations in eating patterns."[2] For fast-breaking Iftars during Ramadan and particularly for Eid, specially prepared foods and sweets emphasize the community and hospitality that are important elements of Islamic tradition, and over time, the focus on food throughout the month has intensified. Modern Islamic scholars continue to view the habit of Ramadan indulgence as a subversion of the original purpose of the fast. Senad Agic, imam at a mosque in Northbrook, Illinois, notes that a "fast should be broken with a moderate meal . . . but that Muslims must not make feasting and food the focus of Ramadan."[3] However, as Seidel argues, there are practical reasons why large quantities of food are prepared: "Should unexpected guests arrive, there should always be enough food to serve them a full meal; this is more likely to occur during Ramadan than at any other time of year."[4] In addition, sending gifts and food to friends and relatives has been a long and widespread tradition among Muslims.

The focus on food during Islamic holidays has opened many doors for food industries that target Muslim communities. Extensive efforts since the 1980s have made halal (from the Arabic word meaning "allowed" or "lawful") food available to Muslims in the U.S. Several of the world's major companies, including Nestlé, Baskin-Robbins, and Campbell Soup, have addressed the growing demand for foods that meet the Islamic dietary code. This code pertains to alcohol, pork, and substances extracted from pork, which Muslims are strictly prohibited from consuming. Any meat eaten must be slaughtered according to Islamic rites.[5] Before they are declared halal, foods must pass inspection by an authorized certifying agency such as the Islamic Food and Nutrition Council of America. Al Safa, a Canadian-based company with distribution throughout North America, specializes in halal food products. With a selection ranging from ground beef, chicken, and turkey to chicken nuggets, frankfurters, and pizza, Al Safa has made available halal versions of many foods. Expressing Ramadan greetings in its holiday advertising campaign, the company identifies itself with the Muslim community. The ads display inviting close-ups of breaded chicken nuggets and beef frankfurters with the logos and names of markets where Al Safa halal products can be purchased. The image is underlined with a message in large bold letters: "Proudly Serving the Muslim Community." The fact that conforming to Islamic dietary codes is a worthwhile investment is evident from Muslim spending on food in the U.S., which tops $12 billion annually, with a reported 70 percent increase in halal food sales since 1998. The international halal food trade is estimated at $150 billion per year.[6]

Many local stores and restaurants also recognize the opportunity to engage the Muslim community by offering special arrangements and discounts during Muslim holidays. At Rezza, a Chicago restaurant serving Middle Eastern cuisine, people often organize private parties for Iftar. Devon Food Market in Chicago specializes in products from many countries of the world, thus attracting customers from

ethnic communities, those with nostalgia for the tastes of their homelands. During Ramadan, the store prepares special packages of food and sweets that can be used for cooking holiday specialties or as ready-made gifts.

On September 1, 2001, the U.S. Postal Service issued, for the first time, a stamp commemorating an Islamic holiday. Part of the U.S. Holiday Collection, the Eid stamp contains the phrase "Eid Mubarak" in gold script on a blue background along with the English translation, "Eid Greetings." While the introduction of the Eid stamp was an important moment for Muslims in the U.S., it was also a clear indicator that Muslim holidays have joined the celebratory circle of mainstream American culture. Asked whether the visual language of other festivities in America has influenced how Muslims observe their holidays, Imam Agic comments that many people invest special efforts in decorating their homes for the holidays, a custom much more emphasized in Western cultures. He notes, "Although Muslims keep and cherish the culture of their roots, the influence of the American culture is unavoidable."[7]

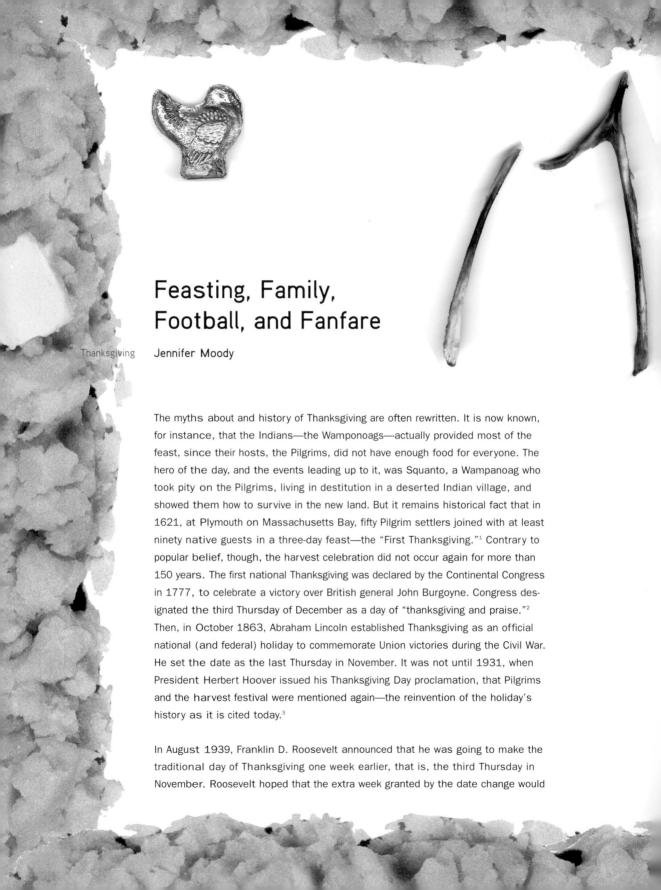

Feasting, Family, Football, and Fanfare

Jennifer Moody

The myths about and history of Thanksgiving are often rewritten. It is now known, for instance, that the Indians—the Wamponoags—actually provided most of the feast, since their hosts, the Pilgrims, did not have enough food for everyone. The hero of the day, and the events leading up to it, was Squanto, a Wampanoag who took pity on the Pilgrims, living in destitution in a deserted Indian village, and showed them how to survive in the new land. But it remains historical fact that in 1621, at Plymouth on Massachusetts Bay, fifty Pilgrim settlers joined with at least ninety native guests in a three-day feast—the "First Thanksgiving."[1] Contrary to popular belief, though, the harvest celebration did not occur again for more than 150 years. The first national Thanksgiving was declared by the Continental Congress in 1777, to celebrate a victory over British general John Burgoyne. Congress designated the third Thursday of December as a day of "thanksgiving and praise."[2] Then, in October 1863, Abraham Lincoln established Thanksgiving as an official national (and federal) holiday to commemorate Union victories during the Civil War. He set the date as the last Thursday in November. It was not until 1931, when President Herbert Hoover issued his Thanksgiving Day proclamation, that Pilgrims and the harvest festival were mentioned again—the reinvention of the holiday's history as it is cited today.[3]

In August 1939, Franklin D. Roosevelt announced that he was going to make the traditional day of Thanksgiving one week earlier, that is, the third Thursday in November. Roosevelt hoped that the extra week granted by the date change would

lead to increased sales for merchants during the holiday season, thus giving an extra boost to the relatively weak economy. Naturally, the move was met with great opposition from the general public, and the day soon became known as "Franks-giving."[4] Twenty-three states celebrated Thanksgiving on November 23, and twenty-three states on November 30. Especially opposed were those people and organizations whose schedules depended on a single date for Thanksgiving—schools, football fans, turkey growers, and calendar makers. Needless to say, the experiment proved chaotic, and it also seems to have failed commercially: retailers reported little change in their sales. Admitting it was a mistake, Roosevelt and Congress reinstated the traditional date in 1941, and Thanksgiving has remained the fourth Thursday in November ever since.

The story of Thanksgiving is continually being revised. Since 1970, the United American Indians of New England (UAINE) has staged demonstrations on Thanks-giving in Plymouth, renaming the day a "National Day of Mourning."[5] Nevertheless, Thanksgiving has remained a cross-cultural holiday—important considering that it started with the idea of accepting others. It has remained a day of giving thanks—for health, family, wealth, and happiness. It has also stayed a home-centered day of leisure. The leisure, however, seems to fall more to the male population. Women bear the brunt of the work—planning, organizing, and cooking.

Since the 1980s, many movies have been made about going home for Thanks-giving family gatherings. Films like *Hannah and Her Sisters, Home for the Holidays,* and *Planes, Trains, and Automobiles* all chronicle some aspect of family unhappiness or dysfunction during the annual feast. With all those trying to get home to enjoy the holiday, it is one of the busiest travel times of the year; the Sunday after Thanksgiving is the most trafficked day of the period. In 2003, an estimated 4.9 million people traveled by airplane and 31.1 million by car over the Thanksgiving weekend.[6] Surveys done since the mid-1980s by the U.S. Census Bureau show that Thanksgiving travel tends to rise every year. Even bus travel squeaks up one to three percent each year. The Bureau of Trans-portation Statistics estimates that, of Americans on the move for Thanksgiving, over 90 percent go by car.[7]

There is a long-standing relationship between Thanksgiving and sports. It started with footraces or "turkey trots"; the goal was to catch dinner. Now, many turkey trots around the country serve as fund-raisers. The Dan Gibbons Turkey Trot, for instance, held since 1983 in Elmhurst, Illinois, raises money for the food pantries of the Chicago Anti-Hunger Federation, contributing $490,000 in 2001.[8] In 1876, the Intercollegiate Football Association, which included Princeton and Yale among others, was formed, and it instituted a championship game on Thanksgiving Day.

Since 1998, when a television broadcast of a Celine Dion performance brought in strong ratings, concerts have also become a Thanksgiving-weekend standard. During a time when families are likely to be watching television together, music programs are both entertaining and commercial, tending to function as long ads for the featured artist: "For musicians and labels, the fourth quarter is a big time of the year when 50 percent of major-album sales are made."[9]

Thanksgiving Day is not a big gift-giving holiday, typically featuring only small sales of cards and flowers. However, there is a significant amount of money spent on celebrating with a big meal. In 2002, nearly 60 percent of Americans said they would prepare a Thanksgiving feast at home.[10] Those who did not probably went to places like the Martinique Restaurant in Evergreen Park, Illinois, where the Thanksgiving Day motto is "Gobble till you Wobble." There is always room for variation—deep-fried turkey, barbequed turkey, and Tofurkey (a tofu turkey). An old Cajun concoction is making a revival—the "Turducken," a chicken in a duck in a turkey, with a layer of stuffing between each bird.

It is unlikely that turkey was eaten by the first Thanksgiving feasters. It is more probable that they dined on fish, goose, and venison. But by the late 1880s, the demand for turkey on Thanksgiving began to grow strong due to the marketing efforts of poultry producers. A substantial amount is spent on turkey at Thanksgiving, and statistics show that Americans are continuing to eat more turkey every year. The National Turkey Federation reports that, in 1974, U.S. consumption of turkey was 8.7 pounds per person per year. This figure grew to 17.7 pounds per person in 2002—a year in which approximately 271 million turkeys were raised, 46 million of which were consumed on Thanksgiving alone.[11] In 1998, the nation's farmers earned over $2.8 billion from turkey sales, compared to $2.5 billion for potatoes and $1.4 billion for apples.[12]

The Macy's Thanksgiving parade is nationally broadcast on the holiday. The commercial pageant began in 1924, but it offended patriotic groups, which disapproved of such a show on a "national and essentially religious holiday." Initially a morning event, the parade was pushed to the afternoon so that it would not conflict with church services. (In the early 1900s, it was common for families to attend church before Thanksgiving dinner.) However, it then provided direct competition for the afternoon football games. By the late 1920s, with pressure from Macy's customers and football fans, the parade was moved back to the morning slot, where it has been ever since.[13] In 1948, the parade was nationally televised for the first time with an estimated 2.5 million people tuning in. In 2002, nearly 2.5 million people lined the 2.5-mile parade route in New York City and nearly 60 million more watched the three-hour spectacle on television. It featured one thousand cheerleaders, five hundred clowns, twenty-five floats, twelve marching bands, ten novelty balloons, four toy floats, and three "falloons" (Macy's hybrid "balloon-floats").[14]

The day after Thanksgiving and the Macy's parade—known as Black Friday (as retailers go from being "in the red," or in debt, to being "in the black," or making a profit)—marks the start of the Christmas shopping season, and so the presence of the retailer is appropriate. In a comparison of Friday-to-Friday growth the weeks before and after Thanksgiving, virtual department stores had large jumps. In 2001, Kmart saw an increase of 227 percent, while Target rose 152 percent and J. C. Penney 86 percent.[15] In 1991, *AdBusters* magazine established "Buy Nothing Day," to be "celebrated" the day after Thanksgiving, in an attempt to encourage consumer awareness. However, even for those who heed the warning, it probably postpones shopping only a day or two as food consumption, football watching, and mall walking continue to dominate Thanksgiving weekend.

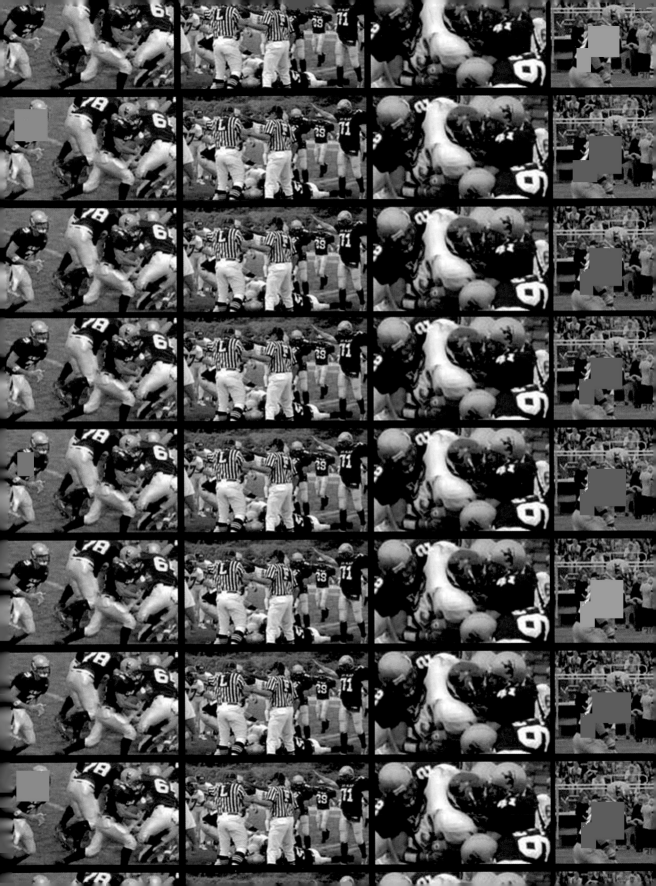

Merry Hanukkah

Hanukkah   Eliza Rosen

Hanukkah, a minor holiday of the Jewish tradition, is now celebrated with a fifteen-foot electric menorah on the White House lawn and a wall of silver, white, and blue paper decorations at the local card store. This hype has little to do with the Maccabees' two-year battle against the mighty Syrians in 165 b.c.e. Rather than celebrating a miracle "derived not from scripture, but from a historical conflict between Judaism and paganism,"[1] as it originally did, Hanukkah has inevitably been converted by big business. Ironically, while the Maccabees fought bravely for the preservation of their culture and beliefs, it took no time at all for American capitalism to transform the holiday into one that celebrates assimilation.

In today's Hebrew schools, young children are told the war tale of the brave Maccabees, who single-handedly defeated their powerful oppressors. From 175 to 164 b.c.e., Antiochus IV, leader of the Seleucid dynasty that controlled Palestine, demanded that his people adopt Greek culture as their own. Many affluent Jews willingly accepted his creed in hopes of advancing their political power and social prominence. However, after Antiochus forbade Jewish worship, declared the Holy Temple of Jerusalem pagan, and ordered the reverence of idols, one hundred Jews (led by Judah Maccabee) rebelled, declaring guerrilla warfare on more than ten thousand Syrians in a courageous effort to preserve their roots. Against great odds, the Maccabees won, and as a sign of God's approval, the small amount of oil used to light the menorah in the temple lasted eight long days. Hanukkah, the Festival of Lights, was born.

The story is an entertaining one, with bold imagery and a dramatic climax. What child can resist a tale of underdogs defeating their evil oppressors? It even proves to be an adequate foil to the story of Christmas; while Hanukkah's religious significance is undoubtedly far less, both stories have the drama necessary to sustain the fourth business quarter.

But Hanukkah was not always so noted. Unlike the High Holy Days and Passover, the festival and its hero, Judah, are not mentioned in the Torah. In fact, it was not until the turn of the twentieth century that the Festival of Lights got its facelift, making it both a true contender with Christmas and the Jewish ticket to the American rite of consumption.[2]

Previously in Europe, Hanukkah was not considered a holiday, merely an observance of God's miracle that would last no longer than the time it took for the candles to burn (about half an hour, rather than eight days). Because miracles were no longer in vogue, it was easy to disregard the story of the oil as fatuous legend. But this would change when a rabbinical ban on the "outside books" was lifted, making the Apocrypha containing the two books of the Maccabees religiously acceptable.[3] Exhilarating descriptions of battles and victories transformed Hanukkah from the ho-hum Miracle of the Oil to the inspiringly climactic Feast of the Maccabees. Craving political freedom and emancipation, modern Jews of the late nineteenth century could heartily embrace a story that exalted nationalism and Zionism.[4]

Rejuvenating Hanukkah was a solid first step for the Festival of Lights as it elbowed its way onto the holiday calendar. What solidified its role, however, was its proximity to Christmas, one of the most significant holidays on the Christian calendar. And according first to immigrants eager to fit in, and then to retailers anxious to capitalize, no American holiday is complete without gifts.

Previously, Hanukkah was not considered a gift-giving holiday. It was not until the seventeenth century that, influenced by the Polish practice of sending children with money for the local teachers, Eastern European Jews began giving their small children Hanukkah gelt, or money.[5] Earlier, Jewish tradition had dictated that gifts be exchanged predominantly on Purim, but because a March holiday does not include Jews in Christmastime festivities, Purim became almost obsolete in America. Hanukkah proudly took its place on the business calendar.

Still, Hanukkah was hardly celebrated at all in America prior to World War II.[6] Indeed, it was far easier for immigrants to be taken in by the rampant holiday cheer and consumption surrounding Christmas. There was really no contest—as the *Yiddishes Tageblatt* reported in December 1900, it was "contended that the ancient struggle of the Jews against the turbulent forces of Antiochus found no better parallel than the struggle between the poor, quiet, little Chanukah lights and the brightly illuminated, dressed up and decorated Christmas tree."[7] Bedazzled by American excess, immigrants considered the giving of Christmas presents a sign that a U.S. resident was no longer a "greenhorn."[8] It was common for Jews to put up a Christmas tree, even though the *Jewish Messenger* implored its people to "try the effect of the Hanukkah lights. If just for the experiment, try it."[9] Soon, the conservative *Yiddishes Tageblatt* conceded and advocated gift giving at Hanukkah.[10] While the pull of consumerism proved too great to denounce, the hope was that at least making Hanukkah gift giving acceptable would deter Jews from celebrating Christmas.

American capitalists in the 1880s and 1890s were happy to oblige. Manipulating Jewish immigrants' desire to fit into American culture but realizing their hesitancy to compromise their faith, businesses expanded on the tradition of exchanging Hanukkah gelt by advertising Hanukkah gifts in Yiddish newspapers. The method was (and largely still is) to combine secular Christmas imagery, such as Santa Claus and holly, with warm Hanukkah greetings. Banking on the fact that the Jewish audience was already accustomed to celebrating a secular version of the Christmas holiday, companies hoped that such effortless montage would instill a sense of inclusion rather than discomfort. The goal was increased profit with no extra expense. Businesses could increase their margin simply by making minor adjustments, such as translating copy into Yiddish and slipping "Happy Hanukkah" onto existing Christmas ads.

Yiddish papers began advertising Hanukkah presents from cars to food to toiletries.[11] As early as December 1897, New York's Ridley's Department Store, a prominent advertiser in the *Tageblatt,* stated, "The spirit with which all Americans wait for the joyous Christmas grows even stronger and stronger with the passage of time, and Chanukah gifts with Christmas presents go hand in hand. There is only a difference in name."[12] This advertisement showed a cross-cultural sensitivity atypical of its time. While expanding on the notion of inclusion, it still left room for individuality.

An advertisement in the *Jewish Daily News* in 1905 took a different approach. A quarter page was dedicated to a traditional Santa descending a chimney with a sack stuffed full of cigars (presumably for all the good Jewish boys and girls, since the text was in Yiddish). The ad was, however, decked with boughs of holly, and the "silent night" backdrop was punctuated by three church steeples that

came dangerously close to indicating the true meaning of Christmas. A 1911 ad for the New York–based Schubert Piano Co. was surprisingly similar in execution. Santa is pictured moving a piano into a young couple's living room; the headline reads, "A Piano or Player Piano for Chanukah."[13] Father Christmas was once again effortlessly recast as the all-encompassing Father Retail.

In the 1920s, Jewish songwriter Irving Berlin (born Israel Baline to a ritual slaughterer in Russia) composed the timeless classic "White Christmas." When asked why, Berlin reportedly said, "I wrote it as an American."[14] Funded by a savvy entertainment industry and businessmen eager to market "a secular version of holiday cheer," Berlin's words spoke to a generation of immigrants so anxious to make the United States home that "I'm dreaming of a white Christmas" became an anthem of pride.

While a few companies may have been ahead of their time, it was not until World War II and the end of the Holocaust that the Hanukkah boom really began. After the war, flocks of Jewish immigrants found shelter in the larger cities of the United States. While these recent arrivals may have had a desire to fit into American culture, this time it was crucial that it not be at their own risk. America responded to this need, and with a surge in patriotism and a climate of acceptance, Jews began to be recognized as a powerful market—one that deserved its own holiday. During the 1940s, Judaica manufacturers expanded menorah styles to encompass both the traditional and the chic. One such company, Ziontalis, marketed forty-seven different styles, many made from chromium, a material that "always gleams, needs no polish and will not tarnish."[15] Larger, more mainstream companies were also quick to seize the opportunity: Hallmark sold its first Hanukkah card in the 1940s.

By the 1950s, newspapers and magazines thick with advertisements began shaming parents into celebrating Hanukkah with parties for their children, home decorations, gifts, and "traditional" meals. Bartons Candy's 1951 introduction of chocolate spheres, "just in time for Chanukah," forever changed children's views of latkes.[16] Over a decade later, Maxwell House encouraged adults to savor a Yule-inspired moment: wrapped gifts are piled beneath a twinkling menorah, Mom pours Dad a warm beverage, and in the background two smiling offspring play with their gender-specific toys.[17]

Ads such as these provide evidence that over time businesses have contributed to reinventing the holiday. And as was typical for a mainstream holiday, colors were assigned. Historian Jenna Joselit credits a Jewish woman from California as saying, in 1951, "Let this be our guiding principle: keeping within the framework of our own tradition, using a color scheme of blue and silver and yellow and gold,

let us adorn our homes inside and outside as beautifully as we can for Hanukkah, enlarging upon the old-time Feast of Lights."[18] Rabbi Shmuel Kaplan, from Potomac, Maryland, speculates that the use of blue derives from the color's traditional appearance in the fringe of the tallit.[19]

So by the late 1950s, it was official. Signature colors, Maccabee-inspired paper decorations, cards, napkins, wrapping paper, ribbons, candy, games, and records: it was the start of a truly American retail holiday. Behind the development of this new market was the idea that everyone would profit—the public would be satisfied and businesses would see a rise in earnings.

Yet Hanukkah and Christmas have continued to blend. As late as 1989, *Suffern Notes*, the community newsletter of Suffern, New York, reported that Santa Claus would be leading a parade to the "Village Hall, where the Menorah lighting will take place" and gift orders for Christmas will commence. A classified ad placed in a 1989 edition of the *Rochester Democrat and Chronicle* reads: "Christmas Tree: 7' artificial. Jewish. Only Used Once. $45."[20] In 1991, Blue Hill Federal Credit Union advertised a Christmas Club account illustrated with a menorah, latkes, gelt, and gifts. By 1997, Jews still pining for Christmas could be enticed by Christopher Radko's "Dreidel of Dreams" ornament, a garish object that "gives the traditional Jewish dreidel a decidedly new spin!"[21] The product is still marketed today.

Clearly, customized Hanukkah decor has not squelched the Jewish yearning for Christmas, even if the guilt over its celebration has heightened. Businesses tend to agree that it is largely futile to produce an entire line of annual products for less than 2.3 percent of the population and that it is far cheaper to promote generic merchandise that fills the required number of shelves and can be used for numerous occasions. So what is the answer? Perhaps it is the new and improved Season's Greetings, which manipulates the Jewish longing to participate in holiday merriment by creating a secular homogenization of Christmas and Hanukkah.

Jack Rosen, a former president of Plus Mark (a subsidiary of American Greetings, one of the giant card companies), admits that catering to such a small population does not make fiscal sense. According to him, Hanukkah remains a minor holiday from the standpoint of the greeting-card industry. He indicates that the industry earns less than $500,000 per year from Hanukkah—very little compared to the $250 million grossed by the Christmas market.[22] The Greeting Card Association offers slightly different numbers, noting $10,000 spent on Hanukkah cards and $2 billion spent on Christmas cards in 1999.

Chain card stores, which rely on volume, promote alternatives to Christmas cards that will not offend. Greeting-card executives market boxed cards devoid of religious symbolism—cards decorated with a generic new "happy holiday" language of snowflakes, lights, candles, and doves, of peace, prosperity, and inclusion. Those who insist on Hanukkah-specific cards can do so, but at a higher, individual price point.

With such a small margin on Hanukkah sales, of gift wrap as well as cards, why do companies bother at all?[23] Carolyn Brookter, spokeswoman for the Colorado Springs Target store, said in a 1997 interview, "The bottom line is we saw that more of our guests are looking for those things. We haven't done any surveys or research to find out if the Jewish population is growing; we just keep hearing from our people in the stores that people are looking for it."[24] Target responded to demand by expanding the Hanukkah selection by 15 percent and stocking the merchandise in all 797 stores.

There are other reasons to provide such relatively unprofitable merchandise. Jack Rosen concedes that the price of negative public relations would be far more costly than the company's meager efforts to appease its customers. In a 2001 interview, Kristi Ernsting, a spokeswoman for Hallmark Cards, claimed: "Jewish customers have been telling Hallmark that they want choices in gift wrap and cards and other products beyond the traditional blue and white and silver."[25] One Hallmark Hanukkah offering features Mickey Mouse. Disney itself weighs in with a full line of Winnie-the-Pooh menorahs, dreidels, and musical snow globes announcing "Happy Hanukkah." Santa may have some competition.[26]

Yet author Esther Jane Ruskay may put it best when she notes that, despite the retail-driven push to include Jews in Christmas revelry, Christmas "gives a zest to life that all the Chanukah hymns in the world, backed by all the Sunday-School teachings and half-hearted ministerial chiding, must forever fail to give."[27] Simply put, it just isn't the same. Once a year, Jews are torn between the desire to fit in and the less merry obligation to defend their heritage—a position that provokes some Jews to find "new annual celebrations that meld Jewish culture with the birth of Jesus"[28] while others try desperately to keep the holidays distinct.

This conflict takes a humorous twist in a small number of competitive cards, such as the American Greetings selections that pit Hanukkah against Christmas. In one such card, the holidays seem to be tied in sentiment and tradition, but Hanukkah garners victory due to its eight full days of gift giving. The "Top Ten Reasons Why Everyone Should Celebrate Hanukkah" suggests, "No big, fat guy getting stuck in your chimney," "In a holiday character face-off, Judah Maccabee could kick Frosty's

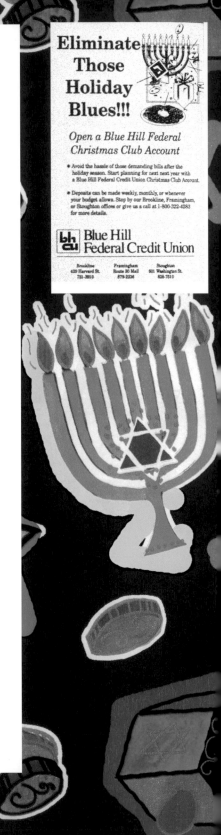

butt," and (number one) "None of that Naughty-Nice crap, everyone gets loot!" Another entrant lists the "Top Ten Hanukkah Songs That Never Quite Caught On"; topping the roster is not "White Christmas" but "Silent Night? I Should Be So Lucky!" One additional greeting card showcases the little elf who opts to read a book by the light of the menorah rather than join his friends, who are undoubtedly celebrating Christ's birth. He feels compelled to justify himself, saying, "What, just because an elf works for Santa, he can't have a private life?"

A Holiday for the Rest of Us

Festivus   **Alyson Priestap-Beaton**

Spending money, socializing with friends and loved ones, taking time off from work, eating, and watching parades are actions we associate with holidays. But accompanying each of the wonderful aspects of the holidays are disappointments and stress: What will we cook for that holiday meal? How will we ever buy all of those gifts on time? Festivus is a holiday for those who wish there was something different, something better—something for the rest of us.

Festivus was invented by the television comedy *Seinfeld*, the 1990s phenomenon featuring the exploits of four self-centered New Yorkers: Jerry (Jerry Seinfeld), Kramer (Michael Richards), Elaine (Julia Louis-Dreyfus), and George (Jason Alexander). In the episode entitled "The Strike," originally broadcast on December 18, 1997, Frank Costanza (George's television father) recalls a moment when he tried to buy a doll for his son. Another man reached for the last one on the shelf just as Frank did. Frank rained blows upon his competitor, and the doll was destroyed in the fight. At that moment, a new holiday was born.

In the Festivus episode, Jerry, Elaine, and George share holiday cards at their local coffee shop.

> **GEORGE:** It's a card from my dad.
>
> **ELAINE:** What is it? (Grabs the card from George. He tries to stop her but fails. She reads it out loud.) "Dear son, Happy Festivus." What is Festivus?
>
> **GEORGE:** It's nothing, stop it . . .
>
> **JERRY:** When George was growing up . . .
>
> **GEORGE:** (Interrupting) Jerry, no!
>
> **JERRY:** His father . . .
>
> **GEORGE:** No!
>
> **JERRY:** Hated all the commercial and religious aspects of Christmas, so he made up his own holiday.
>
> **ELAINE:** Ohhhh . . . and another piece of the puzzle falls into place.
>
> **GEORGE:** (Pleading) Alright . . .
>
> **JERRY:** And instead of a tree, didn't your father put up an aluminum pole? (Elaine starts laughing uncontrollably—and continues to do so.)
>
> **GEORGE:** Jerry! Stop it!
>
> **JERRY:** And weren't there feats of strength that always ended up with you crying?
>
> (Jerry joins in with Elaine's laughter.)[1]

Festivus, celebrated on December 23, allows its celebrants to air grievances—tell their friends how they have disappointed that year—and relieve stress with feats of strength. The symbol of the holiday is a shiny silver pole devoid of any decoration (especially tinsel)—which leaves absolutely nothing to buy. But ironically, this holiday was born in the commercial culture of television. According to Media Research ratings compiled in 2002, 98 percent of households in America have at least one television set.[2] TV-Turnoff Network has compiled statistics that say that the average American watches over four hours of television each day (more than sixty days of non-stop watching per year). By age sixty-five, most Americans will have spent approximately nine years watching television.[3] In 1997, NBC's revenues were about $4.8 billion. *Seinfeld* alone was so profitable that it was worth $5 million per episode to NBC to bring it back for its last season.[4] The 1997–98 Nielsen ratings show that about 31 percent of Americans with television sets turned on were tuned to the series.[5] Much of America's current holiday culture is inspired by television commercials. And designwise, the radiating screen has in many ways replaced the glow of the nostalgic fire. Before too long we could be hanging Christmas stockings from the top of the television. So why shouldn't a holiday come from TV?

This package is being covered up because we were not allowed to show the carton. Ben & Jerry's ice cream company was not able to grant us this Festivus Miracle.

Brown Sugar Cinnamon Ice Cream Loaded with Gingerbread Cookies & a Ginger Caramel Swirl

Seinfeld was classified as a "TV supershow" by *Business Week* magazine in an article describing how the show single-handedly changed the face of the television industry.[6] The authors note that the show "commanded more than $1 million a minute for advertising—a mark previously attained only by the Superbowl." In the article, NBC's top media buyer explains that *Seinfeld* made its money by delivering the "key demographics that advertisers seek." And the show continues to demand prime-time-level ad rates even for its reruns.

The network generated so much money from *Seinfeld* that it was able to improve other areas of its market. For example, the show's success allowed NBC to purchase the rights to events like the Olympics, and it used *Seinfeld* to build an audience for other shows on the schedule. But the most interesting effect was the show's infiltration of the "buy this" market, that is, when the stars and the episodes were used in seemingly unrelated marketing campaigns for, for instance, hair dye or ice cream. In order to capitalize on the show, these other companies must purchase the right to use the name or even a particular episode of the series.[7] Then they attempt to gain *Seinfeld*'s market demographic: twenty-five- to forty-five-year-olds with an annual household income of more than $75,000 and "cultural creatives—people who make decisions in their lives based on their values."[8] Therefore, a hit like *Seinfeld* provides a much broader commercial opportunity.

> **JERRY:** Happy Festivus!
>
> **KRAMER:** What's Festivus?
>
> **JERRY:** When George was growing up . . .
>
> **GEORGE:** (Interrupting) No!
>
> **JERRY:** His father . . .
>
> **GEORGE:** Stop it! It's nothing. It's a stupid holiday my father invented. It doesn't exist!
>
> (Elaine enters while George is exiting.)
>
> **ELAINE:** Happy Festivus, Georgie.
>
> (George leaves yelling out "God!")
>
> **KRAMER:** Frank invented a holiday? He's so prolific!

In 1999, Ben & Jerry's, considered more stylish than other ice-cream companies, developed a flavor called Festivus. Headquartered in Vermont, this onetime small business, started by Jerry Greenfield and Ben Cohen in 1978, has made a name for itself with quirky flavors like Chunky Monkey and Cherry Garcia. As I explored the creation of the flavor Festivus in relation to the popularity of *Seinfeld*, I discovered that Ben & Jerry's habitually piggybacks onto existing markets, but the ride on *Seinfeld*'s was particularly inspired. Any cynical *Seinfeld*-watching twenty- to thirty-something who is shopping around for an ice-cream treat could be tempted by a flavor like Festivus. In fact, at the time of the limited release, pints were selling for a whopping $64.95 for six—certainly not in the anticonsumer spirit of Festivus. Ben & Jerry's eagerly embraced the Christmas buying frenzy. Nearly one-fourth of all yearly sales come from Christmas purchases; in 1999, even supermarkets generated nearly 30 percent of their profits between Thanksgiving and the New Year.[9] These statistics made the prospects for Festivus ice cream even rosier.

The national marketing director at Ben & Jerry's would not grant an interview. So I turned to Rafael Cortez, manager on duty at a Chicago-area Ben & Jerry's. Cortez had first-hand experience selling the flavor since it had appeared in stores. He said that the campaign was relatively unnoticed at first but would pick up whenever "The Strike" was aired.[10] "After the show aired sales were up," said Cortez. He also explained a major motivation for the campaign: slow ice-cream sales during the winter months. Thus seasonal marketing trends go far in illuminating Ben & Jerry's adoption of the Festivus aspect of *Seinfeld*. Cortez pointed out that people actually requested the flavor all year long; they were informed that Festivus would be available only between November and February—another way the company built desire.

Cortez said that the flavor was promoted by offering free samples and by convincing regulars to switch from their usual flavor. Ben & Jerry's also put up store posters depicting a gingerbread man happily holding a Festivus pole.

> **KRAMER:** Frank, this new holiday of yours is scratching me right where I itch.
> **FRANK:** Let's do it then! Festivus is back! I'll get the pole out of the crawl space.

I talked with Festivus flavor developer Rob Douglas about his perception of the holiday as one of new traditions.[11] He also admitted that the flavor was developed just because they thought it would be funny. When I asked Douglas to explain why the flavor was based on gingerbread, he told me that this idea came from a personal tradition. Every year he has a gingerbread-decorating party with his friends, and it is a running joke that their gingerbread men always end up looking like drag queens. Douglas also told me he just wanted the flavor to taste like the holidays. According to Douglas, Jerry Seinfeld knows Ben Cohen and Jerry Greenfield, and the star approved the final recipe.

> (Frank and Kramer enter. Frank is dragging an aluminum pole.)
> **KRAMER:** Well, Happy Festivus.
> **GEORGE:** What is that? Is that the pole?!
> **FRANK:** George, Festivus is your heritage—it's part of who you are.

GEORGE: (Sulking) That's why I hate it.

KRAMER: There's a big dinner Tuesday night at Frank's house—everyone's invited.

FRANK: George, you're forgetting how much Festivus has meant to us all. I brought one of the cassette tapes.

(Franks pushes play, George as a child celebrating Festivus is heard.)

FRANK: Read that poem.

GEORGE: (Complaining) I can't read it. I need my glasses!

FRANK: You don't need glasses, you're just weak! You're weak!

ESTELLE: Leave him alone!

FRANK: Alright, George. It's time for the feats of strength.

(George has a breakdown.)

GEORGE: No! No! Turn it off! No feats of strength! (He gets up and starts running out of the coffee shop.) I hate Festivus!

FRANK: We had some good times.

A varied culture celebrates Festivus. One group, which annually gathers around a Festivus pole, reported being upset that Ben & Jerry's was capitalizing on this noncommercial holiday. But members of the group could not resist the temptation to taste the flavor. A description of the event, in December 2001, is posted on its Web site: "Much scouring of Los Angeles grocery stores yielded nothing. We encountered a Ben & Jerry's store, that had some of the flavor in-stock. We got a pint, and while the clerk's eyes were turned the other way (per our request!) we snagged the poster of the featured flavor! A Festivus Miracle!!"[12] Another group, Jacksonville high school students, celebrated by erecting a Festivus pole on campus and demonstrating feats of strength.[13]

KRUGER: George, we have a problem. There's a memo here from accounting telling me there's no such thing as the Human Fund.

GEORGE: Well, there could be.

KRUGER: But there isn't.

GEORGE: Well, I—I could, uh, I could give the money back. Here.

(Holds it out.)

KRUGER: George, I don't get it. If there's no Human Fund, those donation cards were fake. You better have a damn good reason why you gave me a fake Christmas gift.

GEORGE: Well, sir, I—I gave out the fake card, because, um, I don't really celebrate Christmas. I, um, I celebrate Festivus.

KRUGER: Vemonous?

GEORGE: Festivus, sir. And, uh, I was afraid that I would be persecuted for my beliefs. They drove my family out of Bayside, sir!

KRUGER: Are you making all this up, too?

GEORGE: Oh, no, sir. Festivus is all too real. And . . . I could prove it—if I had to.

KRUGER: Yeah, you probably should.

Ben & Jerry's cleverly captured the *Seinfeld* audience with appealing packaging. First to draw the eye is the company name, then the word Festivus, and finally the *Seinfeld* logo. In addition, Ben & Jerry's has thoughtfully included the story of Festivus right on the back of the pint. Most important, the famous phrase "Let's put the fun into dysfunctional" is prominently displayed. The blatant holiday imagery—gingerbread, Christmas lights, and snow—is reinforced by repetition on the lid.

The ice-cream company included only a small plug for ice cream as a holiday gift: a stamp-sized graphic just above the ingredients flows nicely into a banner indicating air dates for "The Strike." The episode is almost *It's a Wonderful Life* for a younger generation. Festivus debuted on grocery shelves in November 2000 and returned for the Christmas 2001 season, but no Festivus ice cream appeared in 2002, and by 2003, it was listed in Ben & Jerry's "flavor graveyard."[14]

FRANK: Welcome, newcomers. The tradition of Festivus begins with the airing of grievances. I got a lot of problems with you people! And now you're gonna hear about it! You, Kruger. My son tells me your company stinks!

GEORGE: Oh, God.

FRANK: (To George) Quiet, you'll get yours in a minute. Kruger, you couldn't smooth a silk sheet if you had a hot date with a babe . . . I lost my train of thought.

Ben & Jerry's—at least some of the time in some of the years—provided Festivus merchandise and thus, in a way, reinvented the holiday. Present-day celebrants can make up holiday traditions for that day, incorporate some of the original ones, eat some gingerbread ice cream, compete in feats of strength, and take a day to have fun amid the holiday-season hubbub.

FRANK: And now as Festivus rolls on, we come to the feats of strength.

GEORGE: Not the feats of strength . . .

FRANK: This year, the honor goes to Mr. Kramer.

KRAMER: Uh-oh. Oh, gee, Frank, I'm sorry. I gotta go. I have to work a double shift at H&H.

JERRY: I thought you were on strike?

It's a
FESTIVUS MIRACLE!

serenity now

KRAMER: Well, I caved. I mean, I really had to use their bathroom. Frank, no offense, but this holiday is a little (makes a series of noises) out there.

GEORGE: Kramer! You can't go! Who's gonna do the feats of strength? (Exit Kramer.)

KRUGER: (Sipping liquor from a flask) How about George?

FRANK: Good thinking, Kruger. Until you pin me, George, Festivus is not over!

GEORGE: Oh, please, somebody, stop this!

FRANK: (Taking off his sweater) Let's rumble!

(Cuts to an outside view of the Costanzas' house.)

ESTELLE: I think you can take him, Georgie!

GEORGE: Oh, come on! Be sensible.

FRANK: Stop crying, and fight your father!

GEORGE: Ow! . . . Ow! I give, I give! Uncle!

FRANK: This is the best Festivus ever!

(Scene ends.)

Xmas Excess

Melanie Archer

It's a quiet night in Bethlehem. Inside a manger, a newborn baby sleeps, while his mother, father, and three wise men keep watch. An overall feeling of tranquility and peace is punctuated by the brilliantly shining North Star—a guide to where the baby lies and a symbol of the hope and redemption to come. Two thousand years later, at Disney-MGM Studios in Florida, multitudes of people, also guided by the light from miles away, visited Residential Street to view the Osborne Family Spectacle of Lights, all four million of them. Stretched end to end, these lights would cover more than 350 miles,[1] a distance that the average person can walk in just over three and a half days—a journey comparable to the unimaginable distance between the simplicity of the birth of Jesus and the complexity and sheer excess of modern-day Christmas decorations. The tradition of adorning is a long road—one paved with tinsel and icicles, lit by flickering green and red lights, and lined with Mr. Claus, holly bushes, and Christmas trees.

Christmas is America's favorite and most celebrated holiday. Decorative representations of the season are varied and widespread. A happy, eggnog-sipping family may choose an eighteenth-century handblown glass ornament, while an angst-ridden twentysomething may opt for a light-up plastic Santa giving the finger. But the underlying reasons for decorating are the same. Decorations provide a sense of merriment and add depth and vitality to the celebration of a particular feast. They also speak strongly to tradition—memories of loved ones are honored by the placement of a special ornament. The much-touted "smell in the air" at this time of year is actually the smell of nostalgia. For some, decorating is an opportunity to involve an otherwise busy family in a single activity. For others, it is a way to have random strangers stand in awe on their front lawns, a way for their houses to showcase the breadth of their creativity and of their wallets—but most important, a way to give a moment of joy to their viewers. Decorating is also a unifying element within communities. A certain closeness at the end of the year stems from being one part of a decorating whole. Perhaps the most popular reason that people decorate is the indescribable joy provided by a simple strand of blinking red lights. It is, however, retailers in the U.S. Christmas-decoration industry that form the most joyous group this time of year.

In 2001, the industry boasted some $6.4 billion in sales, not a surprising number considering the ornaments that need to be purchased for the trees of 82 million households.[2] But these statistics are just the tip of the Christmas iceberg—since

2000, sales for the entire season have averaged around $200 billion.³ The celebration of Christmas in America is widespread—rather interesting, when it is considered that it is a religious holiday celebrating the birth of Jesus Christ. Not all Americans are Christians; though 76.5 percent of them are,⁴ only 55 percent of this latter figure are considered practicing.⁵ Why does the nation depart from the commonly held notion of separation of church and state exclusively for this holiday? Is it the festivities? The raucous office parties? The presents? More and more, the religious significance of Christmas is being pushed into the background as its gift-giving, mulled-wine-drinking, Christmas-tree-decorating characteristics move steadily forward. Many non-Christian Americans buy and trim trees or sing along to "O Holy Night." If the holidays were a popularity contest, Christmas would be the hands-down winner.

Christmas decorating has turned to excess—in the availability of decorations and the size and shock value of displays, in the live television coverage of tree-lightings, even in the way that modern trends are evident in Christmas decorating. The earliest practitioners of Christmas decorating were Romans, who chose greenery, representing life, to trim their homes.⁶ In the seventh century, a monk from England traveled to Germany to spread the word of God. He found that the Holy Trinity could be represented with the fir tree, and soon, converts began to regard the tree as sacred. In Central Europe, by the end of the twelfth century, this emblem of Christianity was being hung from ceilings at Christmastime. The tradition of decorating the tree followed a few centuries later—the first known instance occurred in 1510 in Riga, Latvia. Martin Luther is also said to have placed candles on a small tree in the early sixteenth century. The lights bore a resemblance to stars twinkling in a dark night and possibly served to illustrate the triumph of light over dark and good over evil, or the presence of the North Star.⁷

Tree lighting, somewhat modified, first became Americanized in New York in 1882 at the home of Edward Johnson—a colleague of Thomas Edison and the owner of the first electrically lit Christmas tree. His neighbors may have thought he was crazy, but the lights seemed magical—and especially so to General Electric, which saw profit in the idea and started to mass-produce the small bulbs by the late 1880s. At the time, decorating with lights was much more complicated. A "wire-man" was needed to connect individual bulbs to separate wires that ran to an overhead fixture. Costing the equivalent of several thousand of today's dollars, this practice was reserved for the wealthy. In 1903, the Ever-Ready Company manufactured the first ready-made Christmas light wiring. The strands were called festoons and came with twenty-eight sockets and bulbs. This type of lighting was less expensive than earlier methods, but it was still unaffordable for many. In 1925,

GE began to promote outdoor lights, which had become possible in 1909 with the advent of all-weather wiring. A community tree on Mt. Wilson in Pasadena, California, was the first lit outdoor display in the United States.

Christmas displays became popular with the middle class after World War II. This trend was in keeping with the sense of celebration and rebirth that marked the end of the war. Like many other items at this time, Christmas lights became smaller and more affordable. Forwarded by numerous magazine promotions and certainly by the manufacturers of the goods, indoor and outdoor decorating became a way to demonstrate the joy that accompanied the season.

The early 1950s saw another notable innovation: ready-made decorations. Union Products made its debut on the Christmas scene in 1952 with the first two-dimensional outdoor Christmas display. The subject? A sleigh with Rudolph and his seven friends. Don Featherstone, vice president of the company, has stated, "They were very spongy and a favorite toy of dogs, who loved to eat them."[8] By 1956, though, styrene—a plastic that could withstand heat—was being used. Styrene engendered the illuminated plastic figures that today adorn many a front yard and rooftop. Around this time, "fake" aluminum trees became the rage, and Christmas decorating became effortless.[9]

Before these conveniences, decorating for Christmas was a time-consuming practice. Women spent many hours making paper flowers, stars, and the like by hand. Today, simple decorating is easy and can be relatively inexpensive—a far cry from the days when tinsel was made out of real silver cut by machine into wafer-thin strips.[10] For those who prefer elaborate displays, there is a veritable barrage of items for self-expression—figurines, wreaths, numerous variations on lights, moving Rudolphs, dancing Santas. But standing out from this chaos is the one item that has remained most popular: the Christmas tree.

Eighty-one percent of U.S. households celebrate Christmas with a tree.[11] Excitement, festivity, tradition, and many, many dollars surround the decorating of the tree. The 1997 Census of Agriculture shows that live trees account for $441.6 million in sales every year, a figure that correlates with the 31 percent of U.S. households that display a real Christmas tree. The best-selling varieties are Scotch pine, Douglas fir, and noble fir. Another 49 percent decorate with artificial trees, opting for the yearly ritual of unearthing the tree from storage and bending and reconstructing it back to believable form.[12] Some artificial trees are more equal than others. Gucci offers a black tree (fondly referred to as "faux fir") for $1,500; the designer rabbit-skin tree skirt is another $1,300.[13] Decorating such a tree noir is simple—it comes with various accessories, including silver, black, and frosted-

glass ornaments, all featuring silver G-logo hangers.[14] While many people instead opt for the average $200 tree, others cannot decide between reshaping and picking up dried pine needles. Two percent of enthusiasts decorate with both a real and an artificial tree.[15]

Certain perils are associated with the seemingly innocent tree. In 1998, Christmas trees were the cause of three hundred house fires, resulting in eleven injuries and $8 million in property damage. The leading causes of these fires were short circuits and ground faults.[16] Additionally, 6,200 people are treated each year in emergency rooms for injuries related to holiday decorations and Christmas trees.[17] Both the National Fire Prevention Agency and the National Safety Council provide tips for safe and happy holiday decorating.

As wonderful as the home tree is, thousands of people visit public trees every year. The televised lighting of the tree at Rockefeller Center in New York City attracts throngs of people. The garden manager scours the nation for the perfect tree, and just like a beauty pageant, much excitement occurs when a winner is finally chosen. A tree, untrimmed except for a star on top and floodlight illumination, was first displayed at Rockefeller Center in 1939. That simple version has evolved into today's showier tree. In 2001, the tree stood eighty-one feet high and forty-two feet wide and was trimmed with thirty thousand red, white, and blue bulbs on five miles of wire. A Norway spruce (the preferred variety), this seventy-one-year-old, eight-ton tree traveled from Wayne, New Jersey, along a specially mapped route in New York City on a telescoping trailer with a 280-ton, all-terrain, hydraulic crane, twenty people, and a police escort. The tree's life extends beyond the Christmas season. The trunk of the tree is recycled to make obstacle jumps for the U.S. Equestrian Team, while the branches provide almost three tons of mulch for the Boy Scouts of America.[18]

A number of other public trees around the U.S. inspire pilgrimages. Many visit the Marshall Field's department store on State Street in downtown Chicago to dine alongside the forty-five-foot tree in the Walnut Room restaurant. But it is the famous Christmas windows that are the big attraction. The holiday windows trace their history to the early days of Marshall Field's. In 1897, forty-five years after the store was established, Field's display manager, Arthur Fraiser, pioneered elaborate holiday window design.[19] At first, the twelve windows were filled with decorations and toys; later the displays became a mechanical multifigure storybook that progressed from window to window. Marshall Field's window themes have included *How The Grinch Stole Christmas, The Night Before Christmas,* and Chicago musicals. Until the 1980s, when secular windows made their debut, the theme was religious.[20]

Today, Steve Didier is the man behind the windows, which still attract holiday crowds. Didier thinks of the windows as Christmas theater at its best, noting, "There is a lot of set building, of lighting, making sure the story is told with just the right touch of snowflakes or candles or lighting."[21] From concept to unveiling, the windows require a team of designers, painters, sculptors, carpenters, and electricians, all sworn to secrecy until the theme is revealed on the first Saturday in November.

Jim Stone, three-dimensional art director for the Larson Company in Arizona, is in charge of making the figures, which are hand-carved from wood or foam and hand-painted by his ten painters. Says Stone, "The hardest part about all of this is making it transportable. We make everything out of the foam, because it's cheap and fast, but it's also very delicate and breakable. It's a trade-off."[22] In mid-October, the figures are carefully trucked to Chicago in four fifty-three-foot trailers. When the display is finally unveiled, always in the evening, an employee at each window ensures that the blinds are opened at the same moment.

Few Christmas decorations have the attraction of an over-the-top light display. Disney-MGM Studios, though, provides just that at the Osborne Family Spectacle of Lights. In 1986, Jennings and Mitzi Osborne of Little Rock, Arkansas, responded to their daughter's Christmas wish; she wanted their family home covered in lights. Jennings began with one thousand lights; by 1993, the display featured more than three million bulbs. In the following years, the scope of the project increased as Jennings bought property adjacent to his to broaden the scope of the show. People from all over Arkansas came to see the array, but the Osbornes' neighbors filed suit against the lights.

Eventually, the Osbornes were ordered to discontinue the display, but in 1995, Disney adopted the lights.[23] Roughly 80 percent of the lights and figurines displayed at Disney-MGM Studios came from the Osborne collection, including a seventy-foot tree, Mickey train, globe, two thirty-foot-tall carousels, and the Flying Santa and Reindeer.[24]

Americans who are touched and rendered nostalgic by public Christmas decorations are increasingly purchasing predecorated ("instant") trees and living room displays. Perhaps the most convenient of all services is the Christmas decorator. One person behind this phenomenon is Jim Ketchum, CEO of Christmas Decor, a Texas-based chain that decorates about forty thousand U.S. homes and businesses every holiday season. People pay from three hundred dollars (for lighting the front of a house) to four thousand dollars (for a jaw-dropping light show). One Christmas Decor job on a thirty-thousand-square-foot Atlanta mansion cost more than twenty-four thousand dollars.[25]

The question of length of display is a serious point of debate among both home-owners and design gurus. One Arizona couple was cited for violating an ordinance prohibiting the display of Christmas decorations more than nineteen days past the holiday.[26] In many households, Epiphany on January 6 marks the end of the holidays. Says Christmas decorator Harold Hand, "I feel very strongly about taking down the decorations quickly. In fact, I'm a believer in getting them down by New Year's Eve. When it's over, it's over. There's always something new to move on to."[27] But there are many people in the Chicago neighborhood of Norwood Park who leave their decorations up year-round in order to reduce the intensive labor needed to re-create some of the displays.

With many feeling strongly about putting away their Christmas goods by January, the year-round Christmas retailer is something of an anomaly. The United States has approximately 1,500 such stores, which bring the newest trends and items to consumers.[28] According to Unity Marketing, the third and fourth quarters represent 20 and 51 percent, respectively, of the annual sales of these Christmas stores. The statistics show that a surprising 29 percent of Christmas sales take place from January to June.[29] Many such retailers rely on purchases by the esti-mated 15 million American families considered to be dedicated collectors.[30] These hobbyists add to their assemblies of ornaments, villages, figurines, nutcrackers, crèches, and dinnerware throughout the year.

The G&L Christmas Barn, a large store in Windham, Connecticut, lures busloads of visitors year-round, especially in the summer. The store owes much of its suc-cess to the sale of collectibles such as the Department 56 house collection and Charming Tails mouse figurines. Lorrie Reid handles marketing and acquisitions and says of the magic of collecting: "It isn't until the customers touch the goods that they become enamored. We call it porcelain poisoning. One touch and you're hooked." Her husband, David, adds that it is "the best legal drug in the world." Fifteen million addicted Americans can't be wrong. Lorrie Reid has concluded, regarding collectors, "Though usage behavior is seasonal, the acquisition behavior is not seasonal."[31]

Christopher Radko knows the ins and outs of this business. With three thou-sand accounts, including Bloomingdale's, Neiman Marcus, Marshall Field's, and Saks Fifth Avenue, Radko is at the top of the Christmas ornament game. His business started in 1984 when his family lost its collection of two thousand handmade blown-glass ornaments in a tree-stand disaster. Since Radko had been responsible for replacing an older stand with a more contemporary one, he vowed to restore the heirloom collection. He ran into great difficulties in locating glass ornaments but eventually began working with a glassblower in Poland. These new ornaments proved so popular with his friends

that they did not make it to the Radkos' tree, so Christopher Radko decided to go into business. By his second year, sales were $75,000. Sixteen years later, he had established a multimillion-dollar business. The Christopher Radko collection for 2000 included more than 1,200 designs, with retail prices ranging from fifteen to one hundred dollars.[32] For the 2002 Christmas season, Radko teamed up with popular bathroom-product retailer Bath & Body Works to produce an exclusive ornament, "The Night After Christmas." This twenty-four-dollar limited-edition hand-blown glass ornament featured Santa Claus, presumably post-Christmas, happily relaxing in a suds-filled tub.

The new retail outlets and acquisitory instincts notwithstanding, collectible sales have been down since 2000. This has prompted several Christmas stores, as well as collectible manufacturers, to turn to the next most lucrative decorating bonanza—Halloween. When the Christmas Joy shop on Cape Cod added scarecrows, ghost garlands, and Halloween ornaments to its merchandise, sales increased and, in 2002, were 10 percent higher than the previous year.[33]

In October 2002, the home-shopping cable channel QVC introduced a show called "Christmas Shoppe." Featured were many hitherto unknown but immediately desirable decorative items. The Snap-n-Glow features fourteen plastic panels with colored lights. Each panel can represent a letter, and consumers can honor changing holiday seasons with different lights or messages. The Bethlehem Lights—a two-foot, pre-lit Christmas-tree stake—also proved popular. QVC sold 968 of the miniature trees in the space of five minutes.[34]

The $6.4 billion Christmas-decorating industry provides incontrovertible evidence that Americans have an ongoing love affair with decorations. Something about tinsel just seems to provide a sense of peace amid the chaos of the everyday. And while lights and Christmas trees may, in the past, have held religious significance, today they are just one of many festive ways chosen to deck the halls.

From Neighborhood Shop to Photo Op: The Evolution of the Department-Store Santa

Liz Connor

In the last decade of the nineteenth century, a dedicated few Santas walked the floors of department stores spreading holiday cheer to the community. Nowadays, thousands appear in almost every mall and department store in America. In addition to spreading cheer to a growing number of shoppers, the professional Santa today sits at the center (literally) of a growing industry known as "event photography."

From the 1960s through the 1980s, taking a picture with Santa meant that a part-timer with a Polaroid camera would stand in front of Santa ready to take a single snapshot of each young visitor. Now it involves a full-blown, well-trained support team with complicated and expensive digital systems that produce the photographs in mere minutes. These images come in packaged sets reminiscent of more elaborate studio portraits. The new arrangement can be found in department stores and malls from Maine to Hawaii.

Nevertheless, what is striking about these photographs are their similarities: a large-bellied, white-bearded, red-suited, smiling old man sits in an ornate chair with a small child (or two) on his knee; the subjects are surrounded by an artificial winter wonderland—a forest, a full-scale Styrofoam workshop full of inanimate elves. But this belies the fact that Santa has not remained unchanged since the beginning of time.

"Santa"
2002

Santa Claus has appeared in varying likenesses and contexts—both entertaining and commercial—since the first decades of the nineteenth century. By the 1840s and 1850s, visual representations of Santa Claus were showing up in children's books and illustrated magazines, and his image graced printed advertisements and store windows.[1]

By the mid-nineteenth century all manner of merchants employed images of Santa in their efforts to lure potential buyers. What began with small toy and candy shops picked up steam over a hundred years until even large national corporations, such as the Coca-Cola Company, commonly used Santa Claus as a pitchman. And it was this commercialization that helped create and solidify the image and mythology of the modern Santa Claus.

When it came to selling goods, one particular Santa myth was chosen from the many versions introduced to the New World by the Old. Santa existed in as many forms as there were nationalities and cultures with the myth of a man who promised rewards for children who behaved. Some histories have depicted Saint Nicholas in his original human incarnation, as a fourth-century boy bishop from Asia Minor; others have illustrated the fearful figure "Belsnickel," a wild man dressed in furs. Until modern times, almost all variations described him as tall and thin.[2] (The jelly-bowl belly that has become so integral to Santa's anatomy began to gain popularity with the publication of Clement C. Moore's poem "A Visit from Saint Nicholas.")

None of these characters seemed the right choice to attract the monied masses, and merchants chose the Santa Claus of Dutch tradition: a benevolent and sprightly peddler with a seemingly inexhaustible supply of gifts. That is, they chose a man in their own line of work. His magical and mythical qualities also helped to quiet concerns about the growth of mass-production and -consumption and fears that the market was replacing the home. It was difficult to argue economics with a historic figure who embodied the generosity and kindhearted spirit that so many feared were lost in industrialization, even if that history was more fable than fact.[3]

In his earliest advertising incarnations around the 1840s and 1850s, when children were the largest market for Christmas gifts, toy and candy shops used Santa most frequently, but it soon became clear that Mr. Claus could do much more. Surely the mythical elf who delivered presents to every household in the world could sell housewares and beverages as successfully as he could children's treats. This is where the unlimited and unregulated use of Santa by American corporations helped his image as much as—if not more than—their own.

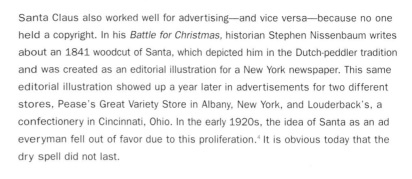

Santa Claus also worked well for advertising—and vice versa—because no one held a copyright. In his *Battle for Christmas,* historian Stephen Nissenbaum writes about an 1841 woodcut of Santa, which depicted him in the Dutch-peddler tradition and was created as an editorial illustration for a New York newspaper. This same editorial illustration showed up a year later in advertisements for two different stores, Pease's Great Variety Store in Albany, New York, and Louderback's, a confectionery in Cincinnati, Ohio. In the early 1920s, the idea of Santa as an ad everyman fell out of favor due to this proliferation.[4] It is obvious today that the dry spell did not last.

Thomas Nast was one of a privileged few individuals who helped create our modern Santa. While Nast's illustrations for Clement C. Moore's "A Visit from Saint Nicholas" set one of the early American standards of Santa Claus's appearance, they were initially a response to his own dissatisfaction with earlier sketches that had accompanied the poem. It is believed that Moore found inspiration for the verse in his Dutch handyman, Jan Duyckinck.[5] Earlier illustrations of "A Visit," including T. C. Boyd's sketches for a booklet published in 1848, often depicted a Santa closely resembling a Dutch burgher. Nast—already with many years at *Harper's Illustrated* under his belt—decided it was his duty to "turn out a better image" of Santa Claus, one more reminiscent of the jolly Pelz-Nicol the German illustrator had grown up with. Nast spent two and a half decades—from 1861 until he left *Harper's* in 1886—revising his image of St. Nick almost every year. Nast's first sketches included the "stump of a pipe" described by Moore. But within a few years Nast had substituted a longer-stemmed, more elegant pipe.[6] And Santa also continued to change in others' depictions. For instance, Haddon Sundblom, the commercial artist behind Coca-Cola's Santa campaigns from 1931 through 1964, never allowed his Santa Claus a pipe of any kind. Sundblom also made sure Santa always appeared plump, a personal reaction to his distaste for the thin, hungry-looking men who found temporary work as department-store Santas during the Great Depression.[7]

It had not always been a position of desperation. James Edgar, owner of the Boston Store in Brockton, Massachusetts, made the first live appearance as Santa in a single store in 1890. He donned a Santa suit for two hours each afternoon, right around the time schools let out, to entertain local children. The crowds were not limited to locals for long, however, and by Christmas Eve, the store had welcomed visitors from Boston, Providence, and even New York and New Jersey. In fact, the response was so great that, by the end of the first week, Edgar put one of his employees in another Santa suit at a second location in the store to meet the demand for visits with Saint Nick.[8]

By the 1930s, though, department-store and street-corner Santas were so common that it seemed almost any man could get a job posing as Saint Nick; the ones who needed the job were usually the worst off. The sad state of the average working Santa led Charles Howard, himself a former department-store Santa, to take matters into his own hands. In 1937, Howard founded the world's first Santa School, an institution still in existence.[9] Based in Midland, Michigan, the Santa Claus School offers an intensive three-day course costing new students $240 and returning students $120. According to its promotional literature, the school "Captures the Spirit of Santa Claus [and] Teaches the History of St. Nicholas and Santa Claus." It also "Demonstrates proper Dress and Make-up use [and] Gives Experience for radio and television Interviews,"[10] responsibilities clearly practical as well as philosophical.

For some, being Santa comes naturally; no weekend workshop is necessary. Brady White, who has come to refer to himself as "Santa to the Stars," has made a living since the early 1980s portraying Saint Nick year-round. During the traditional holiday season he appears live, but the rest of the year companies like Neiman Marcus, Cartier, Filene's, and L. S. Ayres hire him to model for their holiday catalogs. White started his career as many professional Santas do: in a mall.

An out-of-work actor living in Los Angeles, in 1981 White found a job through Cherry Hill Photo, the event-photography company contracted by the Beverly Center in Beverly Hills. He made roughly $4.25 an hour as Santa, lifting children onto his knee, listening to their Christmas wishes, and having his photo taken with each one. That year, the *Los Angeles Herald Examiner* (which has since folded) asked a number of children to scour the city for the best mall Santa. After much deliberation, the group chose White. The next day two talent agents came to call; one pointed out that he would make more money as a "natural Santa" with a real beard. By the following July, he found himself in Austria on a shoot for a Neiman Marcus catalog. He has been asked to play Santa at a Christmas party hosted by Burt Bacharach—making quite an impression on such celebrities as Elizabeth Taylor—and he regularly appears at parties held by the Hollywood elite, the pursuit that earned him his moniker. White still appears as Santa at any number of Santa-arrival parades held by malls across the nation each year, waving and smiling at the gathered crowds, spreading holiday cheer from a distance.[11]

Most people imagine Santa's employers to be like the Mr. Macy of *Miracle on 34th Street,* one of the most beloved holiday movies of all time. One famous scene depicts Mr. Macy growing flustered at hearing that the Santa he hired is sending parents to other stores rather than pushing Macy's overstocked inventory

as instructed. His anger quickly turns to an enthusiastic giddiness when a customer tells him how impressed and touched she is by the charitable gesture. "We'll be known as the helpful store," declares Mr. Macy, "the store that places public service ahead of profits . . . and consequently, we'll make more profit than ever before!"

As it turns out, the formula is not quite that simple. Communications and media representative for the International Council of Shopping Centers Malachy Kavanagh explains that, while the increased traffic created by Santa's presence can sometimes mean small, incremental sales increases for some stores, "That's not really the point . . . [It is] a community service in a lot of respects."[12] Chris Cummins, general manager of Minnesota's Southdale Mall (and vice president of the mall's management company), concurs: "Having a Santa is not a money-maker. He's here for the joy of the visitors."[13] The malls and shopping centers that welcome Santa each year know quite well that having Santa in the mall does not increase sales in any significant way, although that does not stop them from welcoming him. Roughly 95 percent of the nation's more than 1,200 enclosed malls make a place for Santa every year.[14]

In *Miracle on 34th Street*, Macy's hires its Santa directly, but this is generally no longer the case. In fact, supplying department stores and shopping malls with Santas has become a big business in itself. Event-photography companies contract with malls around the country to provide this service. Judy Noerr, cofounder and president of Noerr Programs, a Colorado-based company that supplies photos-with-Santa setups to over two hundred malls, estimates that more than 80 percent of Santa's visitors opt to buy a set of photographs. The one-page sheet of photos Noerr offers (which includes a five-by-seven-inch image and eight wallet-sized pictures) sells for $19.95.[15]

In virtually every case, when mall management contracts with an event-photography outfit, the latter agrees to share a percentage of its photo sales.[16] But the specific details of the contract vary from company to company and mall to mall. Noerr does not offer specific numbers but says that the percentage of revenues shared is negotiated with each individual mall.[17]

Anyone who wants to see Santa today knows where to seek him. Even after James Edgar realized the relationship between stores and Santa Claus, for decades St. Nick could be found in many other places. Retail was not his only home. Banks and other public institutions often hosted a Santa during the holidays. (My own great-grandfather appeared as Santa at the Franklin National Band in Franklin Square on Long Island.) These days, though, the public community spaces of yesteryear have changed into shopping centers and malls. Malachy Kavanagh notes, "For many communities, the mall is the only place Santa Claus has left."[18]

The photography companies that hire and supply professional Santas to malls feel that they are involved with the creation of special moments. Judy Noerr says of most event-photography companies, "Whether they are having their photo taken or not, we are trying to provide [the children with] a magical experience."[19] But as wonderful as the smiling face of a child who has just met Santa, it cannot stop these companies from seeing the bottom line. If the sales at a particular mall are not up to snuff, the photo company may choose not to renew the mall's contract.

San Antonio's Rivercenter Mall lost its Santa in 2001. The company with which the mall had contracted for the previous seven years, Santa Plus in Missouri, decided that the business it did in 2000 was not enough to bring it back. The president of Santa Plus, Paul Rasmussen, says that about 10 percent of the company's contracts were not renewed for 2001.[20]

But most malls can be counted on to provide Santa—and, for a fee, photographic proof of children's exchanges with St. Nick. After all, it is the image that counts. And the more Santa fits our image of him, the more valuable the visit. Brady White is not the only Santa who has been encouraged to flaunt his beard. In 1997, a *Time* magazine poll showed that 95 percent of mall Santas were "naturally bearded."[21] In 2001, *Wall Street Journal* writer Robert Hughes visited malls across the country to take stock of the Christmas displays and, more important, the man (or men) at the center of each. He found that the majority of malls "were placing a new emphasis on a naturalistic Santa": a real beard, no padding, and a convincingly jolly disposition.[22]

Thus, while Americans want the real Santa, many would be surprised to learn how the real Santa came to look the way he does. He looks a little like an old Dutch peddler, and a little like a famous illustrator's handyman, and a little like a soft-drink pitchman. He is a kind of one-man community of images, an amalgamation of many characters, all generous with goodwill—and with goods. He is the perfect embodiment of an American Christmas.

Kwanzaa, Inc.

Kwanzaa   Shayla Johnson

For Kwanzaa, more than for any other holiday on the calendar, controversy over its commercialization has roiled throughout its history. Begun in 1966 by then black nationalist Dr. Maulana Karenga as a separatist, anti-capitalist, anti-Christian, radical affirmation of African ancestry and the mythical power of Africa, Kwanzaa was from its inception celebrated as an anti-consumerist option to Christmas for black Americans. Karenga considered it an important cultural observance for which gifts should be handmade. As it slowly evolved into a mainstream holiday, Kwanzaa shed its anti-Christian stance and became an adjunct to Christmas. Observed on seven nights, from December 26 through January 1, it became a family-oriented way to express racial pride. It also acquired mass-produced props, such as a candleholder, imitation African cloth, greeting cards, and a libation cup; presents not necessarily handmade; and the interest of large corporations. As Kwanzaa grew, so did accompanying debates about gift giving and commercialism. The key question became who exactly was profiting and should profit from Kwanzaa.

As created by Dr. Karenga, Kwanzaa (derived from the Swahili *matunda ya kwanza*, or "first fruits") was based on an amalgam of African harvest celebrations and black nationalist symbolism. Each night a red, green, or black candle placed in a *kinara* (candleholder) was lighted to honor one of the seven principles considered to have sustained Africans and African-Americans in their journey: *umoja* (unity),

kujichagulia (self-determination), *ujima* (collective work and responsibility), *ujamaa* (cooperative economics), *nia* (purpose), *kuumba* (creativity), and *imani* (faith).[1] The holiday culminated with *karumu*—a feast on December 31. Cultural historian Elizabeth Pleck has studied Kwanzaa's transition from a fringe holiday to one celebrated by the black middle class. At first neither Black Muslims nor Christians observed Kwanzaa because it was considered incompatible with their faith, and so it caught on only slowly in the rural South. (Even today, my family in Florida, which makes great efforts to celebrate the holidays that are meaningful to Christians, maintains little interest in Kwanzaa.) In the late 1960s and early 1970s, Kwanzaa spread to cities where black nationalism had a strong presence: San Diego, San Francisco, Chicago, Atlanta, Durham, Newark, Brooklyn, New Orleans, and others. Pleck states, "Kwanzaa became widely adopted in schools and homes only when it shed its oppositional character and came to be redefined as a more familial event."[2] She identifies this happening along with the growth of the post–Civil Rights–era black middle class in the 1980s. As middle-class blacks became more assimilated into the white mainstream, they remained interested in teaching their children pride in their racial identity. And Kwanzaa became one of the vehicles for doing so. (Critics, however, have considered it unnecessary and too fabricated— depicting a type of timeless fantasy Africa and ignoring African-American history.)[3]

Ebony and *Jet* first published articles on Kwanzaa in 1983, and in the 1990s, Kwanzaa continued to grow. In 1999 the *Milwaukee Journal Sentinel* reported, "'Interest in Kwanzaa is sweeping the country,' said Clayborn Benson, executive director of the Wisconsin Black Historical Society Museum . . . 'Some 33 people attended the museum's first Kwanzaa program [in 1986]. That number grew to about 3000 then tapered off . . . as more people began having their own Kwanzaa celebration.'"[4] In 2000, *Ebony* estimated that about five million African-American families celebrate Kwanzaa and that it is a $700 million event nationally.[5]

As Kwanzaa increased in popularity, it became more commercial, and advertisements in turn publicized the holiday. Kwanzaa expositions from 1981 onward showcased holiday goods. Public-school celebrations starting in 1979 and multiplying in the 1980s also spread information about the holiday. An invented tradition, Kwanzaa was ripe for incorporation into the ethnically segmented consumer culture and the multicultural interests of the educational system. However, since it occurred immediately after Christmas, it inevitably took on many of the season's characteristics—cards, wrapping paper, store-bought presents, and even the greeting "Merry Kwanzaa."[6]

In a 1999 *Philadelphia Tribune* article, Dr. Karenga, now professor of Black Studies at California State University at Long Beach, pleaded: "Kwanzaa is above all a cultural practice not a commercial one." But in the same essay he lobbied for

purchases from black artists at Kwanzaa time: "No serious celebrants of Kwanzaa can support a corporate control of the Black community or the economics of Kwanzaa. Nor can they in good conscience drive small-scale community artists, producers and vendors out of business by buying corporate products and aiding their penetration and domination of the Kwanzaa market."[7]

The current arguments concerning Kwanzaa and consumerism are not over the existence of commercialization but rather over who will profit—black-owned and Afrocentric boutiques, artists, and designers or large corporations like Hallmark. (Hallmark started its Mahogany brand, targeting African-American consumers, in 1987 and for 2003 offered ten Kwanzaa card designs.) The principle of *ujamaa* (cooperative economics, in its original black nationalist usage signifying socialism) is today interpreted as a call to support black-owned businesses at Kwanzaa time. Small Milwaukee retailer Daniel Gregory has urged blacks "to embrace the fourth Kwanzaa principle of cooperative economics . . . 'If we practice this principle, we'd be more self-sufficient and better off as a community . . . Why not seek out a cultural gift and buy it from someone of your culture?'"[8] In fact, African specialty stores in Chicago are profiting from the holiday, says Desiree Sanders, president of the Afrocentric Bookstore, which offers Kwanzaa kits, books, stickers, and greeting cards.[9]

Jose Ferrer, spokesperson for New York City's Kwanzaa Fest (usually housed at the Jacob Javits Convention Center), estimates that about half the vendors at the Fest's Afrocentric mall sell handmade goods, the other half, manufactured ones. For many retailers, handcrafted items, whether made in the U.S. or imported (such as authentic Kente cloth from Africa), are simply too expensive.[10] A recent socially oriented product is the MEE (Motivational Educational Entertainment Productions) Complete Kwanzaa Kit—candleholder, candles, unity cup, straw mat, poster of the seven principles, and printed guide and video that emphasize contemporary relevance. MEE director of marketing William Juzang says that he feels the celebration promotes ideals that should be applied in any person's life. The goal at MEE is to

Indeed
The Struggle Continues
It is a thing to Celebrate
Happy Kwanzaa!

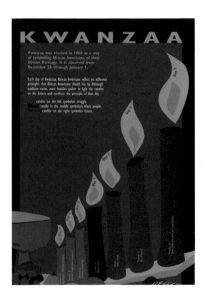

"develop social responsibility and to have a positive impact on the urban community."[11] There lies the heart of Kwanzaa. Retail events and various adaptations reflect a genuine fervor for the meaning of Kwanzaa, providing a solid opportunity to support the African-American community. The observance of Kwanzaa merges cultural pride and celebrations with the dollars that dance around it, so that, even in the new millennium, the struggle of African Americans can provide true promise—and profit.

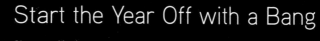

Start the Year Off with a Bang

New Year's Eve   Shannon Hughey

Many corporations in the United States are closed on New Year's Day. It is considered to be a day of rest, remembrance, and resolution after the celebrating of the night before. But for police officers and firefighters, it might be the most challenging holiday of the year. New Year's Day has the highest number of reported crimes of all major holidays. As Chicago fireman Matt Flanagan explains, "Most of the calls we get on New Year's Day are for situations that were caused the night before."[1]

Average Number of Crimes Reported In Chicago

	Average for New Year's Day 1995–2001	Average for Major Holidays
Aggravated assault and battery	114	76
All other offenses except traffic	161	104
Arson	4	3
Burglary	82	86
Criminal sexual assault	34	8
Disorderly conduct	4	3
Drug-abuse violations	89	91
Embezzlement	3	0.8
Forgery and counterfeiting	4	4
Fraud	43	27
Gambling	3	2
Homicide (first- or second-degree)	2	2
Larceny, theft	239	242
Liquor laws	5	3
Motor-vehicle theft	92	81
Offenses against family and children	21	6
Simple assault and battery	340	261
Prostitution	10	12
Robbery	64	61
Criminal sexual abuse	15	7
Stolen property (buying, receiving, possessing)	0.3	0.8
Vandalism	286	175
Weapons	71	20

Compiled from data obtained from the Chicago Police Department Research and Development Division, Research and Analysis Section, Chicago, Illinois, April 16, 2002.

Gun-Related Calls for Service, December 31 (6:00 p.m.) to January 1 (3:00 a.m.), City of Los Angeles

Year	Number of Gun-Related Calls
1992	778
1993	792
1994	650
1995	567
1996	600
1997	613
1998	645
1999	580
2000	500
2001	393

From "Final Report of the 2001 New Year's Eve Gunfire Reduction Efforts"

New Year's Day receives the highest number of reports of the major holidays in ten different categories of crime. Half of all reports of criminal sexual assault committed on all major holidays are filed on New Year's Day. Other categories where New Year's crimes rank the highest in volume of reports are assault and battery, arson, embezzlement, fraud, liquor laws, offenses against family and children, vandalism, and weapons. A good example of crime running rampant on this holiday is the tradition of celebratory, indiscriminate gunfire that starts on New Year's Eve and carries over throughout New Year's Day. Chicago police officer Jack Beningo describes the situation: "At midnight on New Year's Eve, a great number of people feel compelled to fire off their guns. What they don't think about is that what goes up must come down."[2] This custom has been a problem for crime enforcement agencies in many major cities in the United States for several years. Indiscriminate gunfire often results in injury or death to members of the community.

The Los Angeles Police Department decided to take a leading role in addressing this undesirable practice. In 1989, the LAPD developed the Gunfire Reduction Program. This program communicated the dangers of celebratory gunfire to the public and encouraged the community to call the police in the event of such activity. The program hawked its campaign with billboards, flyers, public-service announcements, and newspaper ads. The LAPD also introduced legislation to ban sales of ammunition in Los Angeles prior to New Year's Eve and created a statute to prohibit indiscriminate gunfire. The final steps in the Gunfire Reduction Program were the development of Gunfire Suppression Teams and increased enforcement. Over the years, this program has proved successful in reducing the amount of celebratory gunfire on New Year's Eve in Los Angeles. Police departments in other cities across the United States have developed programs similar to the one developed by the LAPD.[3]

Many factors contribute to the high crime statistics of New Year's Day. New Year's Eve is a holiday that is marketed as purely celebratory, and it caps a holiday season that runs for almost two months. According to the Distilled Spirits Council of the United States, November and December are the two biggest months of the year for alcohol sales. In December 2000 alone, more than 39 million gallons of distilled spirits were sold in the United States.[4] Twelve percent of all distilled-spirits sales occur in December.[5] During the holidays, consumers buy bottles for gift giving and entertaining, and New Year's Eve is the holiday that is most about consumption of, entertaining with, and celebrating with alcohol. Nearly no gift giving, with the exception of a gift of alcohol or other forms of entertainment, is built into the marketing of the new year. Timing is also a key factor that explains the high crime rate. Because New Year's Eve anticipates the stroke of midnight, most of the activity reported on New Year's Day began the night before. It is no wonder the celebration of the new year easily equals mass mayhem after midnight. In general, crime statistics tend to be higher on holidays than on non-holidays Additionally, patterns in crime statistics show that secular and non-family-oriented holidays have higher reports of incidents than religious holidays. Christmas and Thanksgiving rank lowest in reported crimes in comparison to Halloween, St. Patrick's Day, Valentine's Day, and New Year's Eve.

Average Number of Reported Crimes on Specified Holidays in Chicago, 1995–2001

	New Year's Day	Valentine's Day	St. Patrick's Day	Halloween	Thanksgiving	Christmas Eve	Christmas Day	New Year's Eve
Aggravated assault and battery	**114**	64	75	105	70	57	61	65
All other offenses except traffic	**161**	130	122	109	73	80	17	88
Arson	**4**	3	3	**4**	2	3	3	2
Burglary	82	**97**	92	93	73	95	73	79
Criminal sexual assault	**34**	5	6	6	4	3	2	5
Disorderly conduct	4	4	4	**7**	1	0.3	2	2
Drug-abuse violations	89	**136**	121	106	85	73	43	77
Embezzlement	**3**	0.2	0.3	1	0.1	0.2	0	2
Forgery and counterfeiting	4	**7**	4	5	2	5	1	5
Fraud	**43**	35	31	35	12	25	8	25
Gambling	3	**4**	2	2	1	1	0	0.6
Homicide (first- or second-degree)	2	1	1	**4**	1	1	2	2
Larceny, theft	239	267	239	**320**	171	248	139	257
Liquor laws	**5**	4	4	**5**	3	1	1	2
Motor-vehicle theft	92	75	86	**95**	71	74	66	86
Offenses against family and children	**21**	4	3	3	4	5	4	4
Simple assault and battery	**340**	248	277	310	242	207	236	225
Prostitution	10	**20**	18	17	12	9	2	10
Robbery	64	67	58	**77**	45	72	45	63
Criminal sexual abuse	**15**	8	7	7	4	4	3	4
Stolen property	0.3	**1**	**1**	**1**	**1**	0.3	0.2	**1**
Vandalism	**286**	132	120	252	144	124	116	222
Weapons	**71**	12	13	20	8	7	6	26

Bold numbers indicate the category of crime with the highest volume of reported incidents.

Compiled from data obtained from the Chicago Police Department Research and Development Division, Research and Analysis Section, Chicago, Illinois, April 16, 2002.

Holiday Crime versus Average Daily Crime in the Same Month in Chicago, 2000

	Number of Crimes Reported on New Year's Day	Number of Crimes Reported on Average January Day
Aggravated assault and battery	112	58
Arson	9	2
Criminal sexual assault	33	5
Motor-vehicle theft	92	78

	Number of Crimes Reported on St. Patrick's Day	Number of Crimes Reported on Average March Day
Burglary	95	81

	Number of Crimes Reported on Halloween	Number of Crimes Reported on Average October Day
Robbery	68	57
Larceny, theft	336	319

	Number of Crimes Reported on Thanksgiving	Number of Crimes Reported on Average November Day
Homicide (first- or second-degree)	2	4

Compiled from data obtained from the Chicago Police Department's Fourth Quarterly Update Report of Index Crimes for Year 2000.

Notes

The Business of Holidays

1. According to the U.S. Census Bureau, www.census.gov, retail (as opposed to retail and food services) annual expenditures for 2001 equaled $3,167,842,000,000.
2. According to the National Retail Federation, in 2001 November and December sales comprised 23.3 percent of annual merchandise sales.
3. Research by Melanie Archer; Unity Marketing, "The Christmas and Seasonal Decorations Report, 2002: The Market, The Competitors, The Trends," http://www.mindbranch.com/listing/product/R395-0013.html.
4. The five major seasons are based on goods generally sold in department stores. Scott Krugman, publicist for the National Retail Federation, telephone conversation with author, October 2002.
5. In 1999, Americans spent $1.059 billion on Valentine's Day candies, making it the fourth biggest holiday of the year (after Halloween, Christmas, and Easter) for the candy industry. Ruth Lopez, *Chocolate: The Nature of Indulgence* (New York: Abrams, 2002), 126.
6. Nicholas Rogers, *Halloween: From Pagan Ritual to Party Night* (Oxford and New York: Oxford University Press, 2002), 138.
7. Matthew Dennis, *Red, White, and Blue Letter Days: An American Calendar* (Ithaca: Cornell University Press, 2002), 162.
8. Karal Ann Marling, *Merry Christmas!* (Cambridge: Harvard University Press, 2000); Leigh Eric Schmidt, *Consumer Rites: The Buying and Selling of American Holidays* (Princeton: Princeton University Press, 1995); Elizabeth H. Pleck, *Celebrating the Family: Ethnicity, Consumer Culture, and Family Rituals* (Cambridge: Harvard University Press, 2000).

Trimming Thighs, Fattening Wallets

1. Theola Labbe, "Post-Holiday Business Is Heavy at Area Gyms: The Resolute Put an End to Weeks—or Years—of Excess and Inactivity," *Washington Post*, January 2, 2002, B1.
2. Labbe, "Post-Holiday Business," B1.
3. Labbe, "Post-Holiday Business," B1.
4. "Average American Gains 7 to 10 Pounds over Holidays," *CNN Online*, December 25, 1995, http://www.cnn.com/HEALTH/9512/holiday_weight. Recent research from the *New England Journal of Health*, however, states that weight gain is only about a pound. Charles Stuart Platkin, syndicated health and nutrition writer, has observed that seemingly insignificant weight gain can accrue over the years, causing serious health problems. And according to a study by the National Institutes of Health, "While Americans gain much less weight over the winter holidays than is commonly believed, the weight they do gain may be a major contributor to the increase in body weight that often occurs during adulthood." "Holiday Waistline Warning," *Portsmouth Herald Health News Online*, November 21, 2002, http://www.seacoastonline.com/2002news/11242002/health/36962.htm.
5. Labbe, "Post-Holiday Business," B1.
6. Lara Cardon, "Some Say Weight Watchers Promises More than Diets Can Deliver," *University Wire*, January 8, 2003.
7. Kitty Pilgrim, "Business Unusual" (CNNfn), January 26, 2001.
8. "WeightWatchers.com 'Weighs In' with Timely Offerings for Holiday Season Offering New Tools and Resources to Help Every Dieter," *Business Wire*, November 12, 2001.
9. "Jenny Craig Kicks Off Diet Season with Attention-Grabbing Ads and a New Attitude" (press release), http://www.jennycraig.com/corporate/news/122402.asp.
10. Thomas Lee, "Ads Go Hand in Hand with Resolutions: Companies Geared to Lifestyle Changes Reach Out Every January," *St. Louis Post-Dispatch*, January 1, 2003, A1.
11. http://www.ballystotalfitness.com.
12. Aline McKenzie, "Sweating the Details: Before You Sign Up with a Health Club, Limber Up Your Investigating Muscles," *Dallas Morning News*, January 17, 2003, 6C.
13. Ira Dreyfuss, "Exercise Enemy Is Lack of Commitment," *AP Online*, January 13, 2003.

14. Michele Norris, "Interview: Samara Williamson Discusses the Impulse of Many People to Sign Up for Health Club Memberships as Part of a New Year's Resolution but Quit within Six Months of Starting," "All Things Considered" (NPR), January 1, 2003.
15. The ads were designed by Magnet, http://www.magnet.com.

Commerce and Meaning in the Celebration of Martin Luther King Jr. Day

1. Federal law (5.U.S.C. 6103) establishes the following public holidays for federal employees: New Year's Day, Birthday of Martin Luther King Jr., Washington's Birthday, Memorial Day, Independence Day, Labor Day, Columbus Day, Veterans Day, Thanksgiving Day, and Christmas Day.
2. Presidents' Day, as it is commonly called, is designated by law as "Washington's Birthday," even though it officially honors both Presidents Washington and Lincoln and, unofficially, all other presidents who have served or are serving the United States.
3. Michael Eric Dyson, *I May Not Get There with You: The True Martin Luther King, Jr.* (New York: Touchstone/Simon & Schuster, 2000), 225–26.
4. Dyson, *I May Not Get There*, 289.
5. Matthew Dennis, *Red, White, and Blue Letter Days: An American Calendar* (Ithaca: Cornell University Press, 2002), 258; Dyson, *I May Not Get There*, 287–88.
6. Rev. Dorris Roberts, interview by Shayla Johnson, Chicago, June 13, 2003.
7. Dyson, *I May Not Get There*, 260.
8. Dyson, *I May Not Get There*, 273.
9. Dennis, *Red, White, and Blue Letter Days*, 270.
10. Dr. R. L. White, telephone conversation with Shayla Johnson, June 16, 2003.
11. Dyson, *I May Not Get There*, 222, 281.
12. Dyson, *I May Not Get There*, 14.
13. Dyson, *I May Not Get There*, 87–88.
14. Dr. White, telephone conversation.
15. Dahleen Glanton, "MLK Jr.'s Go-To Guy in Own Right," *Chicago Tribune*, January 20, 2003, 1, 17.

Groundhog Money

1. http://www.groundhogsday.com.
2. *Chase's Calendar of Events,* 3rd ed. (New York: H. W. Wilson, 1978), 139.
3. Rick DiMaio, interview by author, Chicago, April 16, 2002.
4. James West, "Making Money with Weather," *USA Today*, June 15, 2000, http://www.usatoday.com/weather/money/wxderiv.htm.
5. DiMaio, interview.

Dim Sum and Dragons

1. http://www.chinesefood.about.com.
2. Elizabeth H. Pleck, *Celebrating the Family: Ethnicity, Consumer Culture, and Family Rituals* (Cambridge: Harvard University Press, 2000), 117.
3. David Johnson, "Chinatowns and Other Asian-American Enclaves," http://www.infoplease.com.
4. Pleck, *Celebrating the Family*, 121.
5. Pleck, *Celebrating the Family*, 122.
6. Pleck, *Celebrating the Family*, 123.
7. Pleck, *Celebrating the Family*, 128.
8. Pleck, *Celebrating the Family*, 136.
9. Sylvia Lovegren, *Fashionable Food: Seven Decades of Food Fads* (New York: Hungry Minds, 1995), 87.
10. Pleck, *Celebrating the Family*, 127.
11. Lovegren, *Fashionable Food*, 87.
12. Lovegren, *Fashionable Food*, 106.
13. http://www.chinesefood.about.com.
14. Grace Ann Walden, "Celebrating Chinese New Year with a Dim Sum Brunch," http://www.sallys-place.com.
15. Lovegren, *Fashionable Food*, 107.
16. Wyatt Buchanan, "Chinese New Year Celebration Tonight," *San Francisco Chronicle*, February 15, 2003, A21.
17. http://www.census.gov/population/estimates/state/srh/srh96.txt.

18. U.S. Bureau of the Census, 2000 questionnaire.
19. Emily Sano, "A Window to Asia," *San Francisco Chronicle,* May 19, 2003, A28.
20. Buchanan, "Chinese New Year Celebration," A21.
21. Patricia Yollin, "Hu's Who of New Year Parade," *San Francisco Chronicle,* Feabuary 16, 2003, A23.
22. Yollin, "Hu's Who," A23.
23. Buchanan, "Chinese New Year Celebration," A21.
24. Yollin, "Hu's Who," A23.
25. Corey Kilgannon, "Firecrackers Make a Somewhat Subdued Return to Streets of Chinatown," *New York Times,* Feabuary 2, 2003, A36.
26. Kilgannon, "Firecrackers," A36.
27. Catherine Bigelow, "Benefits," *San Francisco Chronicle,* January 19, 2003, E12.

Viagra and Valentines

1. Melody Petersen, "Pfizer, Facing Competition from Other Drug Makers, Looks for a Younger Market for Viagra," *New York Times,* February 13, 2002, C10.
2. David Goetz, "Hearts, Flowers and Viagra: Happy Valentine's Day," *Advertising Age,* January 31, 2000, 4.
3. Goetz, "Hearts, Flowers and Viagra," 4,
4. Maureen Groppe, "FDA Slow to Rein In Misleading Drug Ads: Report Finds Review Process," *Chicago Sun-Times,* December 5, 2002, 36.
5. Steven Findlay, "Do Ads Really Drive Pharmaceutical Sales?" *Marketing Health Services,* Spring 2002, 20.
6. Findlay, "Do Ads Really Drive," 20.
7. Melody Petersen, "TV Ads Spur a Rise in Prescription Drug Sales," *New York Times,* March 8, 2002, C13.
8. Peterson, "TV Ads Spur a Rise," C13.
9. Earl Mindell and Virginia Hopkins, *Prescription Alternatives: Hundreds of Safe, Natural, Prescription Free Remedies to Restore and Maintain Your Health,* 2nd ed. (New York: McGraw-Hill, 1999).
10. Peter Carlson, "Potent Medicine: A Year Ago, Viagra Hit the Shelves and the Earth Moved. Well, Sort Of," *Washington Post,* March 26, 1999, C1.
11. http://www.fda.gov/cder/consumerinfo/viagra/safety3.htm.
12. Carlson, "Potent Medicine," C1.
13. Carlson, "Potent Medicine," C1.
14. Carlson, "Potent Medicine," C1.
15. Jack Santino, *All Around the Year: Holidays and Celebrations in American Life* (Chicago: University of Illinois Press, 1994).
16. Art Buchwald, "Roses Are Red, Viagra Is Blue," *Washington Post,* February 10, 2000, C2.

Love, Hate, and Cover-Ups

1. Mary Lord, "A Parent's Guide to Tattoos," *U.S. News & World Report,* November 3, 1997, 67.
2. Angelina Jolie, interview by Barbara Walters, "20/20" (ABC), July 11, 2003.
3. Celeste Busk, "Love Dyes Hard for Stars," *Chicago-Sun Times,* July 23, 2002, 30.
4. Jori Lakars, interview by author, Chicago, April 8, 2002.
5. Henry Lewis, interview by author, Chicago, May 29, 2003.
6. Lakars, interview.

Valentine's Day, Wedding Engagements, and Diamonds

1. Beth Sneller, "Valentine's Day Origins Are Uncertain," *Arlington Heights Daily Herald,* Feabuary 14, 2003, 2.
2. Leah Garchik, "When Fire Turns to Ice," *San Francisco Chronicle,* May 19, 1996, 5Z1.
3. Richard Klein, *Jewelry Talks: A Novel Thesis* (New York: Vintage Books, 2001), 155.
4. Edward Jay Epstein, "The Diamond Invention," April 8, 2002, http://edwardjayepstein.com/diamond/chap7.htm.
5. Alan Cowell, "Bumpy Start for De Beers's Retail Diamond Venture," *New York Times,* November 21, 2002, W1.
6. Jackie Lyden and Michael Montgomery, "De Beers and the Diamond Mystique," November 20, 2002, http://www.americanradioworks.org/features/diamonds/full.html.
7. Epstein, "Diamond Invention."
8. Janine Roberts, "Blood Diamonds: Glitter and Greed and the Romantic Stone," April 12, 2002, http://www.sparkle.plus.com.
9. Lyden and Montgomery, "De Beers."
10. Lyden and Montgomery, "De Beers."
11. David Johnson, "Diamonds Fuel Africa's Ongoing Wars," October 28, 1999, http://www.africana.com/articles/daily/index_19991028.asp.
12. Fatal Transactions campaigns to stop the trade of illegal, smuggled, and "conflict" diamonds that are fueling wars in Africa. As defined by the U.N., conflict diamonds are "rough diamonds which are used by rebel movements to finance their military activities, including attempts to undermine or overthrow legitimate Governments."
13. Johnson, "Diamonds Fuel."
14. Peter C. Mastrosimone, "Al Qaeda Holds $20 Million in Diamonds," *Rapaport Diamond Report,* October 21, 2002, http://www.diamonds.net/news/newsitem.asp?num=7102&type=all&topic=Conflict.
15. Mastrosimone, "Al Qaeda Holds."
16. Amelia Hill, "Bin Laden's $20M African 'Blood Diamond' Deals," October 20, 2002, http://www.globalwitness.org/press_releases/article.php?id=3.
17. Mastrosimone, "Al Qaeda Holds."
18. "De Beers: U.S. Congressional Hearings," http://www.diamonds.net/news/newsitem.asp?num=4046&type=all&topic=Conflict.
19. "De Beers: U.S. Congressional Hearings."
20. "De Beers: U.S. Congressional Hearings."
21. Launched in Kimberley, South Africa, in May 2000, the Kimberley Process is an initiative that aims to sever the link between conflict and legitimate diamond trade. In 2002, the Kimberley Process Certification Scheme for tracking diamonds' origins was introduced, setting an international benchmark for national certification schemes.
22. "Diamond Identification Technology Developed," *Rapaport Diamond Report,* June 28, 2002, http://www.diamonds.net/news/newsitem.asp?num=6631&type=all&topic=Conflict.
23. Christine Tatum, "Anyone Can Sparkle in the Afterlife, for a Price," *Chicago Tribune,* August 20, 2002, 1.

The Patriotism of Spending

1. Art Buchwald, "Sale Away," *Washington Post,* February 20, 2003, C4.
2. Alan Wolf, "Snowstorms Disrupt Presidents' Day Sales," February 24, 2003, http://www.twice.com/index.asp?layout=story_stocks&display=Archives&articleid=CA279345.
3. Wolf, "Snowstorms."
4. Buchwald, "Sale Away," C4.
5. Buchwald, "Sale Away," C4.
6. Buchwald, "Sale Away," C4.
7. John Fonte, "Bring Back Washington's Birthday," *Human Events,* February 18, 2002, 14.
8. Sam Allis, "Upsetting Presidents," *Boston Globe,* February 16, 2003, A2.
9. Fonte, "Bring Back," 14.
10. Allis, "Upsetting Presidents," A2.
11. Bob Levey, "Our Pals at Ford Need a History Lesson," *Washington Post,* March 17, 2003, C11.
12. Matthew Dennis, *Red, White, and Blue Letter Days: An American Calendar* (Ithaca: Cornell University Press, 2002), 194.
13. Allis, "Upsetting Presidents," A2.
14. Allis, "Upsetting Presidents," A2.
15. Angus Lind, "Too Many Chiefs; Presidents' Day Is One Dumb Holiday," *New Orleans Times Picayune,* February 16, 2003, E1.
16. Allis, "Upsetting Presidents," A2.
17. Allis, "Upsetting Presidents," A2.
18. Fonte, "Bring Back," 14.
19. Dennis, *Red, White, and Blue Letter Days,* 216.
20. Dennis, *Red, White, and Blue Letter Days,* 216.
21. Dennis, *Red, White, and Blue Letter Days,* 213.
22. Allan Sloan, "Consumption, Conspicuous or Not," *New York Times,* February 12, 2003, E12.
23. George W. Bush, "Address before a Joint Session on the United States Response to the Terrorist Attacks of September 11," *Weekly Compilation of Presidential Documents,* September 24, 2001, 1347–51.

24. Sloan, "Consumption," E12.
25. Dennis, *Red, White, and Blue Letter Days*, 162.
26. Levey, "Our Pals at Ford," C11.
27. Sze Tsung Leong et al., eds., *Harvard Design School Guide to Shopping* (Cologne: Taschen, 2001), 129–30.

Making Millions on Girls Gone Wild

1. Carol Flake, *New Orleans: Behind the Masks of America's Most Exotic City* (New York: Grove Press, 1991), 5, 6.
2. Kinser, *Carnival American Style: Mardi Gras at New Orleans and Mobile* (Chicago: University of Chicago Press, 1990), 18.
3. Flake, *New Orleans*, 5.
4. Samuel Kinser, *Carnival American Style*, 3.
5. Flake, *New Orleans*, 6.
6. Jay Gibbs, "Soulard Mardi Gras Follows Long Legacy," www.soulard.com/renaissance/mardi97/tradition.html; Myron Tassin and Gaspar "Buddy" Stall, *Mardi Gras and Bacchus: Something Old, Something New* (Gretna, Louisiana: Pelican Publishing Company, 1984), 18. See also James Gill, *Lords of Misrule: Mardi Gras and the Politics of Race in New Orleans* (Jackson: University Press of Mississippi, 1997), 27.
7. Flake, *New Orleans*, 6.
8. Division of Business and Economic Research and School of Hotel, Restaurant, and Tourism Administration, College of Business Administration, University of New Orleans, "Annual Report, 2001 New Orleans Area Visitor Profile," March 2002, 5, 6.
9. James J. McLain, "Mardi Gras 2000: Its Economic Impact," *Louisiana Business Survey* 31, no. 2 (Fall 2002): 2, 4.
10. McLain, "Mardi Gras 2000," 4.
11. Vanessa Grigoriadis, "Inside the 'Girls Gone Wild' Empire," *Rolling Stone*, June 6, 2002, 53.
12. Pacifica Coughing, "The 'Girls Gone Wild' Rollercoaster," http://www.yesportal.com/dev/news.cfm/392.
13. Grigoriadis, "Inside the 'Girls Gone Wild' Empire," 53.
14. Geoff Edgers, "Flash News! Call Them Reality Videos. They Show Young Women Willing to Lift Their Shirts, and 4.5 Million Were Sold Last Year," *Boston Globe*, January 26, 2003, N1.
15. Grigoriadis, "Inside the 'Girls Gone Wild' Empire," 53.
16. Paul Cullum, "Load Warriors: The A-Team Meets Boogie Nights on the Colorado River," *L.A. Weekly*, November 8, 2001, http://www.laweekly.com/ink/01/51/features-cullum.php.
17. Edgers, "Flash News," N1.
18. Dan Cox, "The Mandalay Connection," *L.A. Weekly*, November 8, 2001, http://www.laweekly.com/ink/01/51/features-cox.php.
19. "48 Hours" (CBS), April 17, 2002, http://www.cbsnews.com/stories/2002/04/16/48hours/main506273.shtml.
20. "Girls Gone Wild Producer Wins Lawsuit," Mantra Entertainment press release, June 4, 2002, http://www.avnonline.com/issues/200206/pressreleases/060402_pr5.shtml.
21. "Rueful 'Girl Gone Wild' Files Suit," *Chicago Sun-Times*, January 23, 2002, 50.
22. Grigoriadis, "Inside the 'Girls Gone Wild' Empire," 86.
23. Mark J. Pescatore, "Court Case Brings Privacy Issues Back," http://www.governmentvideo.com/2002/04/video_0402.shtml.
24. "'Girls Gone Wild' Owner Is Arrested," *Chicago Sun-Times*, April 5, 2003, 19.
25. "'Girls Gone Wild' Producer Charged," *Los Angeles Times*, April 11, 2003, A32.

Hot Cross Buns: Ash Wednesday Rising

1. John McCollister, "The History of Easter," *Saturday Evening Post*, March 1995, 44.
2. http://www.rbanet.com/programs/paczki.htm.
3. http://www.rbanet.com/programs/paczki.htm.
4. Claire Hopley, "The Respectable Bun," *British Heritage*, October–November 1999, 8–10.
5. http://www.rbanet.com/programs/hcbuns.htm.
6. http://www.rbanet.com/programs/hcbuns.htm.
7. "Bright Spots in Commercial Shelf for In-Stores," *Modern Baking*, June 1999, 24.

8. http://www.aibonline.org/resources/statistics/instore.html.
9. http://www.rockymountainnews.com.
10. http://www.chowhound.com/boards/crave2/messages/1585.html.

Spending the Green

1. Catherine Bigelow, "Evolution of St. Patrick's Day: Transplanted Emeralds—St. Patrick's Day Has Taken On a Rowdy Life of Its Own among Irish Americans," *San Francisco Chronicle*, March 16, 2003, E1.
2. http://www.geocities.com/RainForest/Jungle/1171/StPats/.
3. http://www.geocities.com/RainForest/Jungle/1171/StPats/.
4. Bigelow, "Evolution of St. Patrick's Day," E1.
5. U.S. Bureau of the Census, 2000 questionnaire.
6. Kerby Miller and Patricia Mulholland Miller, *Journey of Hope: The Story of Irish Immigration to America* (San Francisco: Chronicle Books, 2001), 11.
7. Diana Dretske, "America Put the Party in St. Patrick's Day," *Arlington Heights Daily Herald*, March 16, 2003, E1.
8. Miller and Mulholland Miller, *Journey of Hope*, 5.
9. Miller and Mulholland Miller, *Journey of Hope*, 11.
10. Mike Cronin and Daryl Adair, *The Wearing of the Green: History of St. Patrick's Day* (New York: Routledge, 2002), 65.
11. Cronin and Adair, *Wearing of the Green*, 34.
12. Bigelow, "Evolution of St. Patrick's Day," E1.
13. Cronin and Adair, *Wearing of the Green*, 65.
14. Cronin and Adair, *Wearing of the Green*, 70.
15. http://www.saintpatricksdayparade.com/NYC/newyorkcity.htm.
16. http://www.ny.com/holidays/stpatricks/parade/html.
17. Cronin and Adair, *Wearing of the Green*, 156.
18. Corey Kilgannon, "Pipes, Drums, Flags and Green Take Over Fifth Avenue," *New York Times*, March 18, 2003, B7.
19. Kilgannon, "Pipes, Drums," B7.
20. Sajan P. Kuriakos, "ILGO Quietly: St. Pat's Protestors Stuck in the Clink," *City Limits Weekly*, March 27, 2000, http://www.citylimits.org/content/articles/weeklyView.cfm?articlenumber=295.
21. Cynthia Billhartz, "Man in Minidress Gets the Boot from Parade: Hibernians Cite Complaints," *St. Louis Post-Dispatch*, March 19, 2003, B3.
22. Cronin and Adair, *Wearing of the Green*, 212.
23. http://www.wilstar.com/holidays/patrick.htm.
24. Shamus Patrick Toomey, "Kiss Me, I'm Irish," *Arlington Heights Daily Herald*, March 12, 1999, 1.
25. Toomey, "Kiss Me," 1.
26. http://www.nbc.com/rateit/build/LateNightwithConanOBrien_rateit.shtml.
27. http://www.saintpatricksdayparade.com/NYC/newyorkcity.htm.
28. Karen Matthews, "St. Patrick's Revelers Unfazed: Nation's Parades Are Festive, Despite Prospect of War," *Boston Globe*, March 18, 2003, A6.
29. Kilgannon, "Pipes, Drums," B7.
30. Matthews, "St. Patrick's Revelers," A6.
31. "Parade Leads the Way on St. Pat's Day," *Chicago Sun-Times*, March 11, 1994, 56.
32. "It's Not Easy Getting Green: How the Tradition of Dyeing the River Got Its Start Here," *Chicago Sun-Times*, March 14, 2003, 20.
33. "It's Not Easy," 20.
34. Bill Zwecker, "Celebs Say St. Patty's Day Should Be National Holiday," *Chicago Sun-Times*, March 17, 2003, 36.
35. Zwecker, "Celebs Say," 36.
36. http://www.guinness.com.
37. "Taste-Review and Outlook: Trouble Brewing," *Wall Street Journal*, March 15, 2002, W15.
38. Dick Kreck, "Beer of the Week," *Denver Post*, March 15, 2002, FF6.
39. Kreck, "Beer of the Week," FF6.
40. Cronin and Adair, *Wearing of the Green*, 240
41. Adams Business Research, *Adams-Jobson Beer Handbook 2001* (New York: Adams Business Media, 2001).
42. Mike Beime, "Guinness Taps Irish Luck, A-B Touts Stout," *Brandweek*, February 17, 2002, 6.
43. Dretske, "America Put the Party," E1.
44. Bigelow, "Evolution of St. Patrick's Day," E1.

Palms and More

1. http://www.byzantines.net/feasts/lent/palmsunday.htm.
2. http://www.jsonline.com/lifestyle/people/apr00/braid16041500.asp.
3. http://www.inhisname.com/Palms.htm.
4. Sister Cecilia Schmitt, interview by author, December 2002.
5. http://www.jsonline.com/lifestyle/people/apr00/braid16041500.asp.
6. http://www.jsonline.com/lifestyle/people/apr00/braid16041500.asp.
7. http://www.inhisname.com/Palms.htm.
8. http://www.jsonline.com/lifestyle/people/apr00/braid16041500.asp.
9. Sister Cecilia Schmitt, *Palm Weaving: The Story . . . and the Art* (Minnesota, 1999).

The Mainstreaming of Kosher Foods

1. Ellen Simon, "Kosher Foods Grow More Popular," *New Orleans Times-Picayune*, February 12, 2000, B4.
2. Integrated Marketing Survey, "Communications Inc.," 2003, http://www.star-k.org/ind-advantages-market.htm.
3. Alfred J. Kolatch, *The Jewish Book of Why* (Middle Village, N.Y.: Jonathan David Publishers, 1981), 182.
4. Peter Nathan, "Passover Relationships," http://www.church-of-god.org/cogn/cn0104/passrel.htm. Also, Exodus 20:1–3.
5. *Delaney Report*, November 6, 2000, 4.
6. Deborah Ross, B. Manischewitz Company, http://www.manischewitz.com.
7. "Our History," http://www.manischewitz.com/docs/history.shtml.
8. Jessica Shaw, "Manischewitz Leavens Its Image," *Fortune*, November 8, 1999, 48.
9. Joshua Harris Drager, "Florida Investigates If High Cost of Unleavened Bread Is Kosher," *Wall Street Journal*, April 14, 1997, B1.
10. Arlene Vigoda, "Tiger Beat," *USA Today*, April 16, 1997, 1D.
11. *Reuters Business Report*, April 14, 1997.

Peeps: A Letter from a Fan

1. http://www.marshmallowpeeps.com/history.html.
2. Roula Amire, "Just Born Too Hot to Handle," *Candy Industry*, February 2000, 20–24.
3. Amire, "Just Born Too Hot," 20–24.
4. Jim George, "Hatching a Strategy That Keeps Chicks Ahead of the Commodity Curve," *Business and Management Practices*, September 2000, 37–40.
5. Kim Severson, "Peeps Rule Roost: Easter's Unofficial Marshmallow Treat Now a Chic and Easy Target to Spoof," *San Francisco Chronicle*, April 3, 1999, A1.
6. Teresa J. Farney, "Marshmallow Peeps Achieve Cult Status on Internet," *Colorado Springs Gazette*, April 10, 1998, 1–2.
7. Daniel Harris, *Cute, Quaint, Hungry, and Romantic* (New York: Da Capo Press, 2001), 5. Harris defines cuteness as something we do and argues that "[cuteness] aestheticizes unhappiness, helplessness, and deformity."
8. Severson, "Peeps Rule Roost," A1.
9. In May 1996, Favorite Brands International introduced a marshmallow that does not melt in temperatures as high as 375 degrees Fahrenheit for ten to twenty minutes, as reported by *Food Ingredient News* 3, no. 5. This suggests that some forms of marshmallow may indeed approach the texture of rubber.
10. George, "Hatching a Strategy," 37–40.
11. Amire, "Just Born Too Hot," 20–24.
12. Severson, "Peeps Rule Roost," A1.
13. Simone Kaplan, "Easter in November—Christmas in July," *CIO*, November 1, 2001, 96.
14. Amy Harmon, "'Star Wars' Fan Films Come Tumbling Back to Earth," *New York Times*, April 28, 2002, 2:28.

Let's Make Whoopee! This Is War

1. Leigh Eric Schmidt, *Consumer Rites: The Buying and Selling of American Holidays* (Princeton: Princeton University Press, 1995), 297.
2. http://www.april-fools.us/history-april-fools.htm.
3. http://www.april-fools.us/history-april-fools.htm.
4. Sigmund Freud, *Jokes and Their Relation to the Unconscious* (New York: W. W. Norton, 1960), 175.
5. Freud, *Jokes and Their Relation*, 123–25.
6. Freud, *Jokes and Their Relation*, 113.
7. Freud, *Jokes and Their Relation*, 171.
8. http://www.ssadams.com/zolotow.html.
9. http://www.abcnews.go.com/sections/us/WolfFiles/wolffiles109.html.
10. http://www.abcnews.go.com/sections/us/WolfFiles/wolffiles109.html.
11. Jim Dawson, *Who Cut the Cheese? A Cultural History of the Fart* (Berkeley: Ten Speed Press, 1999), 143.

The Consumption of Cinco de Mayo in the United States

1. Betsy Streisand, "Latino Power: Big Media Tune In to the Nation's Largest Minority," *U.S. News & World Report*, March 17, 2003, 34–36.
2. Streisand, "Latino Power," 34–36.
3. Streisand, "Latino Power," 34–36.
4. Streisand, "Latino Power," 34–36.
5. Maria Puente, "Cinco de Mayo: It's a Cross-Cultural Cocktail But Boozy Emphasis Is in Bad Taste to Some," *USA Today*, May 3, 2002, D7.
6. Joel Millman, "U.S. Marketers Adopt Cinco de Mayo as National Fiesta—Minor Mexican Holiday Revs Up Beer, Food, Card Vendors: Most Avocado Sales All Year," *Wall Street Journal*, May 1, 2001, B1.
7. Puente, "Cinco de Mayo," D7.
8. Madhu Krishnamurthy, "More Than Just a Fun Family Picnic: Cinco de Mayo Festival Puts Accent on History, Culture," *Arlington Heights Daily Herald*, May 6, 2002, 3.
9. Juan Andrade, "United States Owes Debt to Heroes of *Cinco de Mayo:* If Not for the Courage of the People of Puebla, the Civil War May Have Had a Different Outcome," *Chicago Sun-Times*, May 9, 2003, 49.
10. Elizabeth Aguilera and Annette Espinoza, "Heavy Beer Presence at Cinco de Mayo Leave Some in Froth," *Denver Post*, May 4, 2003, A1.
11. Patrisia Gonzales and Roberto Rodriguez, "'The Drinko for Cinco' and the Hijacking of Our Heritage," *Denver Post*, May 3, 1998, G2.
12. Robert Crowe and Jo Ann Zuniga, "Fiestas Patrias Keeps Mexican Culture Alive," *Houston Chronicle*, September 16, 2002, A17.
13. Millman, "U.S. Marketers," B1.
14. Natasha Emmons, "Fiesta Broadway Draws Half a Million," *Amusement Business* (New York), May 13, 2002, 28.
15. Lucio Guerrero, "'The Day That Everyone Is Mexican,' Cinco de Mayo Brings Thousands to Pilsen for Parade, Carnival," *Chicago Sun-Times*, May 6, 2002, 4.
16. Puente, "Cinco de Mayo," D7.
17. Fred Alvarez, "Guacamole Makers Are Superbusy," *Los Angeles Times*, January 26, 2003, B1.
18. Millman, "U.S. Marketers," B1.
19. Alvarez, "Guacamole Makers," B1.
20. Millman, "U.S. Marketers," B1.
21. Courtney Kane, "Marketers Extend Their Holiday Efforts to a Mexican Celebration and Even to Lent," *New York Times*, May 2, 2003, C2.
22. Hillary Chura, "Brands: In Trouble—In Demand," *Advertising Age*, January 8, 2001, 4.
23. Hillary Chura, "Brands," 4.
24. Aguilera and Espinoza, "Heavy Beer Presence," A1.
25. Geoffrey Mohan, "Controversy Brews Over 'Mexican St. Patrick's Day' Holiday: Some Hope to Reverse the Trend of Associating Cinco de Mayo with Drinking," *Los Angeles Times*, May 6, 2002, B1.
26. Mohan, "Controversy Brews," B1.
27. Bill Gallegos and Bernardo Rosa, "Don't Hijack Cinco de Mayo," *USA Today*, May 5, 2003, A15.
28. Aguilera and Espinoza, "Heavy Beer Presence," A1.
29. Gallegos and Rosa, "Don't Hijack," A15.

Sentiment, Guilt, and Profit

1. Joshua Coleman, "Strangers at Our Table: Holiday Gatherings Are Supposed to Be a Time to Eat Heartily and Bask in the Presence of Our Loved Ones. So Why Do Many of Us Leave the Table Feeling Empty?" *San Francisco Chronicle*, November 12, 2000, WB1.
2. Susan Ferraro, "For Some People, the Holidays Can Trigger Depression," *New York Daily News*, November 24, 2000.
3. Eileen Brown, "Mother's Day Brings Annual Gift of Guilt," *Chicago Sun-Times*, May 9, 1999, 39.
4. "Spare Mom Guilt Trip This Mother's Day," *Peoria Journal Star*, May 13, 2001, A4.
5. Brown, "Mother's Day Brings," 39.
6. Elizabeth H. Pleck, *Celebrating the Family: Ethnicity, Consumer Culture, and Family Rituals* (Cambridge: Harvard University Press, 2000), 18.
7. Chris Davis, "What Moms Want: Forget the Commercialism—This Time, It Really Is Thoughtfulness That Counts," *Sarasota Herald-Tribune*, May 9, 2002.
8. William Grady, "Dot-Com Calls In Reinforcements," *Knight Ridder Tribune Business News*, May 7, 2002, 1.
9. Steve Tarter and Anita Szoke, "Putting a Price on Mom—Millions Will Celebrate Mother's Day with Phone Calls, Fine Dining and Flowers, Making the Day a Boon for Many Businesses," *Peoria Journal Star*, May 11, 2002, C1.
10. Yvonne Sam, "History of Mother's Day," *Montreal Community Contact*, May 31, 2001, 4.
11. Leigh Eric Schmidt, "The Commercialization of the Calendar: American Holidays and the Culture of Consumption, 1870–1930," *Journal of American History*, December 1991, 887.
12. Reed Tucker, "Great Questions of Our Age: Did Card Companies Create Any Holidays?" *Fortune*, June 10, 2002, 42.
13. Tucker, "Great Questions," 42.
14. http://pressroom.hallmark.com.
15. Madona Devasahayam, "Hallmark Cards Celebrate Womanhood on Mother's Day" *Businessline*, May 8, 1999, 1.
16. http://pressroom.hallmark.com.
17. Devasahayam, "Hallmark Cards," 1.

The Indianapolis 500

1. http://www.va.gov.
2. Matthew Dennis, *Red, White, and Blue Letter Days: An American Calendar* (Ithaca: Cornell University Press, 2002), 223.
3. Dennis, *Red, White, and Blue Letter Days*, 221.
4. John Dougherty, "Memorial Day Ironies," http://www.worldnetdaily.com/news/article.asp?ARTICLE_ID=15647.
5. http://www.usmemorialday.org/backgrnd.html.
6. http://www.pbs.org/memorialdayconcert/history.
7. Dennis, *Red, White, and Blue Letter Days*, 225, 224, 234.
8. Dennis, *Red, White, and Blue Letter Days*, 226.
9. Donald Davidson, telephone conversation with author, March 2003.
10. http://www.500festival.com.
11. Dennis, *Red, White, and Blue Letter Days*, 220.
12. Davidson, telephone conversation.
13. http://www.va.gov.
14. http://www.500festival.com.
15. http://www.500festival.com.
16. http://www.usmemorialday.org/backgrnd.html.
17. http://www.usmemorialday.org/memorials.html.
18. http://www.indy.org.
19. http://www.indy.org.
20. David Poole, "Racing? It Must Be Indianapolis," August 1, 2002, http://www.thatsracin.com/mld/thatsracin/archives/3779618.htm.
21. http://www.indianabusinessrally.com/Version2/ims.pdf.
22. http://www.speedway.lib.in.us/community.html.
23. http://www.speedway.lib.in.us/community.html.

The Ties That Bind

1. Ralph LaRossa, *The Modernization of Fatherhood: A Social and Political History* (Chicago: University of Chicago Press, 1997), 171.
2. Marney Rich Keenan, "Make Room for Daddy," *Detroit News*, June 13, 1996, E1.
3. Douglas Hanks III, "Pop Culture: Dads Rank Below Moms on Their Big Day," *Knight Ridder Tribune Business News*, June 15, 2003, 1.
4. LaRossa, *Modernization of Fatherhood*, 176.
5. Keenan, "Make Room," E1.
6. Leigh Eric Schmidt, *Consumer Rites: The Buying and Selling of American Holidays* (Princeton: Princeton University Press, 1995), 284.
7. Schmidt, *Consumer Rites*, 283.
8. LaRossa, *Modernization of Fatherhood*, 180.
9. Schmidt, *Consumer Rites*, 286.
10. LaRossa, *Modernization of Fatherhood*, 183.
11. Schmidt, *Consumer Rites*, 286.
12. Schmidt, *Consumer Rites*, 288.
13. LaRossa, *Modernization of Fatherhood*, 184.
14. LaRossa, *Modernization of Fatherhood*, 186.
15. LaRossa, *Modernization of Fatherhood*, 190.
16. LaRossa, *Modernization of Fatherhood*, 191.
17. Schmidt, *Consumer Rites*, 289.
18. Schmidt, *Consumer Rites*, 290.
19. Schmidt, *Consumer Rites*, 286.
20. Jennifer Wirth, "Spending Surges for Father's Day," *Florida Today*, June 2002.
21. Schmidt, *Consumer Rites*, 283.
22. Schmidt, *Consumer Rites*, 284.
23. Clyde Noel, "Father's Day Doesn't Come Close to Mother's Day," *Los Altos Town Crier*, June 12, 1996, http://www.tattooine.fortunecity.com/spielberg/434/dad/1.htm.
24. Noel, "Father's Day."
25. Yvonne Zipp, "Why Mom Gets Roses and Dad a Collect Call," *Christian Science Monitor*, June 18, 1999, 1.
26. LaRossa, *Modernization of Fatherhood*.
27. Keenan, "Make Room," E1.
28. Zipp, "Why Mom Gets Roses," 1.
29. Schmidt, *Consumer Rites*, 283.
30. Nancy E. Dowd, *Redefining Fatherhood* (New York: New York University Press, 2000), 62.
31. "Almanac," *Atlantic Monthly*, June 1997, http://www.theatlantic.com/issues/97jun/9706am.htm.
32. Zipp, "Why Mom Gets Roses," 1.
33. Wirth, "Spending Surges."
34. Zipp, "Why Mom Gets Roses," 1.
35. "Gifts Are More Than Ties and Tools," *Business Wire*, June 11, 2002, http://www.findarticles.com/cf_0/mOEIN/2002_June_11/87071709/pi/article.jhtml.
36. Survey posted June 3, 2002, http://www.nationalretailfederation.com.
37. Wirth, "Spending Surges."

E-Greetings with Love

1. "Who Is Sending and Receiving Greeting Cards?" http://www.greetingcard.org/gcindustry_whoissending.html.
2. "Creative Captures Emotion: Views from Paul Barker," http://pressroom.hallmark.com/barker_creative_view.html.
3. Dan Chrzanowski, telephone conversation with author, March 23, 2003.
4. "Greeting Card Industry General Facts and Trends," http://www.greetingcard.org/gcindustry_generalfacts.html.
5. "The American Greeting Card," http://www.greetingcard.org/thegreetingcard_history.html.
6. "Greeting Card Industry General Facts."
7. "Mother's Day Web Sites Perform Well, But Fall Short on Flower Delivery Fulfillment, According to Keynote," *Business Wire*, May 15, 2001, http://www.findarticles.com.
8. "Nielsen/NetRatings Find E-Mail Is the Dominant Online Activity Worldwide," http://www.nielsen-netratings.com/pr/pr_020509_eratings.pdf.
9. Barry Wellman et al., "Examining the Internet in Everyday Life," http://www.chass.utoronto.ca/~wellman/publications/euricom/Examining-Euricom.htm.
10. Wellman, "Examining the Internet."
11. Susan Polis Schutz, quoted in Markie Robson-Scott, "In a Sending Situation: U.S. Greetings Cards Cover Divorce and Aids," *Independent* (London), April 28, 1991, 21.

12. Stephen D. Solomon, "Go Sell It on the Mountain," *Inc.*, December 1999, 48.
13. Brian Caulfield, "Hallmark without the Revenue?" *Internet World*, February 22, 1999, http://www.findarticles.com.
14. "Greeting Card Industry General Facts."
15. Scott Robinette and Claire Brand, *Emotion Marketing: The Hallmark Way of Winning Customers for Life* (New York: McGraw-Hill, 2001), 163.
16. Solomon, "Go Sell It," 48.
17. Luisa Kroll, "E-Sentiments, Exactly," *Forbes*, December 27, 1999, 276.
18. Neil Orman, "Cash-Strapped At Home Takes a Bath on Blue Mountain," *Silicon Valley/San Jose Business Journal*, September 21, 2001, 17.
19. Linda Staten, quoted in Robson-Scott, "In a Sending Situation," 21.
20. Chrzanowski, telephone conversation.
21. Caulfield, "Hallmark without the Revenue?"
22. John Sullivan, quoted in Bob Tedeschi, "The Possible Sale of Blue Mountain Arts Could Lead to the End of the Free Online Greeting Card," *New York Times*, September 10, 2001, C6.
23. Esther Pan, Thomas Hayden, and Walaika Haskins, "When You Care to Send the Very E-Best," *Newsweek*, August 30, 1999, 14.
24. Solomon, "Go Sell It," 48.
25. Chrzanowski, telephone conversation.
26. "Greeting Cards and the Internet," http://www.greetingcard.org/gcindustry_gcandtheinternet.html.

Icons, Activism, and the Cachet of Pride

1. Terry Miller, *Greenwich Village and How It Got That Way* (New York: Crown, 1990), 41.
2. Miller, *Greenwich Village*, 41.
3. Lucian Truscott IV, "Gay Power Comes to Sheridan Square," *Village Voice*, July 3, 1969, 1, 18.
4. Jerry Lisker, "Homo Nest Raided, Queen Bees Are Stinging Mad," *New York Daily News*, July 6, 1969, 1.
5. "Police Again Rout 'Village' Youths; Outbreak by 400 Follows a Near-Riot over Raid," *New York Times*, June 30, 1969, 22. See also, "The Stonewall Riot and Its Aftermath," *Stonewall and Beyond: Lesbian and Gay Culture* (online exhibition), http://www.columbia.edu/cu/lweb/eresources/exhibitions/sw25/case1.html.
6. "Four Policemen Hurt in Village Raid," *New York Times*, June 29, 1969, 1.
7. "Four Policemen Hurt," 22.
8. Lacey Fosburg, "Thousands of Homosexuals Hold Protest Rally in Central Park," *New York Times*, June 30, 1970, 1.
9. Fosburg, "Thousands of Homosexuals," 26.
10. Mubarak Dahir, *Pride Magazine*, March 2003, 81.
11. Human Rights Campaign, "State of the Workplace 2002," http://www.hrc.org/Content/ContentGroups/Publications1/State_of_the_Workplace/sow2002.pdf.
12. Human Rights Campaign, "State of the Workplace 2002."
13. Cliff Rothman, "Advertising and Marketing: Big Companies Are Openly Courting Gay Consumers," *Los Angeles Times*, May 18, 1999, 1.
14. Rothman, "Advertising and Marketing," 1.
15. Rothman, "Advertising and Marketing," 1.
16. "Gay and Lesbian Milestones in the Media," http://www.religioustolerance.org/hom_medi.htm.
17. Rothman, "Advertising and Marketing," 1.
18. http://www.pridefestkeywest.com/flag.htm.
19. Shelly Rosenbaum, interview by author, Chicago, June 2002.
20. Rosenbaum, interview.
21. http://www.billyworld.com.
22. http://www.billyworld.com.
23. http://www.maccosmetics.com.
24. http://www.maccosmetics.com.

The Nation's Glamour: Fireworks on the Fourth

I thank Dennis O'Brien for supporting me with ideas for this essay as well as with his critical reading of it.
1. Matthew Dennis, *Red, White, and Blue Letter Days: An American Calendar* (Ithaca: Cornell University Press, 2002), 77.
2. Dennis, *Red, White, and Blue Letter Days*, 69.

3. Carol Dingle, "Quotations by Massachusetts Writers of the Past," http://www.intelligentsianetwork.com/mass-1/mass-1.htm.
4. Along those lines, Matthew Dennis has observed the symbolic significance of massive naturalization ceremonies organized by the government on July 4. (Dennis, *Red, White, and Blue Letter Days*, 13–80.) The same day, however, often features attempts to "remember" counter-histories as a way of self-determination. During the 2000 celebration in Boston, for example, native Hawaiians re-created a Hawaiian version of the Boston tea party, not with packaged English tea boxes but with Hawaiian ti leis, to draw attention to the Hawaiian movement for national sovereignty. (For details, see Helen Altonn, "Hawaiians Hold Boston Ti Party," *Honolulu Star-Bulletin,* July 4, 2000, http://starbulletin.com/2000/07/04/news/story2.html.) And yet dissent on the Fourth of July is much less widespread than that on, say, Columbus Day.
5. "Fireworks Light Up Independence Day Finales," CNN.com, July 4, 2000, http://www.cnn.com/2000/US/07/04/july.four.04.
6. "APA Anticipates Banner Year for Fireworks Industry," American Pyrotechnics Association press release, http://www.americanpyro.com/News%20Releases/release6.24.02.pdf.
7. For up-to-date information on state laws regarding the use of fireworks, see American Pyrotechnics Association, http://www.americanpyro.com/State%20Laws%20(main)/map.html.
8. "Zambelli Fireworks," http://www.zambellifireworks.com/home.html.
9. "Fireworks by Grucci," http://www.grucci.com/budgetpg.html.
10. "Facts for Features," U.S. Census Bureau, http://www.census.gov/Press-Release/www/2002/cb02ff10.html.
11. "Facts for Features."

Man, I Feel Like a Woman

1. Rich Collins, "Delicious Decadence," *Gambit Weekly*, September 2, 1997, http://www.weeklywire.com/ww/09-02-97/gambit_swell.html.
2. Keith Darce, "Decadence Kicks In," *New Orleans Times-Picayune*, September 3, 2000, 1.
3. "The Future of Southern Decadence," *New Orleans Times-Picayune* September 1, 2001, 8.
4. Collins, "Delicious Decadence."
5. Darce, "Decadence Kicks In," 1.
6. Ronette King, "Dollars and Decadence: Festival Expected to Be Bigger and Bawdier Than Ever," *New Orleans Times-Picayune*, August 30, 2002, 1.
7. http://www.ambushmag.com/is1902/hot.htm.
8. http://www.ambushmag.com/is1801/hot.htm.
9. Darce, "Decadence Kicks In," 1.
10. "Future of Southern Decadence," 8.
11. "Future of Southern Decadence," 8.

Back to School: Crafting Young Consumers

1. Kathleen Thompson, "Art History for the Holidays," *School Arts*, December 1991, 32–33.
2. Constance L. Hays, "Martha Stewart Company Posts First Loss and Blames Inquiry," *New York Times*, March 5, 2003, C6.
3. Hays, "Martha Stewart Company," C6.
4. Hays, "Martha Stewart Company," C6.
5. Lisa Singhania, "Martha Stewart Living Suffers First Loss," *Associated Press Online*, March 5, 2003.
6. Guy Debord, *The Society of the Spectacle* (Detroit: Black and Red, 1970), 11.
7. Janet Hickey, interview by author, April 2003.
8. Terry Lincoln, interview by author, March 2003.
9. "Focus SA Classic 1958: Issues of the Day," *School Arts*, December 1989, 29.

The Workingman's Holiday

1. U.S. Department of Labor, "The History of Labor Day," http://www.dol.gov/opa/aboutdol/laborday.htm.
2. AFL-CIO, http://www.aflcio.org/aboutaflcio/history/history/mcguire.cfm.
3. Ellen Litwicki, *America's Public Holidays* (Washington, D.C.: Smithsonian Institution Press, 2003), 81.

4. New Jersey Historical Society, http://www.jerseyhistory.org/matthew_maguire.html.
5. U.S. Department of Labor, "History of Labor Day."

Fiscal Flop or Secret Success?

1. Eve Golden and Glen Pringle, "Silent Star of May 1996: Theda Bara," http://www.csse.monash.edu.au/~pringle/silent/ssotm/May96/. See also Ronald Genini, *Theda Bara: A Biography of the Silent Screen Vamp* (Jefferson: McFarland & Company, 1996).
2. "Silent Star of May 1996."
3. John Nangle, "Vamp: The Rise and Fall of Theda Bara," *Films in Review*, July–August 1996, 117.
4. "Sweetest Day Seductions: Romance-Novel Writers Share Recipes for Lovers," *Chicago Sun-Times*, October 16, 1996, 1.
5. "Two Major Candy Events in October—Sweetest Day and Halloween!" *Kettle Talk* (Retail Confectioners International), October 2000, 1–2.
6. John Hargrave, "John's Journal 10/18/02: Sweetest Day, My Ass," October 1996, http://www.zug.com/gab; John Hargrave, "Sweetest Day, My Ass," October 1996, http://www.zug.com/scrawl/sweetest/.
7. FindGift.com, http://www.findgift.com/Holidays/Sweetest-Day/for-Him/for-Boyfriend/p-5/.
8. "Valentine's Day Price Tag: $100; Survey Says Holiday Spending to Be Up 23% This Year," http://money.cnn.com/2004/01/27/news/companies/valentines_nrf.
9. "Floral Gift Market," American Floral Endowment Consumer Tracking Study, 1999, http://www.flora-links.org/marketing.html; American Floral Endowment Consumer Tracking Study, June 2000–May 2001, http://www.flora-links.org/marketing.html.
10. Michael A. Lev, "Bosses Have Day, But Next Day Is Sweeter," *Chicago Tribune*, October 15, 1993, 1SW1; http://pressroom.hallmark.com/val_day_facts.html; http://pressroom.hallmark.com/sweetest_day.html.

Devil's Night in Detroit

1. Photographer Bill Eisner and Detroit Fire Department Squad 3 fire-fighters Larry Gassel, Mike Levin, Walter Harris, Brent Gilbert, Herb Mulford, and DFD driver Eric Jurmo, interview by author, October 28, 2002.
2. Detroit Fire Department Squad 3, "Tale of The Tape," 1984.
3. Eisner, Gassel, Levin, Harris, Gilbert, Mulford, and Jurmo, interview.
4. Eisner, Gassel, Levin, Harris, Gilbert, Mulford, and Jurmo, interview.
5. Helen Irving, interview by author, October 31, 2002.
6. Eisner, Gassel, Levin, Harris, Gilbert, Mulford, and Jurmo, interview.
7. Thomas J. Sugrue, *The Origins of the Urban Crisis: Race and Inequality in Detroit* (Princeton: Princeton University Press, 1996), 6.
8. "Tale of the Tape," 1979.
9. Eisner, Gassel, Levin, Harris, Gilbert, Mulford, and Jurmo, interview.
10. Eisner, Gassel, Levin, Harris, Gilbert, Mulford, and Jurmo, interview.
11. Ze'Ev Chafets, *Devil's Night, and Other True Tales of Detroit* (New York: Random House, 1990), 217.
12. http://www.box42.net/history/shtml.
13. Eisner, Gassel, Levin, Harris, Gilbert, Mulford, and Jurmo, interview.
14. Eisner, Gassel, Levin, Harris, Gilbert, Mulford, and Jurmo, interview.
15. Ben Schmitt, "Fire Truck Is Ready to Roll into Action," *Detroit Free Press*, October 30, 2002, 4B.
16. Erik Lords, "Angels Gathering Yet Again to Squash a Devil's Night," *Detroit Free Press*, October 30, 2002, 4B.
17. Schmitt, "Fire Truck," 4B.
18. Lords, "Angels Gathering," 4B.

Halloween and the Business of Witchcraft

1. Phyllis Curott, interview by author, May 2002.
2. Jenie Carlin, interview by author, May 2002. See also "Bewitched at the Bookstore," *Weekly Standard*, March 4, 2002, 39; Douglas McDonald, "Amazon's Top Sellers Are New Age Based," *Publisher's Weekly*, June 14, 1999, 36; Judith Rosen and Robert Dahlin, "Crossing the Boundaries," *Publisher's Weekly*, May 27, 2002, 25.
3. Lynne Menturweck, interview by author, May 2002.
4. Debra Riley Parr, interview by author, July 2002.

5. Estimates vary from about five hundred thousand to ten million. (The U.S. Census does not track religious affiliation.) Four million is a middle-of-the-road estimate. Extrapolating from book sales to a larger population can be helpful, although those formulas too are open to interpretation. Curott, interview; Llewellyn Worldwide religious-tolerance fact sheet.
6. Covenant of the Goddess 2000 survey, http://www.cog.org/cogpoll.html. See also Ruth la Ferla, "Like Magic, Witchcraft Charms Teenagers," *New York Times*, February 13, 2000, 9:1.
7. Lisa Braun, interview by author, May 2002.
8. Michael Windsor, interview by author, May 2002.
9. Scholars believe approximately forty thousand witches were executed, primarily in the years between 1550 and 1630, and primarily in France, Switzerland, and Germany. Charlotte Allen, "The Scholars and the Goddess," *Atlantic Monthly*, January 2001, 18. In 1693, at the culmination of the Salem witch trials, nineteen people were hanged, one man was crushed beneath stones, and five others died in jail. All but six of the accused were pardoned in 1711, but it was not until 1992 that Massachusetts passed a bill exonerating the rest. "Salem Witches Exonerated," *American History*, April 2002, 12.
10. Diane Purkiss, *The Witch in History* (New York: Routledge, 1996), 283, 276.
11. Fiona Horne, *Witch: A Magickal Journey* (London: Thorson's/HarperCollins, 2000), 283.
12. Alice Cuneo, "Using Halloween to Scare Up Sales," *Advertising Age*, October 8, 2001, 4. Cuneo notes, "[Halloween spending is] still less than gift-giving holidays such as Mother's Day and Father's Day, and far behind Christmas with $194.9 billion in 2000."
13. Theresa Howard, "Retailers Scare Up Strong Halloween Sales," *USA Today*, October 31, 2001, B6.
14. Alice Cuneo, "Marketers Carve into Halloween's Bonanza," *Advertising Age*, October 23, 2000, 76.
15. Curott, interview.
16. On the transformative potential of seeing and experiencing traces of hope in everyday culture, see Ernst Bloch, *The Principle of Hope*, 3 vols. (Cambridge: MIT Press, 1995). On the cultural meanings of Halloween, see Nicholas Rogers, *Halloween: From Pagan Ritual to Party Night* (Oxford and New York: Oxford University Press, 2002). On the commercial culture of Halloween, see David Skal, *Death Makes a Holiday* (New York: Bloomsbury, 2002).

Beyond Baklava: The Consumption of Muslim Culture

1. Nuray Mestci, "Baklava: Flavor Which Conquers the Palate," *Skylife*, Summer 2000, 93.
2. Kathleen Seidel, "Serving the Guest: Food For Remembrance," 1999, http://www.superluminal.com/cookbook/essay_serving_the_guest.html.
3. Imam Senad Agic, interview by author, Northbrook, Illinois, March 16, 2003.
4. Seidel, "Serving the Guest."
5. Jane I. Smith, *Islam In America* (New York: Columbia University Press, 1999), 138. As with kosher foods, obtaining halal certification involves added steps in the food preparation process. The animal's throat should be slit with a sharp instrument, cleanly cutting through the windpipe, gullet, and jugular veins. After the throat is cut, the blood must be drained before the head is fully removed. This method contrasts with the typical American way of slaughter, in which the animal is stunned with an electric shock before being killed and the blood is not fully drained. In addition, the name of God is to be recited during the slaughter, as indicated in Sura 6:118 of the Koran.
6. Mian Riaz, "Examining the Halal Market," *Business News Publishing*, 1999, http://www.preparedfoods.com/archives/.
7. Agic, interview.

Feasting, Family, Football, and Fanfare

1. Brian Awehali, "Inventing Thanksgiving," AlterNet.org, November 27, 2002, http://www.alternet.org/story.html?StoryID=14628.
2. http://www.plimoth.org/Library/Thanksgiving/thanksgi.htm.
3. http://www.plimoth.org/Library/Thanksgiving/thanksgi.htm.
4. Oliver Andresen, "Here's the Story behind Moving Date of Thanksgiving," *Arlington Heights Daily Herald,* November 15, 2002, 3.

5. Mahtowin Munro, "National Day of Mourning: No Giving Thanks for Colonialism," *Workers World*, December 12, 2002, 3.
6. Adam Wilmoth, "U.S. Holiday Travel Expected to Near Levels of Late 1990s," *Knight Ridder Tribune Business News,* November 26, 2002, 1.
7. Travel News, http://www.cnn.com.
8. Harry Hitzeman, "Runners Will Lace Up for Turkey Trot to Help Others," *Chicago Daily Herald*, November 25, 2002, F3.
9. Bill Keveney, "For Dessert: TV Music Specials," *USA Today*, November 25, 2002, D3.
10. Association of Sales and Marketing Companies (ASMC) telephone survey, October 11–14, 2002.
11. National Turkey Federation, "Turkey History and Trivia," http://www.eat turkey.com/consumer/history/history.html.
12. U.S. Census Bureau's Public Information Office statistic quoted in "On Two," *Houston Chronicle*, November 23, 2000, 2.
13. Awehali, "Inventing Thanksgiving."
14. Melissa Grace, "Parade and Joy of N.Y.: 2.5 Million Brave Freezing Temps for Macy's Spectacle," *New York Daily News*, November 29, 2002, 7.
15. "Post-Thanksgiving Online Holiday Shopping Jumps 22 Percent, According to Nielsen/NetRatings' Holiday eCommerce Index," November 26, 2001, http://www.nielsennetratings.com/pr/ pr_011126.pdf.

Merry Hanukkah

1. Andrew R. Heinze, *Adapting to Abundance: Jewish Immigrants, Mass Consumption, and the Search for American Identity* (New York: Columbia University Press, 1990), 71.
2. Heinze, *Adapting to Abundance*, 71.
3. Jakob J. Petuckowski, "The Magnification of Chanukah: Afterthoughts on a Festival," *Commentary*, January 1960, 31.
4. Petuckowski, "Magnification of Chanukah," 39.
5. Heinze, *Adapting to Abundance*, 75.
6. Jenna Weissman Joselit, *The Wonders of America: Reinventing Jewish Culture 1880–1950* (New York: Hill and Wang, 1994), 230.
7. Heinze, *Adapting to Abundance*, 73.
8. Heinze, *Adapting to Abundance*, 77.
9. Joselit, *Wonders of America*, 230.
10. Heinze, *Adapting to Abundance*, 77.
11. Joselit, *Wonders of America*, 233.
12. Heinze, *Adapting to Abundance*, 77.
13. Heinze, *Adapting to Abundance*, 78.
14. Joe Berkofsky, "So Yule Do a Mitzvah . . . Jews Creating New Traditions at Christmas," *Chicago Jewish News*, December 2002, 16.
15. Joselit, *Wonders of America*, 237.
16. Joselit, *Wonders of America*, 239.
17. Maxwell House Advertisement, *Day-Jewish Journal*, November 1964, 3.
18. Joselit, *Wonders of America*, 239.
19. Annie Groer, "Gift Wrap Breaks Free of Color Barriers," *Los Angeles Times*, December 6, 2001, E4.
20. "Spice Box," *Moment*, December 1989, 4, says that Ezra Katzen of Rochester, New York, discovered the original tree listing in the *Rochester Democrat and Chronicle.*
21. Dreidle of Dreams, Smithsonian catalog, August–December 1997.
22. Jack Rosen, interview by author, Cleveland, Ohio, November 2002.
23. It appears that the demand for Hanukkah merchandise is likewise negligible. From 1985 to 2002, American Greetings offered only six designs of wrapping paper, one matching bow bag, one set of gift tags, and one collection of gift bags. Two or three years of inventory were manufactured at one time, and so the already limited designs changed only every third year. In a further effort to increase sales, Hanukkah collections were graced with universal artwork in inoffensive solid blues and golds. In comparison, the Christmas selection featured 600 designs of gift wrap, 75 percent of which were newly designed and which were printed four to five times per season; 400 gift trims sold in packs of seven to eight designs, all changed yearly; 250 gift-bag designs, 70 percent newly designed from the artwork to the shapes and sizes; and 700 box-card designs, 70 percent of which were changed annually.
24. Jane Turnis, "Hanukkah Items More Common at Colorado Retail Stores," *Colorado Springs Gazette*, December 24, 1997, 48.

25. Groer, "Gift Wrap Breaks Free," E4.
26. Julie Hyman, "Holiday Market Niches: Stores Embrace Hanukkah, Kwanzaa," *Washington Times*, December 26, 2000, B9.
27. Joselit, *Wonders of America*, 233.
28. Berkofsky, "So Yule Do," 5.

A Holiday for the Rest of Us

1. http://www.seinfeldscripts.com/TheStrike.htm.
2. Mark O'Keefe, "Giving Up Television Has Added Time to Former Viewers' Lives," *New Orleans Times-Picayune*, November 17, 2002, 18.
3. "Facts and Figures about Our TV Habit," http://www.tvturnoff.org/ factsheets.htm.
4. "Basic Data about Television Watching," http://www.tvp.org/ Handouts%20pages/basic_data_txt.html.
5. Elizabeth Lesly, Ronald Grover, and Jeanne Dugan, "Seinfeld: The Economics of a TV Supershow, and What It Means for NBC and the Industry," *Business Week*, June 1997, 116.
6. Lesly, Grover, and Dugan, "Seinfeld," 116.
7. Lesly, Grover, and Dugan, "Seinfeld," 116.
8. http://www.nielsenratings.com.
9. Lesly, Grover, and Dugan, "Seinfeld," 116.
10. *Seinfeld* is syndicated by Castle Rock Entertainment and Sony Pictures. Sony Pictures sells episodes to local television networks. Ben & Jerry's does not influence air dates but finds out the schedule from Sony Pictures.
11. Rob Douglas, telephone conversation with author, March 2002.
12. http://lever.cs.ucla.edu/yarvis-guests/lianne/Festivus/.
13. Brian Kindle, "Festivus for the Rest of Us," *First Coast Community*, December 23, 2001, http://www.jacksonville.com/community/ cc/neasevertical/stories/122401/12230152228.shtml.
14. http://www.benjerry.com/our_products/flavor_graveyard/ departed_flavors.cfm.

Xmas Excess

1. http://www.wdwplanner.com/spectacle.htm. In 2003, the light display was put on hold due to the demolition of MGM Studios' movie set, home to Residential Street, the site of the show since its inception. It is set to return in 2004 on New York Street with, according to Jennings Osborne, the addition of a million lights. Osborne enthusiastically stated, "We're just going to cover everything down there, we're excited about it." Disney spokesperson Gary Buchanan added, "We continue to work with Jennings on the future of the Osborne Family Spectacle of Lights. We're glad to hear he's still thinking big." "Osborne Family Lights; No Lights for 2003," http://www.wdwinfo.com/holidays/osborne lights.htm.
2. Unity Marketing, "The Christmas and Seasonal Decorations Report, 2002: The Market, The Competitors, The Trends," quoted in "Christmas Decorating Is $6.4 Billion Industry," http://www.casual living.com/news062402.html.
3. "Holiday Sales," http://www.nrf.com/content/press/release2002/ holidaysales.htm.
4. Polling Data, 2001, http://www.religioustolerance.org/chr_deno.htm.
5. http://www.adherents.com/rel_USA.html.
6. Mary Edsey, *The Best Christmas Decorations in Chicagoland* (Chicago: Tabagio Press, 1995), vii.
7. http://www.christmasarchives.com/trees.html.
8. Edsey, *Best Christmas Decorations*, vii.
9. Edsey, *Best Christmas Decorations*, vii.
10. http://www.christmasarchives.com/trees.html.
11. Pam Danziger, in "Christmas Decorating."
12. http://www.usda.gov/nass/events/news/trees.htm.
13. Zena Olijnyk, "O Tennenbaum," *Canadian Business*, December 2001, 97.
14. Jenny Bailly, "Is Black the New Green?: Tom Ford Fashions Faux Fir for Gucci," November 29, 2001, http://www.geometry.net/detail/ celebrities/green_tom_page_no_3.htm.
15. http://www.usda.gov/nass/events/news/trees.htm.
16. http://www.nfpa.org/Research/NFPAFactSheets/ChristmasTree Fires/ChristmasTreeFires.asp.

17. http://www.oph.dhh.state.la.us/injuryprevention/safekids/news bdaf.html?story=152.
18. http://www.rockefellercenter.com/home.html.
19. http://www.wttw.com/chicagostories/marshallxmas.html.
20. http://www.chicago.about.com/library/weekly/aa011501a.htm.
21. Charlyn Fargo, "A Christmas Tradition: A Look at the Window Displays at Marshall Field's in Chicago," *Springfield Journal Register*, November 27, 1998, 5A.
22. Fargo, "Christmas Tradition," 5A.
23. http://www.wdwinfo.com/holidays/osbornelights.htm.
24. Olijnyk, "O Tennenbaum," 97.
25. Brian Sullivan and Martha Neil, "Yule Be Sorry," *ABA Journal*, April 2002, 18.
26. Shawn Sell, "Christmas Decorating Won't Dim This Year," *USA Today*, November 30, 2001, D4.
27. Amy Merrick, "Cashing In on the Creeps," *Wall Street Journal*, October 30, 2002, B1.
28. "Christmas and Seasonal Decorations."
29. "Christmas and Seasonal Decorations."
30. "Christmas and Seasonal Decorations."
31. Jane Gordon, "What a Gift: Christmas All Summer Long," *New York Times*, June 3, 2001, 14.
32. http://www.christopherradko.com/html/history.html.
33. Merrick, "Cashing In," B1.
34. "Christmas Shoppe" (QVC), October 2002.

From Neighborhood Shop to Photo Op: The Evolution of the Department-Store Santa

1. Leigh Eric Schmidt, *Consumer Rites: The Buying and Selling of American Holidays* (Princeton: Princeton University Press, 1995), 130.
2. Webb Garrison, *A Treasury of Christmas Stories* (Nashville: Rutledge Hill Press, 1990), 61.
3. Garrison, *Treasury of Christmas Stories*, 48–50.
4. Schmidt, *Consumer Rites*, 130.
5. Stephen Nissenbaum, *The Battle for Christmas* (New York: Vintage Books, 1997), 169–71.
6. Guy Trebay, "You Get Just One Night Out, You Want Your Own Look," *New York Times*, December 11, 2001, D10.
7. Garrison, *Treasury of Christmas Stories*, 56, 63–65.
8. Karal Ann Marling, *Merry Christmas!* (Cambridge: Harvard University Press, 2000), 211–14.
9. Marling, *Merry Christmas!* 198.
10. http://www.santaclausschool.com.
11. Brady White, telephone conversation with author, November 9, 2002.
12. Diane L. Cormany, "Malls Spend Big on Holiday Displays," *Minneapolis/St. Paul Business Journal*, November 23, 2001, 14.
13. Sandra Lowe Sanchez, "Malls Say Santa Business Not in Red This Christmas Season," *San Antonio Business Journal*, December 21, 2001, http://www.bizjournals.com/sanantonio/stories/2001/12/24/story4.html?page=1.
14. Robert J. Hughes, "Santa's Back in Town," *Wall Street Journal*, December 7, 2001, W1.
15. Cormany, "Malls Spend Big," 14.
16. Sanchez, "Malls Say."
17. Hughes, "Santa's Back," W1.
18. Cormany, "Malls Spend Big," 14.
19. Sanchez, "Malls Say."
20. Sanchez, "Malls Say."
21. Daniel Eisenberg, "Out of the Claus-et," *Time*, December 22, 1997, 14.
22. Hughes, "Santa's Back," W1.

Kwanzaa, Inc.

1. http://www.officialkwanzaawebsite.org/origins.html.
2. Elizabeth Pleck, "Kwanzaa: The Making of a Black Nationalist Tradition," *Journal of American Ethnic History*, Summer 2001, 3–28.
3. Debra J. Dickerson, "A Case of the Kwanzaa Blues," *New York Times*, December 26, 2003, A43.
4. Tanette Johnson-Elie, "Area Stores Benefit as More People Embrace Kwanzaa," December 20, 1999, http://www.jsonline.com/bym/news/dec99/johncol21122099.asp.
5. "Kwanzaa Becomes $700 Million Business," *Ebony*, December, 2000, 42.
6. Pleck, "Kwanzaa," 3–28.
7. Maulana Karenga, "Kwanzaa and Corporate Commercialism," *Philadelphia Tribune*, December 24, 1999, A7.
8. Johnson-Elie, "Area Stores Benefit."
9. Desiree Sanders, interview by author, December 2002.
10. Jose Ferrer, interview by author, September 2002.
11. William Juzang, interview by author, September 2002.

Start the Year Off with a Bang

1. Matt Flanagan, interview by author, Chicago, May 15, 2002.
2. Jack Beningo, interview by author, Chicago, April 7, 2002.
3. Los Angeles Police Department press release, "What Goes Up—Must Come Down! Final Report of the 2001 New Year's Eve Gunfire Reduction Efforts," http://www.lapdonline.org/press_releases/2002/01/pr02009.htm.
4. Distilled Spirits Council of the United States, "DSS Sales Volume Year End Detail December 00," http://www.discus.org/economic/sv.htm.
5. Lisa Hawkins, interview by author, October 2, 2002.

Photograph and Illustration Credits

D. Denenge Akpem: 76–77 top, 79, 288 top right
Melanie Archer: 40, 46, 47
Matt Avery: 216 top
Megan Avery: 15, 216 bottom
Amir Berbic: cover, 1, 2–3, 102–3, 118–19, 210, 211 top, 218
Isak Berbic: 208–11 background
Amy Dale: 242 bottom
Seth Duffey: 110
Bill Eisner: 194–97
Amy Tavormina Fidler: 6, 7, 12, 13, 26, 32 bottom, 34 top and bottom, 83, 82–85 background, 105, 116–17, 126–27, 138–45 background, 188, 206, 208, 212–15 background, 221, 250, 258–59, 260–61, 265, 278 top
Benjamin Finch: 48, 174–79 background
Fireworks by Grucci: 164
Alan Freed: 39
Jennifer Getz: 129, 131
Troy Gregory: 194–97
Mable Hanke: 133, 135, 137
Lianne Hoskins: 232
Shayla Johnson: 255, 256, 257
Eric Jones: 57 top right
James Kim: 31, 33, 35
Jori Lakars: 57 bottom right
Maud Lavin: 60–65 background
Raymond Lee: 92 top, 288 top left and middle right
Rebekah Levine: 16
Jennifer Lilia Lopez: 120, 122, 124
Curtis Love: 57 bottom left
Jennifer Moody: 161, 213
Gerald Posley: 9, 156, 158, 160
Alyson Priestap-Beaton: 10, 14, 22, 23, 58, 59, 62 middle and bottom, 68, 69, 87, 89, 93, 96–97, 100, 101, 112 top, 113, 114–15, 154, 162–63, 181, 182–83, 185–86, 187, 189, 190–91, 207, 226, 231, 234–35, 236, 240 top, 241, 242 top three, 243, 252–53, 262, 267, 277, 281, 282–83, 288 bottom
Jacob Ristau: 60–65 illustrations, 196, 201, 205 illustrations
Sister Cecilia Schmitt: 98
Laurie Shefsky: 172–73
Christian Sheridan: 8, 11, 62 top, 72–73, 166, 167, 168–69, 249 background, 279, 287
Ben Skinner: 278 bottom
Loren Stephens: 77 middle
Jason Warriner: 111, 134, 155, 266
Anne Webster: 239
Cecelia Wingate: 57 top left
Beth Wodnick: 24, 170, 217 top

Historic Image Credits

All reasonable efforts have been made to trace the copyright holders of the visual material reproduced herein. Omissions will be corrected in subsequent editions.

Courtesy Broadway Books, a division of Random House, Inc.: 201 top left

Day-Jewish Journal, **November 25, 1964; Courtesy Library of Congress African and Middle Eastern Division:** 222

© Kevin Flemming/Corbis: 77 top right

Courtesy HarperCollins Publishers Ltd., © 2000, Fiona Horne; copyright for customized version, The School of the Art Institute of Chicago: 203 top left

Jewish Daily News, **December 14, 1905; Courtesy Library of Congress African and Middle Eastern Division:** 222

Kautz Family Archives; Courtesy YMCA: 141, 194

Warren K. Leffler; Courtesy Library of Congress: 30

Marilyn Monroe TM/©2003, LLC by CMG Worldwide, http://www.MarilynMonroe.com: 60, 64

Thomas Nast; illustration from Dover Publications: 250

New York Mirror: 245

http://www.paxchristi.net/symbols/britain.html: 80

Courtesy Smithsonian American Art Museum, Washington, D.C./Art Resource, New York: 246 (St. Nicholas, © 1837, oil on wood, 75.5 x 62.1 cm., by Robert Walter Weir, 1803–89)

Essay Design Credits

Melanie Archer: 40–47, 66–71, 80–85, 102–5, 116–19, 154–61, 170–73, 198–205, 218–25
Amy Tavormina Fidler: 24–29, 48–53, 60–65, 126–31, 138–45, 148–53, 192–97, 208–11, 212–15, 258–65
Benjamin Finch: 5, 36–39, 174–79, 180–81
Alyson Priestap-Beaton: 146–47, 184–89, 226–33, 234–41, 244–51, 254–57
Jason Warriner: 30–35, 54–57, 74–79, 86–95, 98–101, 106–11, 120–25, 132–37, 164–67

Contributors

D. Denenge Akpem is an artist, performer, writer, and educator. Her work has been presented at numerous venues including the Museum of Science and Industry, Chicago, and the Art Institute of Chicago and is shown at www.denenge.com.

Melanie Archer is an artist and writer. Born and raised in Trinidad and Tobago, she is currently managing editor of D.A.P. in New York. She received an M.F.A. from the School of the Art Institute of Chicago and a B.Arch. from Hampton University. She has designed projects for the cities of Conway, Arkansas, and Santa Fe, Roswell, and Truth or Consequences, New Mexico; the Kennedy Group; and Walt Disney Imagineering.

John-Paul Avila is a graphic artist whose academic research revolves around socioeconomic and political issues, the Latino community, and visual-communication education. He is the principal of the Ripe Design.

Amir Berbic is a Chicago-based graphic designer. He holds an M.F.A. in visual communications from the School of the Art Institute of Chicago and a B.F.A. in graphic design from the University of Illinois at Chicago. He has worked as an associate art director of *F News* in Chicago and has contributed illustrations to the *Chicago Tribune*. His work has been exhibited in Chicago, Rome, and Sarajevo. He is a design consultant for the weekly magazine *DANI* in Sarajevo.

Liz Connor designs book jackets for G. P. Putnam's Sons. She has also designed for HarperCollins Publishers, Kralyevich Productions (CourtTV), the Little Gray Book Lectures, www.otherpeoples stories.com, and MSNBC.

Amy Tavormina Fidler is an instructor in graphic design at Bowling Green State University in Bowling Green, Ohio. She received an M.F.A. from the School of the Art Institute of Chicago. Her clients have included the Ravinia Festival, the Evangelical Lutheran Church of America, and Bowling Green State University. She has taught typography and digital technology at the School of the Art Institute of Chicago.

Benjamin Finch is the principal of the Killswitch Collective, a Chicago-based design and multimedia firm. Clients have included Glitschka Studios, the Lake Placid Film Festival, Starmaker Productions, Desan Productions, McDonald's, and New York installation artist Monika Weiss.

Jennifer Getz is a Minneapolis-based designer specializing in Swedish issues. She has won awards for art direction in "The One Show" in New York City and "The Show" in Minneapolis.

Anne Hankey is a graphic designer and visual merchandiser who lives and works in Chicago. She has worked with Banana Republic, Sotheby's, the Junior League of Chicago, and many other clients. She has exhibited in the Charles Addams Gallery in Philadelphia and the Louis Meisel Gallery in New York City.

Shannon Hughey is a Chicago-based designer whose work has appeared in *Chicago Magazine*.

Shayla Johnson is a part-time instructor at the School of the Art Institute of Chicago and specializes in interactive electronic media and illustration. She has worked as a designer and illustrator for the software developer Novient and the Morrison Agency (clients including Idapta, Kodak Print, and Comsys).

Maud Lavin is an associate professor of visual and critical studies and art history, theory, and criticism at the School of the Art Institute of Chicago. She is the author of *Clean New World: Culture, Politics, and Graphic Design* and *Cut with the Kitchen Knife: The Weimar Photomontages of Hannah Höch* as well as critical essays published in the *New York Times Book Review*, *Print*, *Art in America*, *Artforum*, and *New German Critique*.

Raymond Lee received a B.F.A. from the Art Center College of Design in Pasadena and an M.F.A. from the School of the Art Institute of Chicago. He is a freelance graphic designer and has taught design at DePaul University in Chicago.

Rebekah Levine is a Chicago artist whose work has been exhibited at the Museum of Contemporary Art in Chicago. Since 1998, she has been a member of the curating collective Law Office, which has organized exhibitions at numerous venues including DiverseWorks in Houston and Locust Projects in Miami and a performance at the University of Chicago. She works as the Thorne Miniature Rooms Departmental Specialist at the Art Institute of Chicago.

Rebecca Mazzei recieved an M.A. in modern art history, theory, and criticism from the School of the Art Institute of Chicago. She has worked at Detroit's *Metro Times*. Her writing has also appeared in the *Salt Lake Tribune*, the *Outsider*, and *McSweeney's*.

Jennifer Moody is adjunct assistant professor in visual communications at the School of the Art Institute of Chicago. Her professional practice includes design for Rand McNally, the Tribune Company, and McDonald's. Her work has been published in design periodicals and books including *New Postcard Graphics*, *Limited Color Graphics*, and *Typography Now 2*.

Debra Riley Parr is a professor of design and art history at Columbia College Chicago and is writing a book on youth culture and design.

Courtney S. Perkins received an M.A. from the School of the Art Institute of Chicago, where she focused on contemporary Latin American art and feminism. She is working on independent curatorial projects for Bloodshot Records at Old Town School of Folk Music in Chicago and Yard Dog in Austin. She received a J.D. from John Marshall Law School in Chicago and has published articles on art law, concerning in particular art stolen during World War II.

Gerald Posley is a Chicago-based artist and freelance designer. His clients include the School of the Art Institute of Chicago, Thousand Waves Martial Arts and Self-Defense Center, Insight Arts, and Chicago Dance Supply.

Alyson Priestap-Beaton is a freelance graphic designer and photographer who received her M.F.A. from the School of the Art Institute of Chicago. She has worked for clients including Neiman Marcus, Bank of America, CB Richard Ellis, Corgan Associates Architects, and the School of the Art Institute of Chicago. Her recent artists' books are in the collections of Printed Matter, Colette, and the Joan Flasch Artists' Book Collection at the School of the Art Institute of Chicago.

Mary E. Ragsdale received a B.A. in art from UCLA and an M.F.A. from the School of the Art Institute of Chicago. She has worked in creative services and programming with WLS-TV in Chicago and has developed design projects for Salinas Valley Memorial Healthcare System and McDill Associates in California.

Jacob Ristau, formerly a designer for RBMM in Dallas, is an M.F.A. candidate in visual communications at the School of the Art Institute of Chicago, where he is focusing on three-dimensional writing models. His design work has been published in *Graphis Design Annual 2003*, *Communication Arts Design Annual 2003*, *Print Regional Design Annual 2003*, and *Graphis Design Annual 2004*.

Eliza Rosen practices graphic design in Chicago, with clients including Deborah's Place and *Chicago Magazine*.

Christian Sheridan is a graduate student at the Rice School of Architecture. His photographs have been exhibited in the United States and Italy. He has worked with the artist Rick Lowe and Project Row Houses in the construction of the XS House and provided photographs for the documentary "Welcome Home."

Loren Stephens practices graphic design in Flagstaff, Arizona. She received a B.F.A. in visual communications from the School of the Art Institute of Chicago and has worked as a graphic designer for Zande + Newman in New Orleans and the Shedd Aquarium in Chicago.

Zhivka Valiavicharska received an M.A. in art history, theory, and criticism from the School of the Art Institute of Chicago and is currently working on a Ph.D. at the University of California, Berkeley. She is a former Marjorie Susman Curatorial Fellow at the Museum of Contemporary Art, Chicago. Her research interests include identity discourses and theories of nationalism and globalization.

Jason Warriner is a graphics associate at AMR Research in Boston and has worked with the Chicago Underground Film Festival, Tumult Records, and *Skyscraper* magazine. He received an M.F.A. in visual communications from the School of the Art Institute of Chicago. His work has been published in *Select Magazine* and exhibited at Buddy and Heaven Galleries in Chicago.

Maia Wright is a writer and book designer living in Chicago. She won the Shellabarger Thesis Prize from the Program in Creative Writing at Princeton University for her translation work, and she has exhibited at the 1926 Exhibition Studies Space at the School of the Art Institute of Chicago.

Ilivia Marin Yudkin is a Chicago-based designer whose clients have included WGN-TV, the Center for International Rehabilitation, Have a Heart for Sickle Cell Anemia, and the Gus Foundation. She received an M.F.A. from the Art Institute of Chicago and a B.F.A. from the Rhode Island School of Design.

Acknowledgments

This is a collaborative project that has been characterized by warmth, fun, respect, and humor—by many of the qualities we yearn for at holiday celebrations but that do not always appear. We consider ourselves very lucky to have collaborated. Most of us met at the School of the Art Institute of Chicago, which nurtured this book in many ways. We brainstormed the concept in a graduate seminar in visual communication taught by Maud Lavin. And we pursued our collaborative work on culture and commercialism around the holidays in subsequent seminars on design and writing. Graduate students from those seminars continued working on the book long after they received their degrees, and the project attracted additional contributors from outside SAIC. Throughout, SAIC served as a creative and stimulating workshop for the research, writing, photography, and design of *The Business of Holidays;* most important, it reinforced the strong sense of cooperation that has colored the project at every stage. At SAIC, Frank de Bose, chair of Visual Communications, and George Roeder, chair of Visual and Critical Studies, were deeply encouraging. We want to express our gratitude, too, to Carol Becker, dean; Paul Coffey, director of the undergraduate division; and other colleagues at the School of the Art Institute for their support of the book.

Outside SAIC, others provided key help. We are grateful to designer Cheryl Towler Weese, principal of Studio Blue, for her feedback. We also want to thank cultural critic Debra Parr, designer Lorraine Wild, and photographer Christian Sheridan.

We are grateful to editor Andrea Monfried and designer Evan Schoninger at The Monacelli Press for their astute input and invaluable contributions. Our thanks also go to assistant editor Sasha Porter and marketing director Susan Enochs.

The production team—Melanie Archer, Amy Tavormina Fidler, Benjamin Finch, Maud Lavin, Alyson Priestap-Beaton, and Jason Warriner—would like to give warm thanks to the people with whom we eat turkey, spread tinsel, glue Peeps, exchange presents, and trick or treat, particularly Kathleen Archer, Lennox Archer, Paulette Archer, Ephraim Archer, Arianne de Govia, Reishma Seupersad, Andrew Fidler, the Tavormina family, Donna Finch, Paul Finch, Meredith Martin, Locke Bowman, Kris Bowman, David Bowman, Audrey Lavin, Carl Lavin, Matt Beaton, Madeline Beaton, the Warriner family, and Hannah Tashjian.

For help with images, Amy Fidler would like to thank Mark and Jerri Wagner, Rebekah Swanson Wagner, and Andrew Fidler of Unity Lutheran Church (Chicago) for being willing Ash Wednesday models; Gary, Colette, and Gwen Buerk for allowing her to photograph at Halloween and Christmas on location at the Kostume Shop (Perrysburg, Ohio); her parents, Joel and Candy Tavormina, for contributing items ranging from ties to Santa photos; and Beth Wodnick for photographing the turkey. Christian Sheridan thanks David Adicker for allowing him to photograph his sculptures. Shayla Johnson would like to thank Selean Holmes, chief curator, "Kwanzaa: The Exhibit," Dusable Museum of African-American History, Chicago. Jason Warriner expresses gratitude to Hannah Tashjian for her design and construction of the Peeps swimsuit and to Tom Hughes for modeling the swimsuit. Alyson Priestap-Beaton would like to thank all of the photographers who helped her with this book as well as Carl Rottenbucher for allowing use of his photograph as Santa Claus. The group thanks Uncle Fun for allowing photography in his store.

Those of us on the production team are grateful to each other for the creativity and affection we achieved—and the large number of hours we worked together. In addition to the production team, many other writers in the group contributed extra work. A special thanks to Mary Ragsdale for photography research and to Anne Hankey for publicity work. And much gratitude to all involved for a collaboration that has been and continues to be a great pleasure.